THE SECOND-TIME TEACHER

Lessons from Afghanistan

Ian Edwards

Published by I C Edwards

Copyright © 2020. All rights reserved. No portion of this publication may be used, reproduced or transmitted by any means, digital, electronic, mechanical, photocopy or recording without written permission of the publisher, except in the case of brief quotations within critical articles or reviews.

ISBN: 978-0-6488057-0-0

First edition, 2020

Hand carved wooden Afghan prints are used to introduce sections of this book.

For book orders and enquiries,
contact: anneandiane@hotmail.com

A catalogue record for this work is available from the National Library of Australia

For Paul and Ocean

Prologue

You're that Mr Edwards!

— Afghan physiotherapist, Maryam

Paul and Ocean, I am now more confident that I can tell you this story. It may seem a case of too late *and* too soon. You have passed away now, Paulo, and you, little Ocie (pronounced Oshi), are still only able to speak in single syllables. So, yes, there are challenges. But talking about Afghanistan has never been easy, even when the listeners were both alive and old enough to ask questions: 'Oh really, you were there? Wow, that must have been a real eye-opener? Was it dangerous?' I would prepare to answer. It was the thoughts behind the words, rather than the words themselves, which were stammered: 'Well, yes it was … it was … definitely … but … well … we …' The machinery of the conversation would break down, and recourse to another topic or person was a mutual relief. Sometimes, I did get more out in the way of an answer, but the flow of words would peter out quickly; much sooner than it takes us, reading one of your picture books, Ocie, to name the farm animals and make their sounds – always, of course, more than once.

It comes to me now as much the same thing. I have wanted to point to – or compose – pictures of Afghanistan and give voice to the characters and the sounds of their lives in which I participated. I didn't know it then but I do now: it was me who sabotaged and effectively extinguished these conversations. And in doing so I have carried with me a collection of images and stories that has never really been opened. Just why I did this has taken me a while to figure out. Something has changed though. I can now widen the aperture of my imagination when thinking of Afghanistan, whereas for so long, just as for many others who have returned from theatres of war, self-preservation required me to narrow it down or close it off.

Sometimes in the hand a book falls open, somewhere about its middle, at a well-read page. This story, too, opens around its middle, and for the same reason. I have thought much about this. It was a Saturday morning in July 2005, the first day of the Afghan working week. I arrived by taxi at the *Wazir Akbar Khan Hospital* compound in Kabul for the first day of the physiotherapy course I was to teach. Walking up the service road, away to my right, I passed the old garages, fronted by their once-white stucco walls and unpainted, (still) weathering timber doors. It was here that the physiotherapy school had its beginnings. They were being used now – I was able to visit them – as storerooms and offices for an eye-care project. Veering off the main hospital service road, further on and to the right, I was given my first view of the Physical Therapy Institute (PTI) of Kabul. Where I remembered a grassy slope leading up to *Tape Bibi Mahro* – the hill overlooking the suburb of Wazir recently made famous in the book *The Kite Runner* – and where there had been a scattering of fruit trees in the remnants of an ancient orchard, there was now a white two-storey building. The entrance was capped by an impressive sign, in both English and Dari, 'Physical Therapy Institute'.

A byline, 'Supported by the International Assistance Mission', spelled out my original connection with the place.

I made my way inside and was ushered upstairs to the office of Aziz Ahmad Adel, the director. After introductions with him and some of the PTI teaching staff, I was taken to a classroom and introduced to the group of about thirty physiotherapists. It was after my name was announced that a participant physiotherapist, a woman called Maryam, called out, as if she had just experienced an epiphany, 'You're that Mr Edwards! [pause] ... I was in the second course and you gave us the first lecture. And then you didn't come back. They said you were sick [longer pause] ... Are you better now?' It had been eighteen years since those classes and that absence, but her question was put to me as if I had been sick and off work just last week.

Eighteen years is reduced to a few days. *'I Afghanistan ast!'* (This is Afghanistan!) Afghans would say this to us foreigners, sometimes resignedly and sometimes defiantly, as a kind of explanation for the way things would often turn out; especially when we foreigners were puzzled or frustrated, which we frequently were. Ocie, I would like to teach you how Afghans say 'Afghanistan'. In Australia we pronounce all the a's in Afghanistan as though we are saying 'pan'. And it comes out real flat just like a pan. But it's not like that at all. It is a strong, full-bodied, almost intimidating word, in some ways matching the place. Paulo, you would remember how Afghans say it, from the time you spent there in the mid 1970s. And let me say, how irked I still am that you saw more of the country in that month than Anne and I saw in the entire four years we lived in Kabul in the early 1980s. Anyway, Afghanistan. After the initial, easy 'af', tackle the more difficult 'gh', which sounds as if you are trying to clear the back of the throat. Then, after the 'gh', the 'An' sounds like 'gone', as does the final 'An'. It's tricky but try it: afghAnistAn. I have always found hearing it said this way induces a certain awe of the place.

Awe. It's worth saying that Afghanistan was not *awesome* as it has come to be used today. It could be awful. There's no getting away from that. But it was also awe-full (or awe-inspiring). A sort of wonder and respect found its way into each of us. Many others who have lived and worked there say the same. It is something that remains, forever connecting you with the place.

The short dialogue with Maryam, however, still seems like a comedy routine. My answer to her guileless 'Are you better now?' was also deadpan: 'Yes, I am better now, thanks. Sorry to take so long.' But I feel in my bones now that it was afg͟hAnistAn, itself, addressing me: 'Welcome back, no hard feelings, no need for explanations. Ready to get back in to it?' I was very grateful.

During this week of teaching, I was reacquainted with two of my students from the very first course in 1983, some twenty-two years earlier. One was now a physiotherapy teacher and a participant in this course. The other arrived one day at morning tea, having been invited by his son, who was now a physiotherapist and a class member that week. Rahim had been older than the others then. Now he was working in a different field, but I would go on to teach his son, and even teach *with* his son on future courses. This was generational change. Even so, the change was as much within me as it was around me. It had taken the greater part of those eighteen years I had been away for me to become a teacher. And, I suppose, this just raises the question, what was I doing in those first four years, when I was tasked with setting up and running the inaugural physiotherapy training course and school in Afghanistan?

It was you, Paul, who suggested that I write an account of this. Remembering and re-experiencing those times in Afghanistan, and the years following our return to Australia, has not been an easy pursuit.

Prologue

You would be pleased that I am doing it. But I am less sure about what you make of the fact that it was your illness and passing which galvanised me into action. I miss you. A birthday card sits in front of me. You wrote it just a few weeks before your death. On the front is a picture of two feathers, not identical but obviously from the same bird. The green, black and grey colours in each feather blend and give way to form vanes which are beautiful. Exquisite, in fact. But it is what you wrote which still creases my eyes. How fortunate you were to have me as your brother and to have me beside you all these years, were your words. Paul, I can now go back and immerse myself in the past because you were largely there with me. You knew me and my foibles well. And you pushed back, rightly and effectively, whenever I was overly opinionated – that is, in most conversations. I know you will, in our wordless conversations, help me understand now what I didn't at the time.

Ocie, you arrived just a couple of months before Paul left. I was always going to love you, as my granddaughter. But your birth so close to Paul's passing made you even more precious to me. Each time you skedaddle from whatever it is you are doing, crossing the space between us as hurriedly as you can, your arms lifted, ready to be picked up, well, I feel almost God-like. I have your unshakeable trust. It is a view of me that I know will pass. After all, I am not the person of unsullied goodness that you seem to think I am. But even so, there is something pure and right about it. If only all our relationships could be so constituted, and we could live out our lives offering such welcome and trust to others. I contemplate the possibility, Ocie, that as you grow into girlhood, and later womanhood, you will continue to have welcome and trust as a part of your natural posture towards others. But it is not always straightforward.

I was shocked at what my first four years in Afghanistan did to me and how, on my return to Australia, I was a stranger. That is, I was someone other than the person who had left Australia four years earlier. I had trouble recognizing myself let alone being recognized or understood by anyone else. But I am grateful. Becoming a stranger helped me learn the value of becoming a host: that is, one who can welcome others, especially outsiders.

There is an old saying in the aid worker community: see one, do one, teach one. It applies to all sorts of procedures – in healthcare or otherwise. Paul and Ocean, past and future, I now have my second-time teacher's hat on. I have seen the puzzling and even hazardous terrains that can lie between strangers and hosts. I have traversed (done) such terrains, including hostile ones. Now, I want to explain to you how I found my way.

Part One
Kabul 1983–1987

Foreigner

Sometimes a landscape seems to be less a setting for the life of its inhabitants than a curtain behind which their struggles, achievements and accidents take place.

— John Berger

1

There was a gradualness in our leaving Australia on 3rd January 1983: first Singapore, then Delhi, and finally, almost three months later, Kabul. Each was a step further from Australia in distance, remoteness and strangeness. In Singapore we saw the unequal handshake of East and West in a high-rise, squeaky clean city state. In Delhi and northern India – spending eleven weeks there waiting for visas to enter Afghanistan, the previous applications having been lost – we were absorbed into an inexpressibly large human panorama, where people lived out their lives in situations and conditions beyond our sheltered Australian experience. Finally, there was Kabul. It lay beyond the North West Frontier, that mythically wild and ungoverned territory bordering Afghanistan and Pakistan. We flew over it, from Delhi, and landed in Kabul on March 23rd, 1983, two days after the Afghan New Year (*Nao rOz*). We were now *beyond the frontier* and it felt like it – wild, isolated and, initially at least, exciting.

The mountains surrounding the city rose beyond the scale of any we were used to, coming from Adelaide. And no trees on them either. Their rocky bareness was clothed by snow. On the range which bisected Kabul, and which was, itself, divided by the Kabul River, small mud and stone huts had, since the start of the war, inched up its vertiginous slopes. These were the homes of those seeking respite from the fighting in the provinces. The highest were perched, like the eyries of eagles, overlooking the distant valley floor. In Australia it is the well off who are able to pay for the enjoyment of spectacular views from their houses. Not here. The poor were the ones a long way up and away from the amenities of fresh water and electricity. Not that there was a reliable supply of these in the valley below either.

We'd point at things whenever we ventured out from the house into the streets and bazaars. Our hosts would tell us what each was, in Dari. Dari is the Afghan form of the Persian language, Farsi. Like you, Ocie, we would try to repeat what we heard. Before arriving, we had learned a few things about Islam and about Afghan culture and etiquette. For example, how to dress acceptably; which for Ma (Anne) included the importance of covering the head with a scarf, and for me not wearing shorts outside the house. And we knew not to drink alcohol, especially in any public way. This was easier for Anne as she didn't drink. So, we adjusted our lives and habits as best we could.

But growing into this new world would require more than compliance with such etiquettes and behaviours or, for that matter, learning the names of things in Dari.

I heard you the other day, Ocie, warbling like a magpie, putting sounds together like music without any recourse to words. To my mind it was better than cute. It was beautiful. I suppose, apart from trying your new vocal 'equipment' out, you were mimicking how you heard people – us – communicating and wanted to participate in that. I remember at times listening to spoken Dari and suspending any attempt to learn the fragments of words and phrases in favour of listening to its musical rhythms and inflections. It was a production from parts of the throat we don't often use for speech in Australia. It fascinated me in much the same way that I have observed you encountering newness, Ocie. It was like a rest break from the nuts-and-bolts work of learning the language mechanically through the recitation of words and grammar. But I think it was also an attempt to participate more fully in what was happening around me, even when it was beyond my skills to do so. You could say it was *perspective* that I was after – how things stand in relation to each other. But questions about perspective could neither be easily asked nor answered, in the way that learning individual words or expressions could.

Part One: Kabul 1983–1987

My observations of the things around me led to expectations in a deductive kind of logic – if *this*, then *that*. But this logic soon broke down when what I knew from my life at home in Australia no longer seemed to hold true. The interpretive lenses through which I was *seeing* this new world were less reliable and, in some ways, not even useable – like bringing an electrical appliance from home and finding out that you can't turn it on because the plug won't fit local sockets.

In Afghanistan things seemed curtained off to foreigners. And I am talking not just about what might lie behind the 'curtains' of a new and unfamiliar culture or religion. Our disorientation started with simple, natural things like space and time.

My long-ago high school learning had imbued me with the idea that the physical laws which determined space and time were given and unchangeable, although I have heard recently that time and space can be bent or distorted by black holes, gravitational waves and such like. In Kabul it soon became apparent to us newcomers, for reasons other than scientific ones (recent or otherwise), that these laws *could* be tinkered with. Who'd have thought that space and time could be curtained off and reshaped so that they were experienced so differently? Let me give you an example. And Paul, this is a very different Afghanistan in many respects from the one you knew. Before coming we had looked at a map and noted that Afghanistan was a landlocked country. So, we didn't expect to be living on an island. But in the early 1980s Kabul *was* an island. It had been made so by a planned military strategy. Russian helicopter gunships systematically and repeatedly bombed the villages in a 60km radius of Kabul in order to insulate the capital from large-scale attack by the *Mujahedeen* – the Taliban was not an entity at that time. Of course, they unloaded their lethal cargoes more distantly as well. Afghans, most of whom lived as subsistence farmers in villages in the country, had three options in order to escape the sustained violence. They could flee east to Pakistan, west to Iran or into Kabul itself, which they did in great numbers.

Even the airspace above Kabul conformed to the zones of secured space that defined the shores of the *island* below. Planes would bank steeply on take-off and corkscrew their way upwards over the city until they reached what was regarded as a safe 'exit' altitude, upon which the flight path towards destination could be commenced. Many planes added an extra strategy of dispersing flares as they gained height, in order to 'fool' heat-seeking missiles which might be launched from the nearby hills or mountains. In the years 1983–1987 we did not leave Kabul except to fly once or twice a year *over* Pakistan to India. Delhi was our port of call for going into or coming out of Afghanistan. This was because there were no diplomatic ties between the Soviet-backed government in Kabul and the nearer Islamabad.

On the ground the boundaries of the 'secure' Kabul within which we were able to go about our lives would, like tidal movements, come in or go out, depending on the state of the conflict. So, this world of big sky and mountains was simultaneously for us a small world. On Fridays – the day of congregational prayer in Islam – we were sometimes allowed to travel to *Kharga* Lake, 20km west of the city, towards the village of *Paghman*. A contested area during the week, the fighting seemed to quieten on Fridays. How these things worked no one seemed to really know. It was not a truce. We were just told that, with caution, we could stroll on the eastern side of the lake.

The boss of the organization we were with at that time was a laid-back American called George Terry. When we first arrived in Kabul we stayed with George and his wife Pat. George had a small sailing boat. One Friday he announced that sailing was on the afternoon social menu. When I asked him how it was that he had a sailing boat here in Kabul, so far from any seashore or navigable river (*Kharga* Lake being a rare

PART ONE: KABUL 1983–1987

exception) he replied, 'When we first came to Afghanistan it was known as a "fun place"'. And indeed it had been. Not so many years before, tourists and young travellers on the overland route between Europe and South East Asia were drawn to Kabul's famous bazaars and Afghanistan's exotic sights – Paulo, you were one. 'Now', George observed wryly, 'I live in the worst of both worlds. If they don't take me for a Russian then they take me for an American.'

On this Friday afternoon three of us sat in a small boat with an orange sail, gliding across *Kharga* Lake, careful not to venture too close to the western shore. We luxuriated in the space and quiet, taking in the clean subalpine air as though it were oxygen therapy, prescribed and administered to sustain us through the next island-confined week of dust and noise. To the west, the 15,000-foot *Paghman* range rose like a monolith; immense, brown and treeless. Unblemished white snow glistened on the upper ridges, embracing an electric blue sky.

The blue sky. It is no coincidence that the most popular colour in Afghanistan is blue. It is the colour of the domes on mosques and the colour of lapis lazuli, the quintessential Afghan decorative gem. Each represents continuity and something lasting, even eternal. Dutch friends we worked with in Kabul once visited us in Adelaide. Driving home from the airport, one exclaimed, 'What a big sky you have in Australia!' It seemed a peculiar comment. But I understand it better now, having read Aussie writer Tim Winton's interpretation of the Australian sky: 'You begin to feel that you could fall out into it at any moment … It's the scantiest membrane imaginable, barely sufficient as a barrier between earthbound creatures and eternity.'

Seated on a plateau some 6,000 feet above sea level, Kabul was already closer to the sky than any Australian city. The mountains drew our gaze further skywards, away from the plateau and its many problems.

Rather than falling out into it, it felt like this sky *pulled* people upwards and into it. It was less a threat and more a promise.

There is an Afghan proverb *KoA e KAbul be zar bAsha, be barf ne*, which translates as 'The mountains of Kabul may be without gold but not without snow'. The snow, precious beyond measure, melts in the spring and feeds the rivers which sustain agriculture, and therefore life itself, in Afghanistan's valleys. It was like that out on *Kharga* Lake that Friday: life going on, unfettered and guided by a natural order rather than by human activity. The hubbub of conflict was absorbed by the snow-fed lake as a forest might soak up carbon. Further up in the foothills, the small settlements and villages were, from this distance, quiet and silent. But it was the same when approaching Kabul by air: lifeless villages with craters in their near vicinity, like pockmarks on the olive complexion of the dry plateau. From the lake, as from the air, things appeared mundane and peaceful, even resolved. But this was a deceptive landscape. Incongruously settled in our small sailing boat, we drank in a landscape of profound beauty. But it curtained off an immense and as yet largely untold suffering to those outside Afghanistan.

In summer the legendary 'dusty winds' of Kabul (*khAk bAd*) – say 'hawk' (with a huff at its beginning) followed by 'board' to get the sound – would whip the high plateau on which the city stood. *khAk* (meaning dust) is the word from which we get 'khaki' and then use in English to describe a light-brown military or work shirt and pants. Only we say 'khaki' like 'car-*key*'. I include this observation, Ocie, not intending to be pedantic or a smart arse. It's just that language, like so many of our other understandings of different people groups, gets changed in arbitrary ways, and mostly to suit our own perspectives.

Part One: Kabul 1983–1987

When a *khAk bAd* rolled in, what began as a curtain of brown in the air would become a shroud. The dust coated and infiltrated everything: eyes, nostrils, clothes and even the insides of houses. Externally, our horizons would be collectively shrunk for periods of a day or two. Internally, these were times when we felt more hidden and severed from the outside world than we already were. It wasn't relevant then – no one had laptops – but the last time we were in Kabul in 2011, I was given a transparent silicon dust cover by a colleague to put over the keyboard of my laptop. It was a reminder that in a place of volatility and uncertainty there will always be dust – the elemental constant.

The separating curtains were of all kinds and on every scale. The city was divided by a great and ancient wall, built in the eleventh century, starting at the *Bala Hissar*, the original fortress of those holding power in Kabul. The wall still lies like a vanquished dragon, its serrated spine coursing up and over *Sher DarwAza*, one of the two mountains bisecting Kabul. Where we lived in *KArte Seh* (area 3) we would have been outside of the city when the wall had been its defence. In *KArte Seh* there were, nevertheless, high walls of the same mud brick – sometimes plastered over in stucco white – surrounding each house. And these ten-foot walls also conspired to conceal, and even defend, the lives of their occupants.

The private and public spaces either side of these walls were kept very separate. Outside, in the streets, there was little sense of community; open drains ran from underneath the front wall of each house into *joies* outside – large open drains, about a metre deep. Household scraps and garbage were deposited on designated street corners, where it was left to rot and be picked over by gangs of stray, roaming dogs, often fifteen to twenty strong. However, to enter an *aoli* (house yard), beyond the walls, was often a revelation. The relentless dust of the streets and brown panorama of mud bricks surrendered to the colour of flowers, the shade of grape vines and, sometimes, even the softness of tended grass – a retreat from all that lay outside. To move further inwards and enter an Afghan house, when invited, was to receive a fulsome and generous welcome. Hospitality sprung from deep and abiding cultural wells, which in the giving, especially during this time of war, watered and kept alive a sense of what it was to be an Afghan. And to be an Afghan then, as now, was to be constantly pulled between the demands of hostility and hospitality.

'Hiddenness' surrounded us as foreigners and it was carried forward in public. Afghan women, when outside the home, or in the presence of guests, covered their heads either with scarves or *chAderis* (more commonly known in the West as 'burqas'). Mostly blue in colour, and resembling a one-person tent, with the head as its apex, women went about their public chores or business looking out through a front 'vent'. Car drivers had to learn to compensate for a lack of peripheral vision among this group of *chAderi*-wearing pedestrians. Women who didn't wear *chAderis* always covered their heads in public with a scarf.

One day while shopping in Chicken Street in *Shar e Nao*, the new city, which had been a tourist precinct before the war, we noticed two young Afghan women in the back of a Russian jeep. They wore Western clothes and bright red lipstick and had uncovered heads. We could see them drinking and laughing with their off-duty Russian soldier escorts. The group in the jeep were all young and, in one sense, doing something which in another place would have been unremarkable. However, given it was unlikely that either girl would accompany these young men back to Russia as brides, their future in Afghanistan was now extremely bleak. Inevitably they would be found out, exposed and their families shamed on several counts; drinking alcohol and consorting with these hated foreigners and occupiers being the two principal ones. It was not likely that they could or would be forgiven. Lurking behind the bright facade of their young laughter lay another unfolding tragedy.

PART ONE: KABUL 1983–1987

Along with the curtaining of place and people was a curtaining of time. Kabul had a nightly curfew from 10pm to dawn. The streets became quiet after 9pm, except for soldiers standing sentry, guarding designated buildings and bridges, and ready to shoot transgressors. It was wise to stay put wherever you were till the morning. Before it was closed later that year (1983), due to the unexplained disappearances of Afghan staff, there was a staff house in *Shah re Nao*, known as The American Club. Foreigners – at least Western foreigners such as ourselves – could, upon registering, order a burger or club sandwich, play pool, read magazines or newspapers, or see a film. One time we left the staff house, relatively late, on a clear moonlit night in early spring. We had seen a film, *Oh God II*, starring George Burns as God. It was typically escapist Hollywood fare but culturally very familiar, inducing feelings of home. Afterwards we stepped out from the staff house onto the dark city streets. Bazaars normally bustling with people were now empty. Electricity was a scarce commodity in Kabul and so no shops were illuminated and there were no street lights. Snow still lay on the mountains surrounding the city and, radiating their received moonlight, cast a ghostly whitish-blue pallor over the streetscape. In this light the cold seemed more pervasive than it actually was at that time of the year. We drove quietly, surreally, on deserted streets, there being no other vehicles apart from military ones, following the river through the gap in the mountains, towards the suburbs on the other side where we lived. On the way we passed small groups of soldiers, standing out in the freezing night, observing the approach of curfew, the occasional glow of a cigarette signifying a small source of comfort.

I assiduously kept a diary in our first year in the country. About this night I wrote:

Thursday 5th May

It's a puzzling experience indeed to become involved in a Western film; become enmeshed in its value system and ethos only to find that when you step outside afterwards you are in war-torn Afghanistan. Reality and illusion have been reversed.

We had just left one movie only to step out into another. Only the scenario we were now in – a young couple from Adelaide living and working in Afghanistan during the Russian occupation – seemed more far-fetched.

Speaking of far-fetched scenarios, at the time of leaving Australia I was under the impression that I was going to work in a rehabilitation unit in Kabul with an orthopaedic surgeon. I did not know about plans for a physiotherapy training program and school. I found that out in the week before we left Delhi for Kabul. The project leader had to come out to Delhi on business and we met with him. He informed us that there were five nurses, two men and three women, who had been chosen to train in the first physiotherapy course in Afghanistan. I was to deliver a two-year diploma program in physiotherapy. Its beginning would coincide with my completion of a four-month language course learning Dari. This was something of a shock. I had not prepared for this prior to leaving Australia. My previous experience of teaching consisted of leading back-care classes for groups of patients attending our rehabilitation centre in Adelaide. I had little knowledge of what went into such a training course.

As this scenario suggests, communication in and out of Afghanistan was poor in those days. The use of email was still some years away. Letters to or from Australia took a minimum of six weeks and often more. And phones were not commonplace in the city. The time would come when it seemed that almost everyone in Afghanistan had a mobile phone, but at that time very few people even had access to a landline. The infrastructure for a comprehensive landline system was simply never developed. It was like the non-arrival of the age of steam in the country: Afghanistan's industrialization, what there was of it, never included steam trains, in contrast to its neighbours Iran, India and Pakistan. In the years 1983–1987 we never once successfully phoned our families in Australia from Kabul. After a few failed attempts in our first year, I think we simply gave up trying.

The conditions for miscommunication were therefore in place from the start. Perhaps it was considered hard enough to entice a physiotherapist to come and work in this remote and isolated outpost, without the added difficulty of trying to find one that would also take on the start of physiotherapy training and the development of a school. Or, maybe this agreement with the Afghan government, to start a physiotherapy training program and school, had been reached *after* release of the job description to which we responded.

Anne's job plans didn't work out either. She had planned to work in a maternity hospital as a nurse midwife but the supervising staff was Russian and did not want a Westerner present. It would be another twenty-four years before she would be able to use these skills in a neonatal intensive care unit in Kabul.

2

There were not many foreigners in Kabul in the early eighties apart from the occupying troops. Tourists and travellers had left either just before or soon after the Russian invasion. If you didn't count soldiers, most foreigners were embassy staff, United Nations consultants or, like us, members of a very small number of non-government organizations (NGOs). Kabul, during this period, was not a place of trade or investment bringing other visitors. In addition to its military force, Russia supplied Afghanistan with the basics of fuel, flour and sugar. A host of other goods, mostly tinned, came from Eastern European countries.

The initial challenge for any *KhAregi* (foreigner) wanting to venture around the streets and bazaars of Kabul was to make it clear that you weren't Russian. The absence of a military uniform wasn't sufficient for this since there were a number of civilians from Russia and Eastern Europe who were in the country as advisors in a range of fields. Even before formal language lessons we learned a few words of Dari in order to greet others and say thank you. The most important words we initially learned were *ShafA KhAne* NOOR. NOOR was the flagship project of the International Assistance Mission (IAM), the organization we were with. It was the eye hospital, the only one in the country. Its name was a combination of terms meaning 'house of healing' and 'light'. NOOR was also an acronym for National Organization for Ophthalmic Rehabilitation. *ShafA KhAne* NOOR was well known and appreciated by most Afghans in a place where blindness, due to conditions such as trachoma, was endemic. Before the NOOR project, eye care had been almost non-existent. To be associated with *ShafA KhAne* NOOR was like having a passport but one issued and stamped 'valid' by ordinary people.

PART ONE: KABUL 1983–1987

Instead of glares, scowls and even at times being spat at because people thought you were Russian, this passport brought smiles, handshakes, requests for eye appointments and, occasionally, an eyeball brought very close for examination.

Strangely enough, given the sensitivity of Afghans towards foreigners during this time of occupation, there was a kind of good humour offered to us, especially in our local bazaars. A popular name given to foreigners by children on the street, usually boys, was *Mester KachAlu* (Mr Potato). It was often followed by the question either in Dari or barely recognizable English, 'What is the time?' Knowing the time was not the immediate right of everyone then. It had not been that many years since a cannon was fired at 12 noon each day to let the population know the time. The noon gun still sat, now unfired, part way up the flanks of the mountain *Sher DarwAza*, above *Barbur*'s gardens.

There was a nurse from Germany on our team called Martha who used to always wear a traditional nurse's headpiece and grey uniform. The local boys who patrolled the streets of *KArte Seh* addressed her as '*KalA e kAghazi*' (paperhead). And when, noticing the watch on her wrist, they followed this greeting with the usual question regarding the time, Martha's answer was rapier-like and just as mischievous. Whatever part of the day it was, she replied, '*Neem shao*' (midnight).

At the other end of Kabul society, Anne and I were registered with the British Embassy. There was no continuous consular service offered by the Australian government at that time. The British Embassy was in *KArte ParwAn* a few kilometres west from *Shah re Nao*. It was at the bottom of a hill which partitioned this northern part of the city from its south-western suburbs, including *KArte Seh* where we lived. Built shortly after the Anglo-Afghan Treaty of 1921, the main residence was an example of the grand white stucco buildings of the British Raj. Also typical of the colonial grandeur of the Raj was the twenty-six acres of green lawns and gardens, which were partitioned from the outside – or you could say from the rest of Afghanistan – by a high wall. This parcel of land easily accommodated the five detached houses for senior embassy staff and their families. It was, altogether, a micro universe existing within but quarantined from the hustle and urgency of Afghan life beyond; the usual and main tasks of living were to procure sufficient daily food and to secure health and safety for the family. And each one of these tasks was made ever more challenging by the war.

In our first year in Kabul we received an invitation to the British Embassy for Christmas Eve carols. We were ushered into the embassy drawing room and once again I had the feeling of stepping into the otherworldliness of a movie set. It was as much a cultural shock as anything else we had encountered in Afghanistan. Burning candles framed the room with steady cones of subdued, reverential light. Portraits of the English monarchy, past and present, with those of other dignitaries such as Lord Curzon, the Foreign Secretary at the time of the embassy's construction, looked down benevolently upon the gathering. It was as if they, and not the current ambassador and his staff, were the real hosts of the evening. The portraits were joined on the wall by the obligatory stag's head. A magnificent wooden mantelpiece sat above a cavernous fireplace, filled luxuriously with burning logs. Panning downwards, dark-stained and polished timber floors were given colour and warmth by plush rugs.

I was in a choir that sang part of Handel's *Messiah* – another cultural shock for me. The evening concluded with mulled wine and fruit mince pies. I would visit the embassy twice more in four years, once to play squash at the invitation of the second secretary and on another occasion to take part in a cricket match on the expansive lawns.

We were generally made aware of the presence of any other Australians in the city through an informal expatriate grapevine. For a period in 1983 we were the only officially registered Australians in the country. The Australian government rented a house in *Shah re Nao* and an Australian diplomat visited twice a year. A secretary from Pakistan was sent (via Delhi) to Kabul and that person would look us up and, more often than not, we would invite them out for a meal. One Aussie diplomat, Jim, visited us a couple of times. He was personable and friendly. And, enjoyably for us, he had a frankness and humour which was recognizably Australian. The Afghan landlord of a house in *Shah re Nao*, which was rented by the Australian government, and used for one week two times a year, had a strict policy on alcohol which Jim did not appreciate. He was, according to Jim, 'like a bloody Tajik Methodist'.

At his request, we took Jim to the bazaars in the old city. We had an old Dodge which we had found in what was known as the IAM 'graveyard'. The 'graveyard' was a deposition of cars, mostly American, left by expatriates as they departed Afghanistan around the onset of war. The old Dodge enabled us to get around the city, and to shop and carry goods more easily than getting taxis or squeezing onto local trolley buses. Despite the restriction on our movements, and these were well prescribed in each direction of Kabul's perimeters, we savoured a certain freedom in these shopping expeditions. We had confidence in going to these places, knowing that we spoke enough Dari to explain ourselves to those around us.

The bazaars of the old city were found in the streets and narrow alleys leading off *Jadi Maiwand*, a long boulevard on the eastern side of the Kabul River. *Jadi Maiwand* began just beyond the point where two mountains bisected Kabul and ended at the *Jeshan* (exhibition) grounds to the east. On these fields, before the war, *Buzkashi* was played – a game where two teams of horsemen would try to wrest a headless goat from each other. Years later here, as well as on the soccer ground next to it, the Taliban would publicly excoriate, lash or execute persons accused of various crimes. The alleys off *Jadi Maiwand* haphazardly wound this way and that, and its bazaars were an improvisation of different coverings and shelters. The place felt ancient and indeed it was. Our induction to life in Afghanistan had included acquainting ourselves with some of its long history. And the history was here in front of us, in the continuation of a centuries-old trade in spices, dried fruits and carpets that had flourished when Afghanistan was the gateway between East and West Asia via the Silk Road. Trade and movement along the Silk Road had diminished sometime in the fifteenth century when the transporting of goods from Asia to Europe was achieved more quickly and economically via maritime routes. But, here at least, in the old city, the bazaars had remained largely unchanged and undeveloped because of the geographical remoteness of Kabul as well as the isolation brought about by war. And sadly, the same could be said of other aspects of everyday life, such as the healthcare system, which had remained undeveloped and in need.

The bazaars were visually arresting. Wooden bins sat side by side filled with green and black raisins (*keshmesh*), dried apricots and figs, and almonds, walnuts and pistachios. Each *dokandAr* (shopkeeper) meticulously presented their wares to somehow differentiate what they were selling from their neighbour even though the merchandise was identical. It was as if they were male bower birds building the most attractive nest in order to attract a mate. And we were the prospective female 'mates' drawn to the shop which looked the most well presented and clean.

Goods of a certain kind were sold in the same area. Even here in the competitive business of trade, the underlying communitarian influence on social life in Afghanistan, dictating how people were obliged to help each other, was evident. If a *dokandAr* didn't have exactly what you wanted he would often send his *shAgerd* (apprentice) or *mAwen* (assistant) to go and get the item from a neighbouring shopkeeper. Transactions were determined via handheld scales and abacuses (ancient counting beads),

Part One: Kabul 1983–1987

although small Japanese calculators were beginning to find their way into these places. Following the handover of money, more often than not, there was the offer of tea.

Some shops were more recognizable with doors and windows, while others were outside under tarpaulins. And some were no more than carts. It was like being at the yearly Royal Show at home, walking past the various stalls and being called out to along the way. And, if some shops were 'inside' and some were 'outside', there was also an inversion of what one might think of as an 'inside' thing versus an 'outside' thing. In my experience Persian carpets (*qAlinA*) were unambiguously an inside-the-house thing. Handmade in wool, cotton and sometimes silk, these carpets bore the weave patterns characteristic of the province from which they came. The combinations of these weave patterns, in deep reds, blues, browns and white, were exquisite. The family of a patient of mine from *Maimana* (a north-western province) later sold me one that had taken the family months to make. I paid them 30,000 Afs (about $300 Australian dollars). It was in the style known as *fil pAi* (elephant's foot) and had a dark-red pile with black and white oval designs (like an elephant's footprint but much smaller). Strangely, given the beauty and value of these carpets, and the meticulous work involved in their making, some were laid out inside the shops and some were laid out on the road. They were placed there as an 'ageing' technique; a sort of accelerated 'antiquitizing' carried out by the Kabul traffic which obligingly passed over them. The scene resembled public art. We found out later that Afghans would take even their most beautiful carpets to sit on at picnics. So, they were an 'outside' thing after all.

Moving further along these alleys one encountered small birds in wicker cages, blue glassware from Herat, cloth sold by Afghan Sikhs, tools (both ancient and modern), bikes from India and China, lamps, books, iron goods and the ubiquitous tea and kebab shops. There was an electrical bazaar across the river in *Shah re Nao* where I purchased a short-wave radio able to receive the BBC. A second-hand clothes bazaar, the size of a football field, sold Western clothes and shoes, donated from abroad, very cheaply. I once saw an Afghan boy wearing a black tee shirt, the front of which displayed the face of Bon Scott, the then lead singer of rock group AC/DC. Who was Bon Scott to this boy? It didn't matter. Kabul was still a crossroads; a place of cultural cross-pollination. The Silk Road may have become relatively dormant but remnants of shared DNA from those who had passed along its route long ago were still evident: Afghan boys with red hair and blue eyes; Afghan girls with hazel eyes and freckled faces. One could encounter almost anyone and anything in the bazaars of Kabul.

It was not just the exotic, dizzying environment in which these goods were sold but learning how to bargain, a cultural imperative, that was part of the bazaar experience. Bargaining was a ritual that had a prescribed preamble followed by certain assertions for you and your purchase inquiry to be respected. Observing a proper Afghan greeting required patience on our part as Australians, who were used to saying not much more than 'G'day'. The content of greetings generally went something like this: *Salaam Alekum* (Peace be with you), *Chetor asten?* (How are you?), *KhUb asten?* (Are you good?), *SehatetAn khUb* (How is your health?), *Famil chetor ast?* (How is the family?), *Jani jor?* (Are you well?) *Dega chetor asten?* (How are you again (really)?). This series of questions was complicated by the fact that both parties were asking them at approximately the same time. Answering and asking simultaneously took some getting used to. In the bazaar this set of greetings would be truncated depending on whether you knew the *dokandAr* but was, in turn, followed by these questions: *Quimatesh chand as?* (What is its price?) or *Chand Afghani?* (How many Afghanis? – the unit of currency, usually shortened to Afs), and following an answer from the shopkeeper,

PART ONE: KABUL 1983–1987

Quimat nes? (Isn't that expensive?), leading to *Akheresh chand as?* (What is your final price?). This set of questions and responses could go on, cyclically, for some time in order to reach an agreed price. But it was a necessary process if you sought any kind of acceptance as a foreigner.

Anne and I worked out fairly quickly that we did not want to spend much time in diplomatic circles, notwithstanding Jim's friendliness to us. But he was more a visitor to the place than we were. Nevertheless, with constraints on leaving the city and a nightly curfew, we did feel starved of opportunities for exercise and recreation. Sometime later we would become members of the United Nations (UN) staff house, a membership which was not that expensive and which enabled us to use the swimming pool and squash court – a single, free-standing building, which meant it was close to impossible in the cold Afghan winter to get any bounce out of the squash ball.

In recognition of a shared need for both exercise and recreation, games of volleyball and basketball, between small diverse groups of foreigners, took place informally and spontaneously on Friday mornings on courts in a park in *Shah re Nao*. We had an IAM 'team' whose members adapted to either game in a remarkable set of encounters with various national delegations; remarkable not for the quality of play but for *who* was playing. On one occasion, we played a game of basketball with some off-duty Marines from the US Embassy which, not surprisingly, they won convincingly. Another time we played against a team from the Turkish Embassy. More unusual though – let's call it bizarre – was a game of volleyball between our IAM team and members from the delegation of the Palestine Liberation Organization (PLO), which had been given diplomatic status by the Soviet-backed government in Kabul. At the time, the PLO was regarded by the West, and the various governments of our team members, as a terrorist organization. Nevertheless, there we were, members of a Christian NGO, trading serves, 'spikes' and 'digs' as well as broken conversation with our PLO opponents. We shared what we had in common: namely, that we were foreigners in a strange land. It was as if we found a fleeting companionship for the sadness and suffering that awaited all of us.

3

I finished four months of language study in early August 1983. I commenced work, now able to speak conversational Dari (or Farsi) quite well. But I would soon find out that to converse in and to teach in a language were two different undertakings. We had learned spoken Dari via a phonetic system known as Glassman script. Glassman script was an English text version of Afghan words with particular combinations of letters employed to indicate certain sounds. You will have noticed in some of the words that I have used so far there are capital letters in the middle of them. These denote the need for a certain pronunciation, such as '*A*' sounding like the 'o' in 'gone'. Similarly, 'gh' and 'kh' and 'q' have pronunciations not commonly used by native English speakers. I use Glassman script here because I am familiar with it, even though it has now been superseded by an international phonetic system. Learning Persian script, necessary for reading and writing, the practical need for which I discovered upon encountering case notes in the wards of *Wazir Akbar Khan* Hospital, would be another more significant and long-term challenge.

Physiotherapy School Kabul (PSK) was a grand name for something that didn't really exist except as an idea, an agreement between a ministry of the Afghan government and IAM. PSK was a subsidiary of another project called Cooperation for Orthopedic Rehabilitation (COR). The COR project was begun with a vision to provide so-called 'cold' surgery for persons whose ongoing orthopaedic problems were regarded as a lower priority than those requiring acute or emergency care. It was Joshua's vision. He was an orthopaedic surgeon originally from South India but latterly from Edinburgh, Scotland, where he gained his specialist training. He was my new boss.

Patients requiring cold surgery included those with skin ulceration and tissue erosion (sinuses) that had resulted from chronic infections such as osteomyelitis; persons whose previous fractures had not healed properly resulting in deformities of bones and joints; and those who had soft tissue contractures as a consequence of conditions such as poliomyelitis, leprosy and cerebral palsy. Almost always, the people presenting with these conditions had not had access to rehabilitation and this had contributed to the development of these tissue contractures and deformities of limbs and spine. And this was where physiotherapy came into it, to provide belated rehabilitation (often dramatically so) for the patients coming to the COR project. Joshua's original intention was to have physiotherapy services following the surgery he would perform for their previously untreated impairments. However, the Ministry of Public Health had requested him to also begin the training of physiotherapists, a related but separate task and burden. It was something he reluctantly took on in order to be able to exercise his surgical skills and pursue his vision of providing this much-needed cold orthopaedic surgery.

I had three tasks, each to be carried out concurrently. The first was to begin physiotherapy work in the wards of the *ShafA KhAna Wazir Akbar Khan* (WAK) hospital with the five students. The second was to establish and equip a physiotherapy department in order to start an outpatient clinic. The third was to prepare and teach a physiotherapy curriculum. This tripartite development plan would not last long.

WAK was part of a cluster of three hospitals, each adjacent to the others. The *Char Sad o Bestar* (400-bed) military hospital and the children's hospital were both within walking distance from WAK down an access road which branched off the main route from the city to the airport. Later, when it was the turn of the US and its allies to occupy the country, this location would become a frequent target for suicide bombers because it was not far from the diplomatic precinct.

The WAK hospital stood in spacious, park-like grounds, backgrounded by a grass slope which, in turn, marked the ascent of the hill *Tape Bibi Mahro*. Built in 1964 with funding from an Eastern European source, WAK stood four floors high. There was a large glass-panelled room, a solarium, at the end of each floor. Not surprisingly, these were converted into wards as the need for beds was paramount. It was essentially an orthopaedic emergency hospital but it had neither pharmacy nor X-ray departments – their arrival would take another two decades. In the north-eastern corner of the WAK site, about 120 metres from the hospital, lay a small two-storey building within which the COR project and later the physiotherapy school (PSK) were accommodated. This building had five main rooms (three downstairs and two upstairs) plus a storeroom. On its left sat a small windowless outbuilding, the hospital morgue. We came to understand why this was so suitably distant from the main hospital building. In summer, depending on the wind direction and whether there were electricity cuts, the smell of decaying bodies would make its way into the clinic itself.

Behind our clinic building, and further up the slope towards *Tape Bibi Mahro*, was a single-storey prosthetic and calliper workshop. In the other direction, to the front and left of the clinic, was a set of abandoned sheds, including an old vehicle repair workshop, complete with pit where mechanics had once stood, examining the underbellies of 'sick' vehicles. These sheds, unlike the main hospital building, were constructed with traditional daubed mud walls and roofs held together by a skeleton of wooden beams. It was this particular 'complex' which would later become, after considerable cleaning and renovation, the initial physiotherapy school: office, clinic and gymnasium. Before all that, the physiotherapy clinic was allocated – quite fairly – one room in the building used by the

COR project. It had a chair, a table, a filing cabinet and an examination couch. Upstairs, there was a makeshift classroom with some chairs, small writing desks and a blackboard on an easel.

The students of this first physiotherapy program were three young women and two men. One was of a mature age – at least for Afghanistan – in his mid to late thirties. They had been chosen well before I arrived in the country. Four of the five were nurses. The older man, Rahim, was from the police department. Each had been seconded to the physiotherapy program from different hospitals and *shObas* (departments) around the city.

I had begun my initial preparation for the physiotherapy program during language school by writing away for further information. I received three booklets from the World Confederation of Physical Therapy (WCPT) in London. They were 'A Guide to the training of physical therapists in developing countries', 'Basic equipment for rehabilitation centres' and 'Physical treatment in the treatment of leprosy (Hansen's disease)'. They were all very relevant pieces of information but the training guide confirmed some of my fears about the inadequacy of our proposed training program. Our course, as it stood, contained only a third of the content recommended by the WCPT for a basic physiotherapy course. In fact, we weren't training physiotherapists as much as physio aides. I put this to Joshua, who agreed and pointed to the possible future need for upgrading of the course. This was somewhat prophetic. I would find myself participating in the teaching of upgrading courses here twenty-five years later, as a participant in my own legacy.

My first encounter with the five physiotherapy students was disappointing. Where there had been such expectation, watching it fade as I talked made it doubly disappointing.

Part One: Kabul 1983–1987

Monday 15th August

What a discouraging day! In the morning a meeting with the five physiotherapy students to talk about the course proved a flop. What I mean is that their English speaking and reading ability proved much less than I had expected. Also, my inability to speak conceptually in Farsi became painfully apparent as the time went on, punctuated by awkward silences and 'Please say it again'.

The syllabuses which I had prepared for the five subjects were discreetly put in storage. It's back to the drawing board.

I had to quickly shift my focus to working with these students in the wards of the WAK hospital. The WAK was built with a Western design. The Persian term for hospital, *ShafA KhAna*, translates as 'house of healing'. Afghanistan was a place where personal security had for centuries been provided by family and clan rather than by civil agencies, such as a police force or army. The *house*, in Afghan consciousness, was therefore a place of personal safety and security, and a means of having some control over one's interactions with a harsh and sometimes unpredictable world. In Afghanistan it was both refuge and a means to offer hospitality, an obligation at the core of Afghan culture. *ShafA KhAna e Wazir Akbar Khan* seemed neither house-like nor a place of healing. The WAK hospital should have been more familiar to me as a healthcare professional than the old bazaars of Kabul, but it wasn't. It was a forbidding place.

The war which surrounded and periodically penetrated Kabul was often heard – 'Kabul thunder' we called it – but it was not always seen. At least not directly, since we saw the artefacts of war daily in the ubiquitousness of military personnel, with trucks and tanks on the ground and the feared helicopter gunships in the sky. Every Afghan was touched by the war. Friends or relatives were taken, either away to fight or to be brought back, dead or injured, as casualties of it. In the wards of

WAK I was forcibly introduced to it: seeing, touching and even smelling the war through its victims. The violence outside Kabul was no longer hidden by the landscape. WAK may not have been a theatre of war itself, but it was a theatre for watching what the war did to people. Played out on its stage were a bewilderment of strange practices, general misfortune and utter misery.

Despite my relative inexperience – three years of professional practice – I had encountered confronting situations at home before, such as the teenager who had lost most of his hands and feet following meningococcal disease. I had also worked with patients with a host of other conditions resulting from orthopaedic or neurological disease or trauma. So, it wasn't that I was particularly squeamish. What I found difficult here was the condition in which most patients presented.

The entrance foyer at WAK would frequently be choked with waiting patients, laid out on stretchers. The remoteness of the villages, exacerbated by poor roads and lack of transport to the city, was made even worse by the fighting, resulting in delayed treatment. The canvas of the stretchers on which patients lay was a montage of red, yellow, green and brown: the variegated colours of trauma, infection and dirt. Bandages glistened with malevolent moisture. The moaning of distressed patients was heard, only just before the pungent, collective smell of their wounds; wounds that had been festering for days or weeks. It was sometimes an effort of will to enter further in, and not turn around, to retreat to the relative sanctuary of our clinic. One time a Russian tank 'T-boned' a bus full of Afghan families on their way to the city. They were crammed in as usual. No one was sure whether this was a deliberate act or a traffic accident from hell. And I did not inquire further. A triage took place. The bodies, around forty of them, were carried in a procession past our clinic to the morgue while the injured were taken into WAK. We listened to loud wailing of the shocked and grieving families and friends. Wailing was an unnerving and unfamiliar sound for us foreigners. But what we did recognize was the thick, impotent anger that surfaced in our colleagues and students; an anger which was normally well camouflaged.

I tried to put my personal difficulties in coping aside by comparing my situation with the misery of so many of the boys and girls, and men and women, who lay in the wards with legs and arms shattered by bullets and mines. Here were the results of the Kabul thunder that we heard as we lay in our beds each night. I was shocked by what I found in the wards.

> **Saturday 27th August**
>
> A young girl covered with shrapnel wounds and a teenage boy aged about 14, with an above-knee amputation of his left leg and with a pseudarthrosis of his left elbow joint, 'replacing' the real one which was blown away: these are my end of day impressions that I bring home after work today. Of course, there are so many more. Some of the staff struggle hard. Others, unfortunately, have given up. This is understandable; their hopelessness, I mean. But it is to the detriment of those needing care.

I would give up, myself, just a few months later – at least on my attempts to work in the wards of WAK. In my observation of staff 'giving up', I did not yet appreciate the difference in choices available to me and my Afghan colleagues. That we foreigners lived with different realities than the locals I knew on some rational level. But I did not understand what it meant to face all this mayhem and suffering in their shoes. I had stopped trying to give lectures in Dari. It would be another three months before we were able to employ an interpreter. The war always affected plans and people adversely.

So far in the clinic I had not been short of patients. From the very poor who sat waiting on the verge of the dirt road outside the clinic to staff from various embassies, they came because they had heard about a new foreigner helping people with disabilities. Acting on a word-of-mouth referral, I visited a young man about my age on several occasions at his family house. Hamid had been in the army but was now discharged from it and also from his acute medical care. Hamid had been shot in the spine and his spinal cord had been transected at the level of the eighth thoracic vertebra. This left him with paralysis of the lower limbs plus much of his truncal musculature. All he had left with respect to muscle power was the use of his arms. He had been issued with an enormous (and heavy) set of metal callipers and waistband. I worked with him, strengthening his upper limbs and giving him standing practice in a set of home-made parallel bars. Hamid enjoyed the company. Working hard, we were still able to joke and laugh together, even in the midst of his devastation and the fact that walking in his callipers was not going to happen. Sometime later he painted a clay pot as a gift for me, with intricate designs employing the favoured Afghan colours of blue, green and white trim. It sat on the mantelpiece at home back in Adelaide for several years until it was accidentally knocked over by one of our children and fell onto the bricks of the fireplace below. I felt the loss of that hand-painted pot. It had shattered as quickly and easily as Hamid's life had those many years before. We were unable to put the pieces back together.

4

Tuesday 27th September

A low treatment table and metal grating were installed in the physio room today. The table still requires a wooden base and a mattress but even the arrival of this partly finished equipment was an encouragement.

Each afternoon now I am attempting to get an outpatient clinic underway in this physiotherapy room in the COR building. In the mornings my efforts are being directed at becoming involved with inpatient treatment and gradually getting the students caseloads of their own. This would seem to be a priority.

Unfortunately, doctors are not used to physiotherapists working in the wards and therefore don't refer patients for physiotherapy. They don't see the need. They tell the patient to move the relevant part and when the patient is unable or unwilling he or she is classified as lazy. There is much breaking of new ground to be done here.

There is also the question of what relationship I should have with the 'six-week' trained 'physios' who have a department in the hospital. These folk never enter the wards perhaps feeling that apart from the application of hot packs, diathermy and other machines, they have no contribution to make. This department has certainly been 'written off' by those who framed the present physiotherapy course. This seems a real pity and makes for a very confusing situation in the hospital. That is, one group (i.e. myself and the students) working only in the wards and even then only spasmodically because of limited acceptance. The other group, totally separate, works in their own department, physio aides rather than physiotherapists, never leaving it.

Dividing my time between the clinic and the hospital wards, I began by making, altering or buying materials in order to fashion exercise equipment for the clinic. Over one weekend Anne and I made some sandbag weights, using sand from the banks of the Kabul River near our house in *KArte Seh*. Things were moving slowly.

The case notes were, naturally enough, written in Farsi and this was unintelligible to me. There was, therefore, a lack of clarity regarding the diagnosis or current management plan for patients. What I also struggled with was the mystery of what was going on in the wards. Orthopaedic inpatient physiotherapy is essentially based on protocols, often post-surgical ones, such as when it is safe to move joints or limbs, actively or passively, and when it is safe to stand and walk with patients following fractures or surgery to stabilize fractures. Physiotherapy in this context requires – and generally works within – clear guidelines. I had my books, which told me when fractures would unite and later consolidate, but that wasn't sufficient for working in orthopaedic wards where the management was a mystery. You might be able to by chance ask a doctor at the bedside if it was appropriate to get a patient up on crutches (if they had some – they had to get relatives to purchase these in the bazaar – and there were no children's crutches) but that was different to saying to students, with any confidence, 'This is what we do in this case – I will show you now how to do it'.

Added to this, there was also 'an elephant in the wards' (also expressed in the diary entry above): namely, the absence of the physiotherapists from the hospital's own department in the hospitals wards. The existing WAK physiotherapy department consisted of a small number of therapists who had reputedly received six weeks' training in Russia. However, none of these therapists were selected for this first physiotherapy course. I was never able to find out *why*. I did visit there once, met these therapists and saw a room with a line of beds with patients lying on them. There were hot packs, a diathermy unit and an ultrasound machine. There was no exercise equipment or evidence of exercise that I could see. I was told that these therapists did not go into the wards but instead saw patients here in their department. Conversely, I and my five students worked away from this group in the wards. How sensible it would have been to spend more time with the WAK 'physios'; to drink tea with them and discuss, even in the light of their disappointment over non-selection for our course, how we might work together. But I was, myself, in many ways just a *juwAn* (a youth). Instead, I fell in line with Joshua's advice to me, which was to 'work in parallel' – a euphemism for don't get too involved with the politics behind their non-selection for your course.

If the foyer of the hospital could be intimidating, then the shock was not lessened upon entering the wards. They were Spartan. The bare walls, painted *operating theatre green*, were now discoloured as though the Kabul traffic had also driven over them. The hubbub of staff, patients and relatives calling out to each other echoed down the corridors. A din added to by spindly, metal beds scraping granite floors and clanking against metal lockers. It was not a place that I would have wanted to find myself in as a patient.

The wards were not clean.

Tuesday 4th October

The wards in Wazir Akbar Khan are dirty. Helping a doctor dress a patient's leg today, I was surprised to see two cockroaches crawl out from underneath the bandage. In another instance a patient directed my attention to his locker. Inside it was a thriving colony of cockroaches crawling, as they pleased, over food, medicine and personal articles.

Sheets are usually changed weekly and, in many instances, they are soiled, or at least become very dirty before the week is up. One can't blame the staff entirely. There is an attitude of doing only what is strictly one's job. Patients undoubtedly suffer because of this. However, generally resources are low and this fact severely limits the level of patient treatment ... It is also interesting to note how medicinal prescriptions are filled here. The doctor writes a prescription for whatever drug is required and the patient's relatives take it to the bazaar to get it filled. Having brought it back, the medicine sometimes just sits in the patient's bedside cupboard. This is because the patients, especially if it is an injection, don't know how to take it and sometimes the nurses are unaware that the patient has this medicine. After all, the doctor gives the prescription directly to the patient ... there is a trolley from which some medicines and injections are distributed. I'm not sure yet why some tablets and injections are given this way and others procured in the way I've described above. What I am about to say sounds incredulous, but it is true. Usually the nurse stands at the door of the patients' room and cries 'Ki pEchkorI dAra?' which means 'Who is having injections?' If the patient is alert and aware then the problem is not so acute; if not then it is a little more serious as he or she will miss out.

Without diary entries, I doubt that I would trust my memories, even if I no longer want to trust the conclusions I appear to have made from them. It's one problem incurred by reading one's own words written decades ago. But there they stand, expressing my thoughts at that time: I was more judgmental then than I am now, Ocie. Nevertheless, behind these puzzling or, at times, even comical healthcare practices, there was ubiquitous, ongoing suffering. Some images burn themselves into memory. One is the face of a young boy, nine or ten years of age, his dark, shifting eyes, wide with fear and pain, lying in bed with hips and knees elevated by pillows. He had septic arthritis of both hips. A doctor leaned towards me and said matter-of-factly, 'He will be dead in another two days'. How could the losing of a young life be so casually observed? Was it the apparently disinterested manner in which it was said which so disconcerted me? Or, was it the daily juxtaposition of life with death, so familiar and exhausting to Afghans, which I did not understand?

The following year, while on holidays in Nepal – it was wise policy that we had to exit the country for our leave, given that we were confined to Kabul with its multiple restrictions – Anne and I visited a small hospital in a rural town called Tansen. After our tour the medical officer said, 'What do you think of our hospital?' I was overwhelmingly impressed with how clean and orderly it was and told him so. The doctor laughed and said, 'That is not what our guests usually say. Most people would say the opposite or, at best, "How rustic this place is!"'. We had come from Kabul and not from Australia, recently at least.

Joshua was a shy man and he had learned his own strategies, as project director, for dealing with the political machinations and changing demands of the Ministry of Public Health. I was naïve. Joshua was around fourteen years older than me and was used to, even inured to, ways of doing things in this part of the world. He once told me, making clear the sardonic humour of what he was about to say, that there was no corruption in India, as it had not been defined as such yet. Joshua had therefore learned to be suspicious and guarded in his decision-making. He had a reputation for being difficult to work with. It was suggested to me one day that some of this may have been the result of racism he experienced during his specialist training in the UK. In any case, there was a recurring theme in our meetings. When I detailed my frustrations, he would respond along the lines of, 'You think you have problems?' What he said, from his experiences as project director, was probably true but it didn't offer me much in the way of encouragement.

There was no readily available way, at least that I could think of, to demonstrate the effectiveness of physiotherapy in the wards, especially in relation to introducing mobilization and exercise in patient management. Physiotherapy and its methods, particularly active exercise, did not fit well with an Afghan approach to healthcare which emphasized passively administered medicines and visible procedures. Even Joshua, when we were discussing what fees (if any) patients should be charged for physiotherapy consultations in our clinic, remarked with a suppressed laugh how difficult it would be to ask people to pay 'just to be told to move or straighten their knee'. I knew then, in the matter of introducing active physiotherapy in the WAK wards, that I was largely on my own.

Ocie, I once saw a documentary about some wildlife researchers who were studying brown (grizzly) bears in a remote Alaskan wilderness. They were 'dropped in' to this lonely place by a seaplane landing on a pristine, glacier-fed lake. Over a period of several months, they observed at close quarters the social and hunting behaviours of these fascinating but physically intimidating creatures. They were soon able to name and recognize each of the bears, together with their dispositions and habits. What so intrigued me was how these bears would go about their daily activities seemingly oblivious to the presence of these foreign observers who were in such close proximity, often just metres away. This was what it was like for me working over these months in the wards at WAK. I was seen and tolerated but, for the most part, I was just as foreign to the staff on the wards as were the wildlife researchers to the bears. Like the researchers, I was perceived to be neither harmful nor threatening. And so, I became part of the scenery. The doctors and nursing staff mostly went about their business as though I was not there. Although, unlike the bears, who may or may not have communicated their impressions of the human observers to each other, I did once hear a doctor say to another, '*Farsisha shirin ast*' (which literally translates as 'His Farsi is sweet'). However, this was only because I had used *Lutfan* (please) and *ShumA* (you) when I had asked a patient to lift her leg off the bed. Staff did not

Part One: Kabul 1983-1987

generally use *Lutfan*. And they employed the singular *Tu* (you) rather than the more polite plural *ShumA*. *Tu* implied familiarity of the subject and an authority of the speaker, emphasizing that the patients were more on the level of children. And so, even this was less a compliment about my language and more just another marker of my foreignness.

Arguably, I understood less about what I was observing in WAK than those wildlife researchers did of the Alaskan bears they studied so closely. It was like a shadow play. I saw the various characters and their actions in WAK's daily drama like shadows on a curtain. Their actions were visible but the motivations and intent behind them remained largely hidden from me.

A retired British orthopaedic surgeon by the name of Gerald Golden arrived, almost unannounced, and became involved in the work of COR and PSK. He was very supportive of me, and knowledgeable concerning physiotherapy. Gerald was, remarkably, for someone choosing to come and work in Afghanistan, in his early eighties. And both his experience and longevity were on display when he told me he was a peer, and encourager, of the person in the UK who founded the Stoke Mandeville Hospital for rehabilitation of persons with spinal injuries. This was just after the Second World War. Stoke Mandeville was well known not just for its breakthrough rehabilitation methods but for being among the first healthcare institutions to demonstrably value the team approach of doctors, nurses, physiotherapists, occupational therapists and others. The textbook I had brought from Australia by Ida Bromley on rehabilitation following spinal injury was based on the Stoke Mandeville experience. I wished that I could have also brought their ethos of team work and collaboration with me.

Gerald would write to me some three years later regarding the continuing challenge of establishing physiotherapy in the Afghan health system.

PSK

22nd November, 1987

Dear Ian,

We were very sad to receive your cable telling of your further delay of three months on medical grounds. Together with your colleagues here I greatly hope that you will continue to progress and will be able to return in January. No doubt you are aware of the date when your present visa expires. You are much needed here. Hope Anne and the children are doing well …

One of my chief matters for concern is how to publicize the need for physiotherapy in every branch of medicine and surgery among the young Afghan doctors and nurses. This is needed as much as the provision of well-trained therapists. At present very few of the doctors and nurses have any conception of the position occupied by physiotherapists and occ. therapists in the Western world, and indeed in many other developing countries.

The new school buildings are growing rapidly. … It will be a very substantial and well-planned base for your work – in sharp contrast to the present state of gross overcrowding and shortages.

Looking forward to seeing you both in January. With affection and prayer, Gerald

In 1983 I saw Gerald as someone in turbulent water sees a lifejacket. I spoke earnestly with him about the difficulties I faced and what I thought needed to change. He listened attentively before responding, 'Ian, it is you that has to change'. I had no idea what he was talking about. His words were as intelligible to me as the grunting of a bear foraging in the Alaskan wilderness.

5

During this period, having been in the wards of WAK in the mornings, I worked each afternoon to get an outpatient clinic underway in the small room that had been allocated for physiotherapy in the COR building. Here, I was more 'on my turf' and felt, somewhat perversely, that I could act more properly out of my training and its professional standards. It *was* like acting, too. Commonly, I did not know what I was really doing. I had never, to cite one example, encountered the dreaded disease of poliomyelitis because it had been eradicated in Australia in the 1950s. Parents would bring their children, often just toddlers or babies, each with a different combination of flaccid limbs and paralysed muscles. Sometimes it was just one limb, an arm or a leg, which was affected. Other times the disease had affected several limbs and even included the truncal muscles, which made the level of disability very severe. The parents would say something like, 'My child was sick with a fever and now this. Will they get better?' Sadly, once this stage of impairment had been reached there was usually little recovery in the function of the muscle and it was now a matter, therapeutically speaking, of maximizing limb function and preventing later onset of even more debilitating deformity, through splinting and the use of callipers. Older children and adults who had contracted polio earlier in their lives, and who had not had access to rehabilitation, presented with debilitating tissue contractures which had developed over time. These contractures resulted in severe physical, and socially isolating, deformities. This was all new physiotherapy territory for me and it took some scrambling on my part to develop even a basic level of competence and confidence to assess and treat these patients, let alone teach others to do so. I continued to feel isolated and somewhat of an impostor. I had no physiotherapy peers to discuss these challenges with, not even by phone.

The fighting not only killed or maimed people, it also delayed or halted much-needed public health programs such as polio vaccination. In rural areas the war made the existing isolation and remoteness from services worse. It was dangerous to travel by public roads. For indigent and remote villagers, seeking reliable healthcare was almost impossible. Even in the relative safety of the capital, the uncertain nature and general scarcity of the electricity supply affected health and healthcare, making it harder, for example, to safely store vaccinations. I saw some children, brought to me in the clinic, who had received vaccinations for polio but because these had not been adequately stored, the children contracted the disease anyway. Part of me was traumatized and near defeat: a selfish thing to say in the context of the suffering around us. But we weren't quarantined from the misery which accompanied almost every person to the clinic.

I remember seeing them through the window; a father and son coming down the dirt track towards the clinic. It was late afternoon and I was writing at my desk. It was not an uncommon sight; a patient being piggy-backed by a friend or relative. There were few wheelchairs then and the terrain of ordinary thoroughfares, potholed dirt roads, broken paths and *joies* (open ditches carrying waste water around a metre deep on the sides of most roads), did not lend themselves to making much progress with them. Most people simply carried their disabled. They were first seen by my boss, Joshua, who then brought them in to me. 'Can you help us?' asked the father. Shifting my gaze to the son, a boy of about eight or nine, I saw a face pockmarked by small, partially healed shrapnel wounds, some still exuding pus. One eye had been removed. The other, although present, was blind. This had taken place when he had unknowingly come across and picked up an unexploded shell.

It was commonly suggested at that time that these were 'toy bombs': small bombs deliberately camouflaged and hidden in the guise of children's toys. Unbelievable? Shocking? Certainly. But we were becoming inured to such possibilities.

Like raising a curtain, the boy's father lifted off his son's overly large coat, and only now did my eyes take in the full extent of this tragedy: both of his hands had also been blown off and his arms had been amputated just below the elbows. The boy did not offer a word or a sound. His face was impassive. He sat quite still. It was as if he were somewhere distant within his body. He was alive and conscious but was so far in retreat that he could not be summoned. Touch and sight, two of the most important means by which we function in and connect with this world, were inexorably gone. The loss of one or another would be tragic enough; the combination of the two was a catastrophe.

Revered religious figures, especially in Asia, are often celebrated for their capacity to be silent and still; qualities considered as the outward expressions of an inner peace. I suspect that the silent stillness of this boy's countenance was born of terror. To live in Afghanistan as a poor person – and most people are indigent – is to live in a severe world. Each morning we would pass the day labourers who would congregate near *Pul e Surkh* (the Red Bridge) not far from where we lived in *KArte Seh*, hoping to be chosen to work for the day, in order to have food for the evening: an ancient, biblical image still played out in twentieth-century Afghanistan. For others, the more pressing need was to evade the ongoing and ubiquitous violence enveloping them. This boy had not managed to do that. His severe world had now become a strange and hostile one. The catastrophic combination of his losses, eyesight and touch, made this certain. He could not hold a cane and so could not go outside by himself lest he fall into a *joie*. He could not feed himself. He could not wash or toilet himself. He could not dress himself. He could not pick anything up, to feel and explore with the sensibility of turning fingers. One could go on. He was utterly powerless and had understandably retreated as far into himself as he could, his old world now totally unmade and his new one intimidating and hostile.

A French philosopher by the name of Emanuel Levinas once wrote, somewhat enigmatically, 'The face speaks'. And that is just what this boy's face did. In its silence and inscrutability, his face called us to respond. We were the foreigners, but he was the stranger in need of hospitality. Joshua and I stood there, impotent. Neither we nor our small orthopaedic workshop at that time had anything to offer the boy or his father that would help him use what was left of his arms. We referred them to the blind school which we knew about. The father simply thanked us, picked the boy up, put him on his back and left; he carried him back down the road to an unknown place, a family somewhere, which would that night receive further disappointment. We stood wordlessly on the porch together and watched them go back down the gravel road. It was as if we were consoling each other over what we had just witnessed.

In the ensuing months and years, more than one Afghan would furtively confide to me that, because of the ongoing Russian occupation, it no longer felt like *their* country any more. They were like strangers in their own land. I began to understand that we can each be strangers and we can each be hosts – wherever we are.

Notwithstanding my own sense of inadequacy, it became increasingly clear just how important the contribution of physiotherapy could be to the lives of Afghans. I was beginning to develop passion and conviction for this task of developing physiotherapy and what it could offer the country.

PART ONE: KABUL 1983–1987

Ocie, the whole thing – coming to Afghanistan – really started with your Ma. She had always been one for adventure. After graduating as a nurse midwife she had set off to work on Saibai Island, a remote settlement in the Torres Strait, at the northernmost tip of Australia. On her return to Adelaide our paths fortunately crossed and, just over a year later in October 1981, they joined. One day not so long after our marriage, Anne suggested, in harmless conversation, that we consider contributing our skills in some, but no particular, under-resourced place in the world. We were part of a small Christian community at the time, living in an area in Port Adelaide of low socio-economic status, alongside and supporting people who were socially disadvantaged and isolated. Several of these people lived in local boarding houses in the Port and Semaphore area. Government policy had recently been changed to move people with mental health problems out of institutional care and into the community. One unintended consequence of this was that these people, under-resourced and often lacking social support, naturally found the cheapest accommodation available. This was in boarding houses, which in their heyday were holiday destinations for those who wished to sojourn by the beach but were now more often like ghettos. They provided basic food and shelter requirements but turned residents out each day to wander the local streets and shops. We had gotten to know a number of the boarding-house residents. We visited them and provided some opportunities for shared meals and company.

Anne and I turned towards the idea that our healthcare training, together with our shared convictions about the nature of disadvantage, and the need of vulnerable people for social justice, should be harnessed and applied in some place where healthcare was even less accessible for ordinary people. Sometimes it's the singular, innocuous comment that'll slip under your guard and make its mark. Anne's did. About fourteen months later we found ourselves en route to Afghanistan: an Afghanistan we knew very little about.

Our departure, at the beginning of 1983, fell in the middle of the cricket season, and I recall my teammates from the Port Adelaide Uniting Church cricket team telling me that they did not consider our going to Afghanistan, and its Russian war, a good idea at all. This grade of cricket had many ageing warriors who played on well into their 40s and beyond. 'Stiddo', my captain coach, was one of these. He declared, in the manner of a mentor, 'The Russians are there you know. That means you're going behind the Iron Curtain. You're out of reach then, you know, anything could happen!' His words were an amplified version of the questions and concerns our parents also had but which they admirably, even courageously, kept in check and largely to themselves.

The name for physiotherapy used by Afghans was *massAge*. It was only an approximation as most Afghans had not heard of physiotherapy. Like other things the English term 'massage' had been adopted into Dari. There were other examples of this commandeering of English. For example, *esh-teer-ing* was the steering wheel on a car and *lAshtique* was elastic. *MassAge* also reinforced the particular understanding of physiotherapy as a thing you had done to you; a passive rather than active encounter.

There were physiotherapy-like traditional physical methods for pain relief in Afghan culture. One was known as *dAgh*, which involved the application of burning pitch onto the skin over a painful area. It functioned as a kind of *counter irritation*; a principle used in the application of some physiotherapy modalities too. But *dAgh* was very harsh and I remember silently gasping at the extent of some of the scars that I saw on skin after this procedure. In the villages there were also 'bone setters'. They would align and, at times, even refracture bones in order to reset them.

The results could be either okay or disastrous for the patient, depending on the location and nature of the fracture. I encountered some dramatic limb deformities and loss of function in patients as a consequence of this practice.

My teaching problems, therefore, did not start with having to decide what to teach and finish with the language challenge of how to teach it. There was a wider problem of orientation: how to introduce physiotherapy in a medical system which had little knowledge of what it offered and to a society which had distinctive and definite cultural beliefs about the nature of health and disease. Layered upon the challenge was the fact that the English of these Afghan physiotherapy students was, at that time at least, more limited than my Farsi. Even though I had reached an adequate conversational language level it was not sufficient for teaching. There was also an issue of endurance. Talking for ten minutes in Farsi required significant concentration and expenditure of my cognitive resources for the right words and right way of putting sentences together. After an hour or more, and certainly well before the end of the day, my Farsi would fragment with fatigue.

When I did find myself on familiar clinical ground, I was so concerned with finally appearing competent and knowledgeable to my students that I managed to turn it into a 'non-teaching' situation. Or, should I say, I taught what I did not intend to teach. Because I was *here* in the clinic and not *there* in the WAK wards, I spoke and acted more dogmatically than I otherwise would have. This time it was my students and patients who observed *me* and could only wonder at the thinking hidden behind my words and actions.

An Afghan man in his mid forties, late middle age in Afghanistan at that time, was referred to me because of pain and stiffness resulting from osteoarthritic change in his knees. The diagnosis was plain enough. Indeed, so was the intended physiotherapy course of action in terms of exercises and advice. I was not prepared, however, for the questions he began to ask me regarding the types of food he would or would not be allowed to eat: could he eat tomatoes, yoghurt or watermelon? One of my students hastily explained to me that in Afghan culture there was a system of 'hot' and 'cold' foods (not related to their temperature) and that these had different perceived effects on the body during sickness or ill health. Various foods should not be eaten at certain times. For example, one didn't eat 'hot' foods when you had a fever. It is a system which I later learned has its origins in Ayurvedic medicine. I listened to this and assured the man that, apart from having a balanced diet, not an easy thing to achieve in Afghanistan for most people, there was no evidence that abstinence from certain foods would play a major role in his recovery. Appropriate exercise and avoiding certain postures of the knees were much more important. My best recommendation to him was to follow the strengthening exercises and postural advice, which primarily was that he not sit with his buttocks on his heels during *namAz* (prayer) five times a day. The look let me know that the initial awe he had in seeing a foreign health worker had just deflated like a punctured bike tyre. Even the student observing this session was caught between two loyalties: respecting her teacher and, at the same time, coping with his ignorance as a foreigner in this matter.

I had requested early on that for six months I be allowed to work without having to prepare and deliver lectures. I hoped that progress in two of the three areas (starting up a clinic and learning to work in the wards of WAK) would be made and the physiotherapy course could start on a better footing. I felt sad for the students. They had waited many months for this new direction in their lives and work to begin. And, more often than not during this time, they had been at a loose end, without instruction or encouragement. My eventual arrival and commencement of work had so far not demonstrably changed this for the better.

6

The energy for work was always in competition with that required to cope with the state of our health. In a city of wells, many of which were not deep and coalesced with seepage from human waste pits, finding clean water for drinking, without either having to boil it or use iodine tablets, was a challenge. Similarly, with the unreliability and shortage of electricity, keeping food safely in a fridge could not be assumed. To make a mistake or to be careless in consuming water or food inevitably led to some form of gastroenteritis. Anne had been troubled since beginning language school by stomach upsets and diarrhoea. She had been put on Flagyl and Ampicillin in anticipation of it being amoebic dysentery. A joke did the rounds of the expatriate community: 'There are two kinds of cross-cultural workers – those that know they have amoeba and those that don't.'

There were choices to be made about what you would eat or drink when you were a guest at an Afghan's house. And this was not easy to do without giving offence. Nevertheless, Anne and I enjoyed being invited to eat with Afghans. We had to learn, however, to eat more slowly than we were used to. If your plate appeared empty or nearing that state, then the words '*Ech nAn naKhOrdEn!*' (You haven't eaten anything!) would be exclaimed – paradoxical, given that you had just eaten the first serving – and another small mountain of *pillau* (a rice dish with slivers of carrots, raisins and meat, usually chicken or lamb) would be heaped back onto it.

My diary records bouts of food poisoning (diarrhoea, stomach cramps and vomiting) on August 31st, September 11th and 15th. This continued episodically:

Friday 7th October

My stomach has been knotted last night in spasm, my bowels working every twenty minutes. During the night hours I hardly knew where to put myself. Most unpleasant to say the least. This has been a strangely frequent occurrence in the last month. I had been largely free of such trouble in the previous nine months.

Pain is such a strange phenomenon. Sometimes it is like a drug which enables one to see new perspectives: that is to leave one's sense of well-being and appreciate again the suffering of others. Security is a great anaesthetic to the appreciation of others' need. It seems paradoxical but sometimes I feel that when all is 'going well' with me then I'm in greatest danger of abandoning my involvement in God's plan both for me and for the world. As much as I have hated the last 24 hours, if it redirects some of my priorities and actions then it will have been not a totally senseless experience.

As you can see, Ocie, I used to think about my life and its priorities during these difficult times. I think reflection is a good thing and I hope you will find time to do this in your life. I had also begun to wonder whether some of these stomach episodes were related to the tensions at work. It is equally true, then, to say that I sought ways to escape the tensions and not just find meaning in them.

Tuesday 18th October

Stomach ache woke me again last night at about 3.15am forcing me to spend the time until morning engaged in reading 'The Code of the Woosters' by P.G. Wodehouse. It may be nonsense but his writing is wonderfully funny.

Over time I would read a lot of P.G. Wodehouse in order to relax both my thoughts and the various muscles of my alimentary system.

However, even in Wodehouse's idyllic world, which avoided real life altogether (to use his words), applications to life in Afghanistan, and the harsh experiences it offered, were never far away:

> It was a confusion of ideas between him and one of the lions he was hunting in Kenya that had caused A.B. Spottsworth to make the obituary column. He thought the lion was dead, and the lion thought it wasn't. (*Ring for Jeeves* 1953)

At times it seemed that the comic Wodehouse I read at night mirrored my work by day. The staff from the wards at WAK, had they the chance to come over and watch me, might have been gratified to know that, here in the clinic, I could also perform the comical in healthcare. One morning I asked a patient, a man complaining of buttock pain, to take off his pants and get onto the treatment bed. I took the opportunity to momentarily write down some details of his history. On turning around, I saw that the patient was not lying or sitting but *standing* on the examination table. Filling my immediate horizon, about a foot and a half away, was a bared Afghan bottom. And this bottom was not merely bared. A thin, rustic hand held each buttock, and had spread them as quickly as a rumour. Having accomplished this, one hand was now redeployed and pointed to a spot further inwards – his anus – as the source of his symptoms. With a now familiar resignation regarding the ups and downs in my ability to communicate in Farsi, I asked him to come down from his lofty standing position on the treatment couch. We established that his problem had more to do with haemorrhoids than referred pain from his back and I sent him back to the doctor.

Slowly, I pieced together a clinic with the help of local Afghan employees. Anne had helped me make some weights and slings. A low treatment bed with overhead grating – to suspend ropes and take the weight of weakened or paralysed limbs during exercise – was made in the bazaar and installed in the room. The first electrical physiotherapy equipment arrived on November 10th, three months after commencing work. It consisted of refurbished ultrasound and short-wave diathermy machines from America, one of each. They each used different voltages, 110 and not 220. It would take another couple of months before we could find an appropriate electrical socket for the transformer. This delay was another example of what Kabul's isolation entailed in those days. Things moved slowly for various reasons, small and large. We continued to get things made locally.

> **Monday 28th November**
>
> Accompanied by Mahmoud Ali, a new employee of COR ... I went down to the Irongari (iron bazaar) off Jadi Maiwand (the main thoroughfare through the 'old city'). This is a bazaar where all kinds of iron implements are made such as spades, chains, axe heads, and other implements which I did not recognize. The bazaar is about 200 metres long down both sides of a winding dirt alley. In this part of the city the streets are quite crowded. ShAgerDA (apprentices) assist their masters, other boys play, or fight, among themselves; a favourite pastime of Afghan children. Soldiers patrol, other folk like ourselves but not quite like us, for foreigners don't come often here under the present circumstances, browse and shop. Our task today was to pick up some pulleys, 'S' hooks, handles and 'D' rings that one khalifa (tradesman) had made for me. These were items for exercise equipment.

Mahmoud Ali now acted as interpreter in the classroom. I had recommenced, despite my earlier request to be relieved of lecture delivery, some classwork teaching with the help of my language teacher who provided good translations of lectures. Joshua had continued in the previous two months with periodic anatomy and physiology lectures.

Mahmoud Ali interpreted in the clinic (as needed). But his interpreting was just as valuable in the bazaars, in describing some of the weird and wonderful things we would ask *khalifas* to make for our physiotherapy department. 'S' hooks and 'D' rings were not as unusual as some other items. And their ingenuity was further on display when we asked them to make things of which they had little or no conception. A wobble board is a circular disc, big enough to stand on, which has a hemispherical 'ball', underneath, as its base. As rehabilitation equipment, it is designed to present an intentionally unstable surface which requires the person standing on it to constantly regain, and therefore retrain, their balance. For the carpenter commissioned to make a wobble board for us, it could have been a piece of abstract art for its apparent lack of use or application in the life he knew. And yet, I have a picture of him proudly holding his finished product. He stands smiling, still not really knowing much about the product he had skilfully made. I, on the other hand, had a growing vision for the 'finished product' regarding the physiotherapy course but, unlike the carpenter, less idea or skill on how to make it happen.

The following sequence of diary entries documented my participation at the other end of the 'developing physiotherapy' spectrum.

Saturday 1st October

This morning I attended a four-hour meeting convened to discuss the building of a 900-bed rehabilitation centre. I had designed a physiotherapy department of sorts and answered questions on this. During the meeting I had mentioned the need for an occupational therapy unit. I was therefore asked on the spot to tell the group what such a department required in its construction. How interesting it was to sit there and design an OT department off the top of my head! OTs forgive me!

Sunday 13th November

I attended a meeting today with Joshua and Gerald at the university where we were to advise on the setting up of a traumatology unit. I met my first Russian advisor, whose proposal, after careful consideration, we dismissed. This was for a good reason. He required a large section of this unit as a changing room for sports, for his medical students. It was thought that an outpatient department for patients might be, overall, more beneficial.

Thursday 29th December

Joshua received a report from a 'select committee' which recommended immediate alteration of the current physiotherapy course along the following lines:

1) The course should be enlarged to 20 students

2) The course should change from being just a physiotherapy course to offer a broader scope. That is, it should be a multi-purpose course encompassing training for OT and rehabilitation nursing.

Under the circumstances and considering my inability to cope with the course as it already is, I do not need to write down my reactions in detail.

On the one hand I would go to the bazaar – which I didn't mind – to get the most basic rehabilitation equipment made by local tradesmen in order to equip a modest physiotherapy outpatient department. On the other hand, I was contributing plans for a physiotherapy department to serve a 900-bed rehabilitation hospital, while being asked to train occupational therapists and rehabilitation nurses.

It was as if, on a daily basis, I was playing the role of A.B. Spottsworth; the one who had misinterpreted, with fatal consequences, what state his shot lion was in. Only, in my case, the 'lion' was the Afghan healthcare system. It, too, bit back. Just when you thought you had something figured out – a process, a custom or a practice – there was always another perspective or a point of view, unexpected and even fanciful, to stymie what you had decided to do. P.G. Wodehouse doesn't tell us how old A.B. Spottsworth was when he made the obituary column. I was twenty-eight years old, turning twenty-nine. My current job activities took me well beyond the scope of things I would have been doing as a physiotherapist at home in Adelaide. They had certainly taken a different turn to the job description, 'physiotherapist required to work with an orthopaedic surgeon in a rehabilitation unit', which had brought us to Kabul. I suspect that it was this discrepancy which sustained my ongoing antipathy to Joshua, along with his apparent lack of support to me in my various challenges. Where I was concerned with what the students were, or were not, learning in our training program, he had let me know early on that it 'is more important that the course finishes and is seen to be finished' (diary entry, September 6th). And this was the viewpoint I was being asked to adopt.

Our unhappy relationship continued on like a grumbling appendix – manageable but with occasional flare-ups. Once, in conversation, he told me I was 'squealing like a stuck pig'. Ten years later Anne and I and our children – we had three by then, Nick, Coby and Bronnie – spent two months in a rehabilitation project in a remote Mexican village called *Ajoya* in Sinaloa state. One morning we listened to a pig being slaughtered next door to the cottage where we were staying. It was a terrible sound, as much desperation as it was suffering, and just metres away. The doomed pig's squealing seemed to fill the whole village. Later on, I shifted my thoughts from the animal to myself: *Were my complaints to Joshua really that bad?* It made me wince. Joshua and I did eventually make peace, a good peace, with each other, Ocie, but I will tell you how that happened a little later. What I do want to let you know now is what has just come to me as I read my diary once more and write about those times: it was Joshua, as project director, who had to take the heat, often on my behalf, and respond diplomatically to these ministerial demands in a way that saved me from further unreasonable assignments. I did not give him credit for this at that time.

Even with the immediacy of these work-related challenges, including problematic relationships, the war had not gone away or released its grip on the population of Kabul. One afternoon after a morning trip with Mahmoud Ali to the bazaar, I was writing at my desk in the clinic when there was a single, enormous 'boom'. It was not like the distant, almost muffled sound of bombing we were accustomed to hearing. And what was also distinctive about it was the 'after noise' following the actual explosion. It seemed to go on for ages: a raining sound, but of bricks, stone, steel, wood and whatever else that had been projected skywards by the explosion, now falling back from a great height and clattering onto streets, buildings and people. It was a car bomb, left adjacent to the Indian Airlines office but also unfortunately next to a kindergarten. It was a massive blast and many lives, including the very young, were lost. Mahmoud Ali and I had driven down that street and past those offices just a couple of hours earlier.

Alterations went on in earnest towards the conversion of the old motor mechanics' garage into a physio gym. The flurry of activity and abundance of workmen and materials was encouraging enough for me to think that we may get something of a viable physiotherapy department underway after all. Little breakthroughs now occurred regularly. The mechanics' pit had been filled in and cemented. The walls and doors were now in place. The new windows needed glass still. But things were definitely taking shape.

PART ONE: KABUL 1983–1987

The physiotherapy room in the COR clinic building, despite the progress, remained dark and drab. We needed curtains between the two treatment cubicles for privacy. Anne and I looked around the bazaar and found some colourful material which she made up into curtains that could readily slide on rails. They were bright yellow and, in our opinion, lent the place some vitality. I asked Nasima, one of the physiotherapy students, what she thought of them. She did not hesitate in communicating her disapproval. She did this with a slight click of the tongue combined with a subtle shake – just once – of the head. Having deciphered her body language, I asked her why she did not like them. She told me that in Afghan culture yellow was the colour of malice and envy.

For goodness' sake, they were only curtains! Couldn't I even get such a minor decision right? Apparently not. But I could see that getting this feedback had its good side. In a place where it was considered sensible to tell foreigners what you thought they *wanted* to hear, it was both refreshing and somewhat revelatory for me to have an Afghan tell me what they really thought. I took the yellow curtains down. At least we were now able to talk about curtains. They not only divided the two treatment cubicles but our different views of the world.

7

On Sunday 27th November you arrived Paul, with Lizzie, on your way to settle back in Australia. You had been away a long time. Anne and I were excited about your plan to travel from London to Adelaide via Kabul. It was unquestionably out of the way, as well as being a strain on your time and your budget. Like others, you had to wait in Delhi to receive your visas, even though they had already been applied for and granted. But you got here. I was able to take a couple of days off work and we took you to the bazaars and drove around Kabul, avoiding the usual proscribed areas. We talked and talked, not having seen one another for some five years. I remember the boil you had on your forehead – who could miss it? It required lancing by one of the team doctors.

On Friday morning we went to church. Well, not you Paul. We tried to explain that there was no expectation on you to *do* anything there. You didn't even have to pretend to enjoy it. Nor, we reassured, in possible contradiction to church teaching, were you placing yourself in danger of anything *happening* to you. It was just our small expat community gathering together. But you weren't going. I knew why. You had been well and truly inoculated against Christianity from our time as schoolboys at Trinity Grammar. Despite Mum's and Dad's good intentions, and the sacrifices they made in sending us there, it was the wealth and hypocrisy of the place that did it. I had a partially successful vaccination, remaining suspicious of the institutional church to this day. But I had gotten to the point where I now chose to be a Christian. By the time we got home from church, you had chopped all the wood in the woodpile, in what I can only surmise was a case of residual protestant guilt. (I so wish you were still around and I could brace myself for the push-back on that little piece of analysis!)

And all of this only makes your gift to me, on learning that I had become a Christian, all the more remarkable. It was eight years before meeting up in Kabul. You were passing through Adelaide at the time and you went out and bought me two books. The first was *Christology* by Dietrich Bonhoeffer and the other *The Meaning of the City* by Jacques Ellul. I received them politely and we talked. I spoke in binary terms: either *this* or *that* – you're either saved or you're not. You listened for a while before saying, 'Geez Ian, that's the stuff of religious wars'. I don't know precisely when I came to my senses and realized that relationships are more important than dogma. Thankfully, it was not too long after that conversation, and certainly well before we came to Kabul. I also came to appreciate the choices you made in these two books. The scholarly nature of each reflected your genuine respect for the direction I had taken. I still have them.

We watched you fly out six days later. Anne and I sat and drank tea in the terminal with our general services officer, Richard, waiting for your flight to take off. We looked through the glass at the military machines coming and going, as though we were in front of a giant screen. The helicopter gunships were the most prominent, landing and taking off in twos every couple of minutes, as was their rule. In the space of a couple of hours, we saw several Russian MIG fighters blast along the runway. And then, amidst the military traffic, your Indian Airlines flight took to the sky and you were gone.

After the two days off, I didn't go back to the wards at WAK. In having the two days off from work and enjoying once more the absence of stress, I was like a hiker who stops for a break and finds it hard to get going again. Joshua supported this decision, and from what I can tell he didn't go back to WAK either. He had been doing some orthopaedic surgery in WAK but he now focussed on the day surgery at the COR clinic. As we had almost finished converting the mechanics' garage into a physiotherapy gym, we relinquished the classroom upstairs and it became a short-term post-operative ward instead.

The year 1983 drew to a close and Anne and I experienced our first winter in Afghanistan. I had frolicked in snow back in Australia but had never watched the first snowfall of the season. It was a thrill. I arrived at work, after my Farsi lesson, mid-morning on Wednesday 21st December just as it was beginning. Gradually the ground became white; the delineation between earth and concrete was lost. The snow kept falling all day. It was your birthday, Paul.

The mountains gradually took on their mantle of snow, the reverse of a receding hair line, as the snowline crept lower and lower down their slopes. What my father called a 'lazy wind' – it went through rather than around you – would rise in the late afternoons when the sun had lowered, snap freezing most things in its wake. We had installed locally made *bukhAris* in our houses. They were mostly fuelled by diesel, and large-diameter pipes rose from the heater, snaked across the ceiling and into the wall cavity, giving our living rooms an industrial ambience. But we were warm, even if many local people were not, without having the 'easy' access to fuel we did. My sister Jane had sent me music cassettes. Bruce Cockburn expressed our feelings of isolation in wintering in Kabul: 'You're not even here, on the coldest night of the year.' The water, which pooled in drains at the bottom of downpipes on the northern or shaded side of buildings, remained perpetually frozen until the following spring.

There was an IAM Christmas party where I contributed a song on guitar. I sang, with an Australian ocker accent, about learning Farsi: a subject near to everyone's heart. Marja, the language and orientation director, was a friendly but serious-minded Finnish woman. However, she was not without self-deprecating humour, telling me that in Finland, 'even our happy songs are played in a minor key'. She asked me if I would sing the 'learning Farsi song' to the Afghan language teachers at the language and orientation school. I did that and the frivolity was a welcome counterpoint for all of us.

This tumultuous year, however, had not yet finished with us.

Saturday 31st December

It was about 4.30am this morning when Anne and I were awakened to a violent shaking and rattling of our surroundings. All was motion and for a moment we just sat in bed wondering what was going on. Eventually, that is after about a further 20 seconds, we realised that it was an earthquake and, unlike other tremors, this was not subsiding. At this stage sitting on our bed felt like riding on the back of a truck on a rough country road. Without putting on any extra clothes or shoes we raced outside even though there was snow on the ground. It would have been sensible to have put something else on but our insecurity about being inside had risen rather rapidly by then. Thankfully, the quake subsided soon afterwards and we were able to go back indoors.

When I arrived at work this morning all talk was on the quake and everyone agreed it was the strongest they had experienced – these were Afghans speaking. Some buildings, including the hospital, had been damaged but overall Kabul seemed to have got off lightly. Overseas news programmes tonight (short-wave radio) said that the epicentre of the quake was in Northern Pakistan and that widespread loss of property and life had occurred.

8

If 1983 had finished with tectonic unrest, the beginning of 1984 was no less inauspicious.

In October of 1983, Anne and I had moved to a house in *KArte ChAr* (area 4), just across the river from *KArte Seh* (area 3) where the majority of team members lived. It was just over two years since a couple, from Finland and Holland, the Barendsens, had been murdered in their house in *KArte ChAr*, in front of their small children. The motive for these murders had never been established: was it a robbery gone wrong or were they targeted (mistakenly) as being associated with the Russian occupation? Together with a family from Scotland, we were the first team members to move back into the area. This move didn't bother us. Our Afghan neighbours, on one side at least, were very friendly indeed and it was only a short walk to the local bazaar.

In early February 1984 Anne and I returned from a month's break in India and Nepal to a house newly damaged by shrapnel. It had happened one night. Our upstairs neighbours from Scotland were in bed when there was the sudden splintering of glass as shrapnel struck the western wall of the house, shattering their bedroom window, and lacerating the wall above their bed. We were always having to make decisions based on the interpretation of events or actions whose origins were either unknown or unreliably known. The important question in this episode was whether it had been a targeted attack or stray fire. After a couple of nights staying elsewhere, it was decided that it was the latter and life was resumed in *KArte ChAr*.

On an almost daily basis, we would walk to our local bazaar. From shops on carts we bought whatever fruit and vegetables happened to be in season. In winter, there were carrots, onions and potatoes together with mandarins and bruised 'travel weary' bananas from Pakistan. In summer, however, the bazaars bulged with the bounty of the orchards and fields from Afghanistan's fertile valleys. There were several varieties of melons, stone fruit, mulberries and grapes. From other, lockable, shops we also bought tinned foodstuffs such as instant coffee, porridge and powdered milk, which were examples of 'fixed price' goods. Drinking instant coffee with imperfectly dissolved lumps of powdered milk was an unfortunate fact of life. But our options were limited and, given the very real risk of tuberculosis, we dared not have fresh milk.

Something we never tired of was fresh nan; flatbread the shape and size of a small skateboard. Together with rice and tea, it was a staple in the Afghan diet. I used to enjoy walking to the nan shop a couple of blocks from our house, placing my money under the carpet, saying how many pieces I wanted, standing in line with others, and watching the nan being prepared. There was a team hard at work, particularly near meal times. There were dough preparers and shapers towards the back of the shop. Then there was the 'main man', face and head covered by cloth to protect him from the heat, who had to reach down and stick the uncooked nan to the side of the tandoor oven, while 'gaffing' the cooked nan out with a hooked metal pole, like landing a fish onto a boat. Finally, there was the person up front, taking the money and passing the nan over. I counted it as a kind of acceptance that my money was taken and placed under the edge of the carpet with everyone else's, while I waited my turn. No being served first because I was a foreigner and no making me wait because I was a foreigner. As foreigners we were generally highly visible. It was gratifying in this situation not to be different.

When we first moved to *KArte ChAr*, the next-door neighbours to our left were very welcoming to us.

The Second-time Teacher

Tuesday November 22nd

Our neighbours are very friendly and there is a young fellow, slightly younger than me, who is a sports teacher at Khair KhAna. Habib comes over and his ambition seems to be to beat me at table tennis, while mine is to beat Anne.

Friday December 9th

Our next-door neighbours came and had lunch with us today. There were ten of us forming a merry little party. There was no pretence of liking the first course which was soup. Most of the bowls came back half empty. However, the stew seemed to be genuinely enjoyed as second and third helpings were partaken of. Later Habib was overjoyed at beating me at table tennis. He came back to earth, however, when Anne 'whipped him' in a couple of games.

I can still see Habib with an index finger pointing to his temple, gleefully shouting '*Tark-teak!*' (an Afghanized version of 'Tactic!') whenever he would win a point against me. They invited us to a relaxing, long lunch at their house. Then it stopped. Habib told us that they had been warned not to spend time with us.

As Westerners, we were also under regular surveillance by *khAd*, the Afghan secret police. Young men in black leather jackets often sat, languishing it sometimes seemed, in Russian-made Lada cars at the end of the street. Thankfully, they never bothered or harassed us. We knew that our letters were opened and read prior to their delivery, adding to the minimum six-week journey from Australia. Once I was sent a birthday present, the novel *Schindler's List* by Thomas Keneally, and when I eventually got my hands on it there were several sections which had been blacked out with a marker pen – sections which mentioned Russia or communism, as far as we could judge by the surrounding text. The compression of space and time in which we lived now extended, or so it seemed, to the compression of our thoughts. At the risk of blatant opportunism – or, the literary equivalent of a 'dad joke' – I still have to say it: 1984 *was* an Orwellian kind of year in Kabul, both for us and the local people.

Anne was, in March 1984, some six and a half months pregnant with our first child. She became really sick with a high fever. I came home at lunch to check on her one day and the bed sheets were wet with her sweat. Joshua was very helpful in arranging reliable blood tests and confirming a diagnosis of mononucleosis (glandular fever).

In mid April of that year, Anne left Afghanistan to go to India to have our first child. We decided, given the curfew and the unpredictable conditions in the local hospitals, that should there be some emergency it would be wiser for this first labour to take place somewhere more peaceful and predictable. This place was the Landour Community Hospital in the foothills of the Himalayas, north of Dehra Dun. It was a lot cooler than Delhi at that time of year and there was a nearby guesthouse. I followed a month later, fortunately arriving three days before Anne commenced labour. The birth went well and we returned to Kabul at the end of May with our new son Nicholas. In one respect, the curfew was then less oppressive, as the three of us spent a lot of time together. I also ceased writing my diary. Between work and the extended responsibilities of helping look after a baby in Kabul, there was now less time to write at night.

When Nick was born our *chaukidar* was seemingly as thrilled as we were at the arrival of this new human being. *Chaukidar* literally means 'one who has a chair' and refers to the person who answers the front gate or door. This is not a foreigner's word but goes back to the idea that in this part of the world security has traditionally and generally lain in the strength of one's family or clan ties (rather than a civil service such as police). Since houses all have walled compounds of different sizes, the front door is actually the front gate. Unlike other parts of the city where there were boom gates, checkpoints and armed guards for protection, we had our unarmed, middle-aged *chaukidars* to answer our doors. Some foreigners had a day *chaukidar* and a night *chaukidar*. We had one, just for the night. He would arrive at around 4pm. He had modest sleeping quarters with heating and cooking facilities, and the keys to the house. There had been rumours of the *chaukidars* being pressured to hand over the keys to our houses.

When we brought Nick back from India and introduced him to our *chaukidar*, he asked us the child's name. We replied, 'Nicholas'. Now, there is a difficulty here. The Dari verb *budan* – 'to be' – uses '*as*' for the word 'is'. For example, '*u darakht as*' means 'that is a tree'. So, he formed the idea, quite understandably, that in replying 'Nicholas', we were saying 'It is Nicol'. Despite our efforts to clarify this, he maintained his choice of aesthetic sensibilities, deciding he liked the sound of 'Nicol' rather than 'Nicholas'. As a baby and then a toddler, he would stroke Nick's hair, cheek or hand over and over, repeating '*Nicol AghA*', '*Nicol AghA*', '*Nicol AghA*' (Mister Nicol, Mister Nicol, Mister Nicol) tenderly, as in a song.

In January while in Delhi, I had purchased some exercise equipment for our converted garage now physiotherapy gymnasium. It took further time but the students and I were eventually able to move in and begin work with patients using the exercise and training equipment that we had procured locally and from afar.

The patients came. There was a man we used to see in the bazaar. He had cut off parts of tyres as pads for his knees and hands and he would crawl from one parked vehicle to another, before kneeling upright and begging from each driver. He arrived at the clinic and Joshua and I assessed him together. We concluded that to 'straighten him up' surgically, followed by the fitting of callipers and use of crutches, might make him more upright and therefore more 'normal', but would probably also take away his income. This was a time when people with disabilities were not generally given opportunities to work, or otherwise participate in society. Paradoxically, it was, economically speaking, more secure for him to be disabled, and to be seen to be disabled, in the way he *was*. The man agreed with these unhappy conclusions. But such decision-making did not always enlighten the students on the principles of rehabilitation. Understandably, demonstrable progress was also necessary to sustain their interest and attendance. It was not always possible to provide this.

Another man came in on a tricycle where the chain was connected to the wheels by a hand crank. He had contracted polio some two decades earlier, which had partially paralysed his legs. His arms were fine. Now, when he disembarked from his bike, which provided his mobility, he could only squat on the ground, knees up under his chin. When asked to move, he could manage a form of waddling like a duck but obviously much less efficient. Joshua wondered whether physiotherapy, and a regime of gradual posturing and stretching, might improve the man's hip and knee contractures prior to surgery, which, in turn, might allow the use of callipers and crutches. Unfortunately, even after our attempts to carefully stretch them out, the hips and knees could only be straightened to 90 degrees, a long way off what would permit successful surgery in this context.

There were many such cases which came wrapped in issues of justice and ethics. And unwrapping these was, at the time, well beyond the scope of teaching my students practical physiotherapy techniques, procedures and protocols. And my own understanding of the conditions in which the people with these disabilities lived, and the particular challenges which they faced each day, was still very superficial. I saw similar dilemmas in the village of *Ajoya*, rural Mexico, some years later. A young woman was brought to me for an opinion. Bonita, twenty-seven years old, had contracted poliomyelitis at an early age and, not receiving treatment until she was much older, had developed severely disabling muscle and soft tissue contractions. Her spine was sharply curved in the lumbar region and her hips were stuck, unable to be straightened out by more than 10 or 20 degrees. What made the situation worse was that these contractions were pulling her spine into an ever more curved position, not only causing increased back pain but a real risk of spinal cord and nerve root damage. Bonita was an otherwise attractive young woman of marriageable age and she was very concerned that her time and opportunity for happiness in this regard was rapidly passing.

It was apparent that physiotherapy treatment alone could not alter such longstanding structural changes. She could be sent for orthopaedic evaluation in a provincial centre some six hours away by bus. The advice received from local health workers and another expatriate health worker was that there were, unfortunately, many unscrupulous surgeons in that part of Mexico who would be only too happy to take the money, if it could be raised, and perform tenotomies (tissue lengthening procedures), leaving the patient with whatever the result. Tenotomies might straighten Bonita's legs but would they lead to more function? Tenotomy without careful and appropriate splintage and diligent follow-up might place shortened nerve trunks in grave danger. If Bonita were to lose sensation on top of her present problems the result would be devastating. Poliomyelitis is a terrible disease but its one redeeming feature is that it leaves its victims with skin sensation intact. Even so, the hip and knee contractures were really of less importance than the severely tilted pelvis and lordotic spine. This needed expert and wise evaluation prior to any surgery. Bonita, with her double disability, the first the result of her polio, and the second her poverty and existence in a remote village, had no money for private orthopaedic opinion in either Mexico City or the US. Not having had access to relatively simple rehabilitation measures when she was young had left Bonita in a seemingly hopeless position. For those who were poor it was often like that.

Ocie, I am confronted with a juxtaposition of images: of you and the young ones I used to see in physiotherapy. As physiotherapists we have the privilege of touching and handling people's bodies. I can remember gently lifting and examining the flaccid limbs of babies and infants who had contracted polio. I have also coaxed the stiff, sometimes contractured arm or leg joints of children, following injury or wounding, towards some useable freedom of movement. And I have positioned the limbs of children with cerebral palsy whose muscles were overworking unreasonably with high tone so that the antagonist muscles had a chance to work better and permit function.

At playgroup come story time I sit cross-legged on the floor. Often, but not always, you back up and sit down on my crossed legs, which seem to make the perfect armchair for you. As your Pop, during the story or the singing afterwards, I get to wrap my hands around your knees and feet, count your toes and fingers, and generally luxuriate in the mystery and beauty of a healthily developing little body. I am, in some ways, still doing what I did as a physiotherapist, handling and palpating little hands and feet, but my heart is, understandably, more involved. I see the precious life behind the bending, little fingers and toes. Perhaps this is what they mean when they say to have a heart for the poor is to see the important, if not precious, life behind the problems of the presenting sufferer. There were times I forgot this.

One lunchtime I was watching a game of volleyball in the grounds of WAK. The men were arguing, verging on fighting – was this a way of letting off steam? A young man beside me noticed my bewilderment and said, '*MA mardum e jangi astem*' (We are a fighting people). 'If the

Russians were not here we would find something else to fight about,' he added. It was an unsolicited explanation but not unlike the one, denoting resignation or defiance, depending on the context, which I mentioned earlier: *I Afghanistan ast!* (This is Afghanistan!). It was one thing for Afghans to say this. However, it was quite another, when we foreigners found ourselves starting to say it, dismissing a place and its people, as though we had run out of patience with them.

One afternoon there was a knock on the door of the physiotherapy clinic. On opening the door I was handed an appointment card, no other actions or words. The holder wore a *charderi* (burqa) and, in this state of anonymity, she stood there awaiting my response. Her appointment was for that morning. It was now mid-afternoon and I had a line of patients, sitting outside (there was no waiting room) waiting to see me. I now gave her my response, spat out at her like a slap: 'What do you expect me to do? Can't you see all those people out there waiting to see me? Why are you late anyway?' She replied that the bus had not turned up that morning and that she had been travelling ever since in order to get here by mid-afternoon. It was a not unreasonable scenario but it did little to quell my vexation at an impossible workload just made worse. 'All right, go out there and wait. I don't know what time it will be before I can see you.'

As she turned, she handed me a plain brown paper bag. Further irritated by another 'complication' to this encounter, I barked, 'What's this?' 'It is for you,' she said. I took and opened the bag. It contained biscuits. It was a gift. And I felt like I was in an episode of *Fawlty Towers*, where Basil, unable to cope further with a morass of confused interactions and injudicious responses, sees a trunk, into which he climbs and pulls the lid closed after him.

At around that time, I was introduced to the Minister for Rehabilitation, Dr Sunaram. Upon shaking my hand he exclaimed,

'So, you're the angry young man with the red beard that I have heard about'. Hmm. Telling. Obviously, I was a serial offender. What was it that my lunchtime companion had said about the hospital volleyball players – including the rest of Afghanistan? It seemed that I had become *'mardum I jangi'* (a fighting person). To be taken by circumstance beyond the boundaries of one's capabilities is a severe challenge to anyone. Apparently, Ocie, my time in Afghanistan was now changing me for the worse or, alternatively, it was exposing who I *really* was but had managed to camouflage in more favourable circumstances at home.

My father died in 2008. Anne and I were in Afghanistan at the time. We rushed home to Australia to be with our family and to prepare for his funeral. In helping prepare Dad's eulogy, Mum told us a story which I had never heard before. It is not an uncommon thing for the children of returned servicemen to hear such stories post mortem. This one was about an experience my father had as a prisoner of war in the Second World War. He had been a fighter pilot, flying Spitfires, and seconded by the RAAF to a British squadron, when he was shot down while flying a mission over northern Italy. Thankfully, he survived. However, he sustained facial injuries and a damaged shoulder. Following medical care and hospitalization he was, with other POWs, to be transported to a prison camp in Germany. The prisoners were waiting outside to board a freight train in the freezing northern Italian winter. Due to his injuries my father had been unable to put his 'greatcoat' on properly. An Italian guard, noticing this, reached over and fastened the top button of my father's coat.

I have since wondered, when it came the guard's turn, whoever he was, to have his life evaluated and expressed in eulogy, whether his family and friends would like to know, perhaps be amazed to know, that the story of what he did for my father would be remembered and retold in another land, on the other side of the world, by another generation, remembering him and his simple act with gratitude. Similarly, this Afghan woman might like to know, and also be surprised, that her gift of biscuits is being thought of and written about some thirty-five years later. As it turned out, her hospitality trumped my hostility. Eventually I would come to understand the reasons a person might be late, even several months late, for their physiotherapy appointment. Snow blocking mountain passes was one of them.

I have already said that 1984 was an Orwellian year, so I may as well refer to a comment George Orwell once made in an essay. He didn't trust memoirs unless, perhaps, they are like the one you are reading now, replete with anecdotes of disgrace:

"Autobiography is only to be trusted when it reveals something disgraceful. A man who gives a good account of himself is probably lying, since any life when viewed from the inside is simply a series of defeats."

Ocie, I don't believe that a life is simply a series of defeats. Nevertheless, I think there are more than enough of them to go around.

We developed a partnership with another project run by Dan Terry, a fellow IAM team member. Dan was working with young people who had been injured by the war and whose employment prospects as a consequence were also dashed. He was teaching metalwork skills to this group and so we contracted them to make us children's elbow crutches as these were not available in the bazaar in Kabul. Children with conditions such as polio and cerebral palsy, who had only ever gotten around either on someone's back or by crawling, were now walking independently for the first time.

Again, it was *the face* which spoke so clearly. We would take the children out of the garage, aka physiotherapy gym, and encourage them to walk with their new aids on the gravel road outside, in the sun, and in public. Reticence and shyness quickly gave way to exhilaration. They were able to encounter the world in a new way: upright and away from the dust. And they learned to do this in our modest physiotherapy garage-cum-gymnasium by means of the physiotherapy the students and I had provided, together with the children's crutches made by Dan's group and the callipers made by the workshop staff. It was a source of joy and celebration for all of us.

As the work became better known, so the crowds came. A child was brought to the clinic by his father, an army officer. He demanded to be seen before others who had been waiting patiently with their children. I saw him as a queue jumper and told him to wait his turn. I could see that my Afghan workmates were uneasy with this action. They quietly, but hastily, advised me that, while they could see *why* I was doing what I was doing, it was nevertheless not a wise course of action. 'This man could cause a lot of trouble for us,' Mr Ofiani, a genial administrator in the project, told me. He had offered me advice before. Once, hearing me mouth off about something or other, he took me aside. 'Take it easy, Ian *KhAn*. You got to look after yourself, you know,' he said in gently broken English. I could be wrong about this. But I think he saw me as someone whose heart was in the right place even if I was easily 'set off'. It was a simple pastoral care for my life in Afghanistan. For my part, I appreciated his concern at the time without knowing quite what to do with it. In this situation with the army officer, however, I interpreted his comment as meaning 'trouble for the project' and therefore 'stuck to my guns', an unfortunate metaphor, I know, for this place. My concern for fairness, however, was not putting me or my well-being under pressure as much as it was the well-being of my colleagues. I was a little too certain of my own virtue.

9

Electricity unavailability was a fact of life. We cooked our meals on a small diesel stove, just as if we were camping. And, if power had been off for a few days, the first thing we did when it came on was to activate water pumps and fill our water tank. Not long after that, our priority was to turn on the washing machine, wash some clothes and then, an hour or two later, wash ourselves under a warm shower. There were often fuel shortages too. We were mostly quarantined from these at the hospital and, to a certain extent, as foreigners in comparison with local people. We each had a 44-gallon drum of diesel at home. But every morning as we drove to work there were long lines of people waiting for diesel.

Sometimes while driving to work we became stuck behind trucks carrying Soviet troops. I could scarcely believe it as I watched these fair-haired teenage boys ride along together; so very young and normal looking. Sitting idly on the back of these trucks, they would eye us off casually, perhaps wondering who we were. This hadn't been in my calculations at all; their youth, I mean. Instead, I had expected some kind of emotionless iron men. And it wasn't difficult to form this view, having imagined them at the controls of the helicopter gunships that left and returned to Kabul on their deadly patrols, sometimes buzzing very low over our houses. At such times, it was more than a buzz. Their approach started off as a low hum before becoming a vibration which would build to a strong, insistent shaking of discrete items, such as plates and glasses. A crescendo of noise and compression followed. It was like an earthquake, but one of and from the air as the gunships passed over, sometimes only 15 or 20 metres above us. It was an 'airquake'. We have never lost our dislike of helicopters – any helicopter.

Part One: Kabul 1983-1987

In late spring there were eight days in which Kabul was without fuel and we were forced to ride our bicycles across town, through the centre of the city, from *KArte ChAr* to *Wazir Akbar Khan* and back again after work. This is a journey which would be almost unthinkable in Kabul today given the volume and intensity of traffic and the current poor security situation for foreigners. There were not many privately owned cars in Kabul in the early 1980s, hence the reason we could contemplate riding our bikes to work across town and back. In general, there were government-owned, mostly Russian-made cars, and there were imported vehicles used by embassies, the UN and NGOs. The upper echelons of the Kabul government also used imported makes such as Mercedes Benz. Military vehicles such as jeeps, trucks and tanks, often in convoy, ceaselessly moved men and equipment (Afghan or Russian) from one place to the other. Civilian trucks were also common, stacked with goods and people, the latter balancing precariously on the very top of the load. Buses transported ordinary people around the city, and to the city, from the surrounding countryside. The city buses usually leaned over to the right, even on the few occasions they were not packed, evidence that the suspension had finally succumbed to the collective weight and habits of commuters who could be seen standing on steps, grasping at rails and handles, overflowing the doors of the bus. And the roads contained other traffic. There were horse-drawn carts, with the poor animal's ribs usually prominent beneath the harness. And there was the stereotypical beast of burden, the donkey. Donkeys were a common sight, bowed down under loads of almost anything: wood, bricks, bales of wool and, of course, humans.

All of this made for a heterogeneous arrangement of road traffic in terms of the variable space and speed of vehicle or user. While nothing like the gridlock of car traffic which can be found on Kabul's overpopulated roads today, there was, nevertheless, a further difference between road users in their aggression and urgency. In general, military vehicles were both the most aggressive and the largest, providing them and their drivers with a de facto 'right of way'. However, size still mattered for the rest of us in determining right of way, and it appeared that this unofficial rule was in play the day a passenger-carrying bus collided with our car. Anne, I and our infant son Nick were driving back from town, heading for our house in *KArte ChAr*. A bus came up beside us on the inside, endeavouring to overtake us on the 'wrong' side. I was driving in the main flow of traffic. There were no lanes as such. The bus, in seeking to pass us, avoided some slower traffic to the right (it is left-hand drive in Afghanistan). It moved laterally in our direction and collided with our vehicle. The impact forced us sideways, moving us off our line and dangerously close to the oncoming traffic. Enraged, I accelerated, calling upon the considerable horsepower of the project vehicle I was driving. I overtook the bus and then, pulling in front of it, brought our vehicle to a sudden halt causing the bus to also stop – it had nowhere to go. I jumped out, ran to the steps of the bus, climbed aboard, grabbed the shirt of the driver in a clenched fist and, in front of the bewildered passengers, shouted at him in Farsi, 'What the hell do you think you are doing?' or words to that effect. He was aghast; eyes wide open in fear and only able to hold his upturned palms out to me. Reason made some return and stopped me from going further in either word or action. I swivelled on my heel, alighted from the bus, with anger giving way to shame, and returned to the car where Anne and Nick were waiting. If I thought the bus driver's expression had been one of shock, then I realized now that his was only surpassed by Anne's. She was horrified by my actions, letting me know how despicably I had acted. There was silence between us for the rest of the day and evening, and into the next day.

In an enforced reflection, as I only had myself for company for a period, I saw how cowardly my actions had been, regardless of the provocation. For all the bus driver knew, I could have been a Russian advisor (non-military personnel who worked in various ministries) in which case the chances of prison or death were both real for him. At best, I was another foreigner wielding, in that instant at least, an illegitimate power and rank in his country. And once again, it was a question of my not understanding the dramatically different perspectives of others in these encounters in Afghanistan. If I, as a temporary resident and able to leave Afghanistan if I chose, was carrying such anger and hostility as a result of my exposure to life here, why should I be surprised that local people also carried anger and hostility among the more docile and acceptable postures of suffering and grief? Their choices were few or nil. This was part of their tragedy. My choices were always still there.

But these are retrospective thoughts. I didn't really understand my anger and hostility at the time. I just remember the visceral experience of being angry. Once, I was so upset by something that happened at work that I drove the project vehicle home, through the crowded bazaars, at breakneck speed. It was – I was – reckless.

It was not easy to escape or get away for recreation, to experience another place, with space, or the companionship of other people who weren't fellow team members. One couldn't just leave Kabul for the weekend. Because it was an 'island' we had to take any kind of holiday or break outside the country. But exit visas had to be applied for. This took several weeks. I continued to regularly wake in the early hours with stomach cramps. This was different from the acute discomfort and diarrhoea associated with amoebic dysentery which was also a periodic event.

Anger usually needs a target or a focus. I guess this allows it to become valid or justified, or at least appear to be so. Just about everyone said how hard Joshua was to work with. He was introverted, acerbic and stubborn.

I, on the other hand, rested the case for the soundness of my character on the fact that I had been well liked and not troublesome in either of my two previous places of employment as a physiotherapist. It wasn't hard, then, for him to be my target of anger, and to blame him for most of my difficulties. Or, at least, to blame him for the problems at work being more difficult than they need have been. Gerald's words about it being me that needed to change had not yet penetrated my thinking. Joshua and I had, at different times, tried to get along. This included external mediation. Nothing had really worked.

One morning I approached Joshua. It was at church. I was willing to try anything to change the dynamics of my work situation and, in turn, my deteriorating health. We went to a side room and I apologized for my attitude towards him. This wasn't just any off-the-cuff apology. It was born of exhaustion and desperation. One could argue that 'confession' and 'forgiveness' were central to our shared Christian worldview. However, it had not previously been clear who should do which, let alone who was willing to do either. I had agonized over this, not willing to concede any culpability on my part for what had gone wrong. But I *had* resolved to apologize for what had become my poisonous attitude towards him. He listened to my apology. When he did respond, I was gobsmacked: 'I know that I am not an easy person to work with. If it wasn't for my wife, we wouldn't have any friends.' He offered me his hand.

The way in which we had previously positioned ourselves with each other, how we had attacked, defended and attitudinally jousted, suddenly changed. I heard an interview the other day with Richard Flanagan, the Australian novelist. He spoke of his dad as a generous and kind man who embodied 'the power of an unguarded heart'. I think, Ocie, that it was a moment of unguarding that enabled Joshua and me to touch each other's vulnerability. It was not unlike trusting a doctor, or a physiotherapist for that matter, to respectfully, even tenderly, examine an acutely sore part of the body. Joshua's response went even further. It lanced some infected, space-occupying pathological process within me. Where life in Kabul had been characterized by compression of space, time and thought, there was now a relieving and healing sense of decompression. I went home and, strangely enough, didn't sleep that night. It felt like I had a fever as I went over and over this encounter in my mind. I wish I could say that, from this point on, everything changed at work. It didn't. I am not telling a fairy tale here. But in the following two and a half years, Joshua and I never had another argument, and the once palpable tension between us was gone.

I think of that short conversation with Joshua as one of the better things I did while in Afghanistan. I have talked a lot about curtains and what lies hidden or obscurely veiled behind them. If I have applied the comic writing of P.G. Wodehouse to my situation then I don't think that it is any less a liberty, Ocie, to take the more serious words of the English philosopher Iris Murdoch and apply them to it as well. She wrote that 'virtue is the attempt to pierce the veil of selfish consciousness and join the world as it really is…' A veil had hung between Joshua and me, preventing us from seeing each other, except in a certain jaundiced way. On that morning it was pierced and fell away. In a place like Afghanistan where *choice* was regularly desiccated, even 'sucked dry', by horrible circumstance and 'a confusion of ideas', here was something that represented 'un-confusion': something clear and reliable, like a virtue.

Mr Ofiani came in to work one day ashen faced. His sixteen-year-old son had gone missing. The first and most likely explanation was conscription into the army. Conscription, in the manner of the day, saw army trucks driving around the city collecting boys and young men off the streets. No goodbyes or farewells, just 'You're coming with us'.

Mr Ofiani needed time off work to try somehow to confirm, or otherwise disprove, this dreadful hypothesis. He spent several hellish days going to army locations, asking questions, begging for information about his son. Of course, the great and realistic fear was that these young recruits, some called 'fodder', would be sent to a fighting front such as the Panjsher Valley. For these young recruits this was regarded as tantamount to a death sentence. He was only a boy after all. The anguish on Mr Ofiani's blanched face was the unrelieved suffering of a parent who does not know the fate of their child. As misery goes, it rivalled anything I had witnessed in the wards of WAK. We felt the stab of inadequacy once more.

Nasima was the student who took me to task over my choice of yellow curtains. She was a good student, being especially gentle, kind and compassionate to the patients. I knew that she had been through a tough, grieving time recently. She had lost five of the male folk in her family in the previous month due to the fighting. One day she sought me out for a private conversation. Her parents had found a husband for her. But all she could see in their future was further death. The prospect was unbearable. She would not agree to this marriage and told me of her plans to escape the country. She would travel by horseback, a dangerous journey, escorted through back roads and over high mountain passes, until she reached Pakistan. There is an Afghan proverb *dewAlA Mush dAra, mushA gOsh* (Walls have mice and mice have ears). In a city under constant and pervasive surveillance by secret police and their allies, Nasima had endowed me with a great honour. She had confided her plans *before* she had carried them out. Her leaving was not only a loss for the physiotherapy school, it was yet another incalculable loss for the country.

I found out some time later that Nasima eventually made it to Germany, married and had a family. As I understand it, Ocie, Nasima's decision to leave the country was not a rejection of her cultural or social world, where arranged marriage is the norm; it was the prospect of further loss, through staying and marrying, which she was unable to face.

Sometimes, we asked ourselves whether we should be working in Afghanistan at this time. A viewpoint, occasionally suggested by some people at home in Australia, was that we were indirectly supporting a totalitarian government, held in place by a foreign Russian occupying force, and therefore we should not be working here. One of the visiting consular staff from the Australian Embassy in Islamabad, not Jim, said as much. It was undoubtedly true that our presence as Western aid workers sometimes brought unwanted and stressful scrutiny on our neighbours and workmates, due to the harsh surveillance activities of the regime. Interestingly, even surprisingly, ordinary Afghans, that is our work colleagues, our neighbours and the people we met in the bazaar, almost always had a different view. They would often say that it was good that we were there, in such close proximity, seeing what was happening to the Afghan people. We had not anticipated any of this when we came to Afghanistan.

10

One night, not long after we had turned in, and were settling for sleep, Anne flung back the bed covers exclaiming, 'I've just been bitten by something'. On the bottom sheet, stationary and probably wondering where to withdraw to, was a scorpion. We had been told, as part of our induction to life in Afghanistan, to be extremely careful not to be stung by a scorpion. The Afghans spoke of *gazhdum* (scorpion) in solemn tones, quickly adding the adjective *khatarnAk* (dangerous). A couple of team members had shared their experiences: 'Like a red hot poker in my hand for 24 hours' was one report and 'Just as bad as childbirth' was another. We eyed each other ominously. Anne rushed to the kitchen, cut an onion and rubbed it over the area: we had heard that this was a useful thing to do. I tried to find the scorpion, which had quickly changed policy and scuttled across the floor. We then waited, as though it was the onset of an approaching labour. Anne had the same anticipation of the waves of pain to follow.

Over the next hour it became apparent, surprisingly, that Anne had escaped the normal effects of a scorpion sting. Maybe she had been able to react to the touch before it had properly gotten into action. Or maybe, miraculously, given the sudden movement of Anne's leg, it had perceived no threat and so did not sting. Anne and I had been sleeping on a mattress on the floor. Nick had not been a good sleeper. And he had been in bed with us at the time. We were very relieved that *he* had not been stung. In the next few days we found a bed with legs. And each of those legs, using a strategy we had heard about, stood in a can partly filled with water. The general level of scorpion-watch was raised as Nick, and later our daughter Coby, grew and learned to crawl around the floor of the house.

A lifeline for us, easing our isolation, was Radio Australia. On our short-wave radio we could listen to news about Australia. We heard about the 1983 Ash Wednesday bushfires devastating the hills near our city, Adelaide, and parts of Victoria. We listened to Australia winning yachting's Holy Grail, the Americas Cup. And, occasionally, on a Friday, during a Kabul winter, I could listen to coverage of test cricket. It was mundane but very comforting to temporarily bridge the thousands of kilometres distance between us and home. Hearing news about Afghanistan on our home news services, however, was disorientating, as it was generally a week or so after the event. One time we climbed up on the roof to watch as an ammunition dump, around seven kilometres from our house, spectacularly blew up. It was a sort of Kabul son et lumière. We heard this reported on the news a week later. It was better to hear the test cricket live, anyway.

There were two fourteen-year-old Afghan boys who used to visit us, though not together. They seemed to be immune from the harassment that our neighbours had reported. The two were a study in contrast. Not so much physically, as both were skinny kids, but in what the Germans would call *sitz im leben*; their situation in life. Abdul went to school and also worked. In the absence of his father, he provided, together with his mother, for his family, which consisted of six younger siblings. Daoud was somewhat of a xenophile. He loved chatting and learning jokes. He had a high-pitched laugh. Daoud was always asking questions – nothing strategic, like what we earned or what we thought about the government. He just wanted, it seemed, to inhabit our world for a while. He also used to ask us if he could have the stamps off our letters and parcels. He was harmless, but I found him a bit of a pain in the arse. This is not the best nor fairest way to describe someone, I admit, Ocie. It was how I felt at the time.

I preferred Abdul for his gravitas and sense of responsibility. Abdul brought his family for lunch one time and it was strange for us to see a fourteen-year-old boy directing his younger siblings in their manners and behaviours. He was respectful to his mother, in a society that relegated her authority, but we nevertheless admired him for his willingness to step up in the family. He had no choice, if they were to survive. They were Hazara and already disadvantaged by being at the lower end of Afghan society.

In the late spring of 1985, a container of physiotherapy equipment arrived at the clinic. Its origin was the World Health Organization and it had been ordered, in a general way, sometime prior to my arrival. What I mean by 'general way' was that it was mostly electrotherapy equipment, ordered for a typical physiotherapy department, without evidence of any thought given to our specific needs or context in Afghanistan. The four remaining physiotherapy students, who were now based in their *shObas* and came periodically to the school for classes, were fascinated by the array of equipment. They helped me unload the container and unpack each item. Because it was the correct voltage, we could switch it all on like Christmas lights but not all at once. And it was a bit like Christmas. My willing assistants peppered me with questions, as we unpacked and catalogued the equipment over the next couple of days. The most frequent question being '*I chis?*' (What is this?) Even the container did not go unused once emptied. Kabul was like a black hole for the world's containers. They brought things into the country, but Afghanistan, not being big on exporting goods, simply appropriated these large delivery boxes and they became shops, storage sites and even houses.

I had been asked to design a new, purpose-built building for the physiotherapy school. Using the WCPT booklets I had received two years earlier, especially the first two on training of physical therapists in developing countries and basic equipment for rehabilitation centres, I extrapolated and came up with ideas and drawings, which led to meetings with Joshua and Ministry of Public Health officials. After that there were more drawings which others produced based on those meetings.

It was not long before we were standing out in the field beside the COR clinic in the summer of 1985, within the precinct of the *Wazir Akbar Khan* Hospital. The Minister of Public Health was in attendance with his entourage. We, the school and clinic staff, as well as a number of others witnessed this sod-turning ceremony for the new, the first, physiotherapy school in Afghanistan. The speeches given by the various VIPs proclaimed, each in turn, what a great day this was for the people of Afghanistan, especially for the many Afghans, children and adults alike, who had disabilities. We all went home as happy and contented as if we had been to a picnic. The following day brought unexpected and unwelcome news from another ministry, the Ministry for Foreign Affairs. It was that the visa applications had been rejected of a Dutch and an English physiotherapist who were coming to teach in the physiotherapy school. The confusion of ideas this time was between the left and right hands of two ministries not knowing what each other was doing or, if they did, having different motives for their respective decisions. We were discouraged but no longer shocked by this kind of incongruence.

We continued on with the work of teaching and the running of the physiotherapy department from our converted garages. He arrived, unannounced, one morning with a ball of string and some short pieces of wood. He said he was an architect, sent from the ministry, to lay out the foundations of the new physiotherapy school. He was as young as or even younger than me, for goodness' sake! I hoped he wasn't as inexperienced as I was. My moral imagination didn't extend, however, as far as considering that these same sentiments were probably what most Afghans thought as they were introduced to me. And now, here was this fresh-faced, enthusiastic architect and he wanted me to go with him to the field next to the clinic and help him mark out the foundations. Now physiotherapists, in general, don't know a lot about constructing buildings. There may be exceptions I admit. However, what we physiotherapists do know about is 'angles'. Among other things we learn to look at the angles of joints and limbs, measuring them either by 'eyeballing' or by using instruments. We do this all the time. And I could tell, therefore, quite early in the piece, that the lines of string my young architect had laid out, denoting the corners of the intended building, were not 90 degrees. This discovery was disturbing, like a prognosis for what lay ahead. The chasm between what I had before me, in the form of string between posts, going in various directions and angles, and a finished, new physiotherapy school seemed too great to contemplate. I needn't have worried. The site was to stand idle for a few more years. Stacks of bricks, forming a perimeter around the site and later given their own roofs by the snow, marked the change of seasons and passing of time over the following two years.

Construction would not take place in my time there. The building was erected in 1988, supervised by a retired Adelaide engineer, Tom Fowler. Over ensuing decades, it would be the site for the successful training of many cohorts of physiotherapists. It still carries, however, a legacy of my inexperience from that time. It was me, and not the young architect, who would have the honour of having their mistake preserved in perpetuity. There is a large 'room' which forms one end of the Physical Therapy Institute, Kabul. Originally, it was intended to be the hydrotherapy department as suggested by my WCPT pamphlet. However, at some late stage, when it was finally subjected to proper scrutiny and consultation, it was deemed culturally inappropriate, too expensive to run and wasteful of water in a city of wells – what was I thinking? Now, the non-existent hydrotherapy department is a space, which although not used on a day-to-day basis, is still handy, nevertheless, for occasions such as prize-giving, graduations and events such as the Congress of the Afghan Association for Physical Therapy (AAPT), which I would attend years later in 2008. Increasingly, it is used for indoor sports. An original decision, let's call it a mistake, has been adapted for another purpose and life goes on.

In September of 1985 the first course limped to its finish line. The prescribed two years had passed and the students, the four that were left, had persevered despite the frequent and improvised changes in teaching arrangements. On the final day the students arranged a morning tea to celebrate the end of the course. I had been up during the night with yet another stomach upset and didn't go in to work that morning. At the time I didn't give this much thought. It felt to me, anyway, that there was not much to celebrate in the course itself. It was so very incomplete. But this non-attendance was churlish of me. It would have been much better on that morning to look past all of that and just focus on the students themselves.

On balance, I am glad that this not particularly dramatic event of thirty-four years ago has eventually and circuitously been brought to my awareness. It does not change anything concerning the event or the students. Instead, I am left with an unfulfilled obligation to myself about what I might do *now* in lieu of what I didn't do *then*. The learning from this constructive conversation is not just a general moral exhortation to 'do the right thing next time'. It is more specific than that. It is the realization that the students experienced my shame of the course and my own role in that as my being ashamed of them.

I make this sad conclusion now as a second-time teacher. I am sure that there would be first-time teachers who would have this kind of sensitivity regarding their students. I just didn't happen to be one of them.

The visas were eventually granted for my two physiotherapy colleagues and their partners. One was English and the other Dutch. Olive and Ditte. They arrived with their partners late in the summer of 1985. I didn't really get to know either of them that well. Ditte and her husband would visit us in Australia a few years afterwards and we would stay with them – more than once, in 2005 and 2011 – in Holland. Olive and Ditte's first obligation, as it was for all of us, was engagement in the four-month full-time language course. It was during this period that they announced their pregnancies. And each had advised us of these intentions prior to coming to Afghanistan. The news was a cause for celebration but at the same time would diminish their capacity to share the load in the teaching and running of the school. There were no childcare centres, and staying healthy for both mother and child always required significant practical effort.

On the IAM team we were from many parts of the world, and the cultural differences existed between us foreigners, and not just between foreigners and Afghans. Ashton and Natalie, a retired couple from the US, arrived in the summer of 1985. Ashton was a physiatrist (a US term for a medical specialist in rehabilitation). Having worked in Iran for some years, they were given some reprieve on language learning, and soon started work at PSK, Natalie as a receptionist and Ashton as a consultant/teacher. Early on, I received a referral from Ashton to apply '1.8 watts/cm ultrasound for 3 minutes to the tendons around the lateral epicondyle of the left elbow'. This was like a red rag to a bull. And remember, I *was* the angry young man with the red beard introduced to Dr Sunaram.

In Australia, physiotherapists had already achieved, via parliamentary legislation, first contact practitioner status, which meant that *we* worked out such dosages and treatment progressions. I told him as much. Ashton was both apologetic and easy-going in his response, saying that at home in the US he was required by law to refer in this prescriptive manner. It was not dissimilar with my new physiotherapy colleagues. They had different training backgrounds and had learned different approaches to treatment than I had. Not that we had much opportunity to work together.

Anne and I took home leave in the first half of 1986. This was one reason for not commencing a second course straight away. I would not be there for the next six months and the level of staffing was just not sufficient to run it. Anne was expecting our second child. And Coby, a Dutch name, was born in the February of our home leave. While on leave in Australia, I had an endoscopy. The results were okay but a small area of erythematous (reddened) mucosa in my stomach was reported. I noted this with my doctor, but no particular action was required.

We luxuriated in the spending of time with our families and friends. Among our friends, however, the topics of conversation and the issues which preoccupied each of us were very different. We felt like visitors passing through. Despite being on R&R, our thoughts were still centred on our lives in Kabul and enmeshed with the people we worked with and the tasks ahead. In the meantime, we soaked up our families' attentions, to us and the children. I doubt that we ever appreciated the often hidden costs which they had to bear because of our choices. Mum related to me many years later how, on their return from the airport, having farewelled us on our trip back to Afghanistan, Dad retired to the bedroom, closed the door and sobbed.

11

On our return to Kabul in June 1986, we found other team members had left and weren't returning. This included our Scottish neighbours with whom we had shared a house in *KArte ChAr*. We moved house again, back across the river to *KArte Seh*, so that we could be nearer the IAM school. Things were always changing. We settled back into life with two children. Nick and Coby enjoyed each other's company and we enjoyed theirs. I bought poles – poplar wood – from the local wood yard and, having fashioned two A-frames with a beam between them, made a swing for the children. We had new neighbours and developing friendships. There was another family from Scotland with whom we gelled. Donald was an ophthalmologist at NOOR. He and I could pay each other out, not only *not* causing offence but doing so to the immense enjoyment of the other. It seemed that we both brought a love of being silly to the relationship. Perhaps it was the counterpoint within me for the times I was so intense and angry. Donald and Emma became godparents for our daughter Coby, a role which they have never forgotten.

On return from leave, one of the two physiotherapists had given birth and for the other it was imminent. Regardless of the lack of expatriate teaching staff, the promise of a new physiotherapy school building was a visible and expected outcome of our project agreement with the government. Yet, I was acutely aware of how the first physiotherapy program was compromised and incomplete. I felt the responsibility of it, hanging uncomfortably and heavily. The reasons were manifold and had their genesis in my own unpreparedness for this job as well as the adverse context into which both the program and I were launched. I wrote a report to our board which recommended consolidating the work with a more grassroots approach to developing physiotherapy. It seemed to me that a new building and school, while desirable for its better accommodation and facilities, would, at the same time, demand a particular focus of energies and priorities. Despite the work that I had put in to help design it, I recommended not proceeding with the building of the school in the immediate future. Instead, it was my view that we should concentrate on establishing working relationships and placements with a few strategic hospitals in Kabul and using our students, who would have further consolidation of their training, to staff such an enterprise. It seemed better than putting up a building and there training physiotherapists who were, to that point at least, not well connected with the existing Afghan healthcare system. Gerald's letter to me, written some six months after I commenced sick leave, and which I shared earlier, reiterated the centrality of the ongoing challenge of educating Afghan doctors and nurses about physiotherapy and its role. My report was an attempt to convey the lessons which I felt I had learned in the 'what' and the 'how' of the development of the physiotherapy school and the teaching so far. I did not want to repeat the mistakes of the past few years. I was not sure, at an existential level, that I could survive repeating them anyway.

This was a stressful period. And to put this in context, Ocie, is to say that this stress was another layer added to the usual level of stress experienced by living and working in Kabul. There was a reliable, albeit roundabout, way of identifying the surreptitiousness of 'normal' Kabul-induced stress – and being able to see what you had been carrying for long periods. It was experienced only after exiting Kabul and landing in Delhi. Team members shared their own versions of it. But they each went to similar ideas: to arrive in and then walk on the streets of Delhi, with its polluted air and crowded spaces, was to find oneself breathing more easily, paradoxical as it sounds. It just felt lighter as though gravity had different properties here compared with Kabul. Without any conscious decision, an inbuilt level of sustained vigilance was suddenly relaxed. It was its release, rather than its presence, which brought the realization of just how taxing and how heavy, on mind and body, was the ongoing vigilance required to live in Kabul. Now in Delhi, the heavy cloak of war was temporarily removed. The relief was as tangible and welcome as afternoon monsoon rain rinsing hot and dusty air towards the end of summer.

In my mind it was as if the acceptance of the recommendations in my report and my ability to continue in the job were somehow enmeshed. The executive secretary, no longer the American George but now the Canadian Richard, met with me and let me know that the report was accepted with thanks but it had been recommended to proceed with the building. I was very disappointed, even distraught. But as the dust settled on this decision, I could see that reneging on agreements with the ministries of a host government was probably not a fruitful short-term or long-term strategy for fostering ongoing cooperation and work in the country. Despite my misgivings, I did therefore agree to a request from Richard to prepare and commence a second physiotherapy program, with another cohort of students.

Recalling the order of events at the time of my getting sick is hazier than my memory of other things that occurred much earlier. Ocie, I had long believed that as a foreigner I was confronted with a series of curtains in Afghanistan which obfuscated the motives and intentions of others. But the hardest curtain to draw, to let light and understanding in, was the one that veiled an awareness of myself.

I am not sure just when it was that I began to be unwell: when the periodic stomach upsets, associated with parasitic hosting of bugs such as amoeba, a fact of life for all expatriates living in Kabul, became something different. It was sometime in the months after my interview with Richard.

Kabul was a difficult place to get definitive diagnoses. For example, there was no facility for endoscopy. And during the Russian occupation, it was not a good place to have any kind of medical emergency. Sometimes it is the little things which collude to shape a narrative. Like the endoscopy I had while on home leave the year before. The minor findings were now enough to sow seeds of doubt in my mind. These seeds were inadvertently watered by the laconic Ashton who, in social conversation at work, recalled the story of an expatriate colleague, an engineer he had worked with in Iran some years earlier. This person had experienced persistent stomach pain, and was always chewing antacids, only to later die of complications from a perforated duodenal ulcer. This seemed to capture my imagination for all the wrong reasons. No longer could I give any symptom the benefit of the doubt; each became a threat and further fed my rising stress levels and inability to relax or sleep. I was soon exhausted. Kabul's isolation fed the process.

In April 1987 the second physiotherapy course began. I did give a lecture according to my Afghan colleague Maryam, whose corroboration came some eighteen years later with, 'You're that Mr Edwards!' But I don't remember this now at all. As my stomach pain became more constant, I became more and more distracted. There was a sense of no longer having control over events, or my body. It was decided by the IAM leadership in May 1987 that I should go on three months' medical leave in order that proper investigations could be conducted. I was spent and by then just wanted to get out of Kabul and escape what seemed like four years of captivity.

On the morning of our departure Joshua drove early across town to our house to say farewell. I was glad to see him. His short, unannounced visit was a sign that not everything had gone wrong during our time here, even though I was then of the mindset that it had. Richard took us to the airport and we underwent the ritual of the numerous security checks. Three-year-old Nick shouldered his brown corduroy backpack. Coby sat calmly in a pusher. Anne and I lumped our mixed bags and over-limit emotions between the various security checkpoints and searches. Finally, we said our farewells to Richard and walked out onto the tarmac and the Indian Airlines plane. Then we were corkscrewing our way upwards over Kabul, prior to setting safe course for Delhi.

When Richard got back to the office there was a message to say that a team member had been rushed to hospital. It was our Swedish neighbour, Gunilla. She had gone to work, complained of a severe headache and then collapsed. She died from a subarachnoid haemorrhage not long after. It was our first news of Kabul after returning home.

Part Two

Adelaide and Mexico
1987–2004

Other

Foreigner and Other are two faces of the Stranger ... the Foreigner is the stranger we see, the Other is the stranger we do not see.

MICHAEL KEARNEY AND KASCHA SEMONOVITCH

12

You never got to hear what I said about you in your eulogy, Paul. Mum's were the best stories. I started with those. They were essentially survival narratives in which she savoured the fact that you and she both got to the other side of your growing up. Our first home was above the chemist shop, one in a block of several shops, just down from the railway station at Wentworthville. Dad was the pharmacist, I was the baby, you were the toddler and Mum, well, she was the one with the awesome responsibility of keeping us, here read *you*, alive.

There was some renovation work being done around the back of these shops, including the living quarters, and you would meander in the vicinity of where the men were working, watching and listening, probably with much the same acuity that I have earlier attributed to Ocie. Mum described herself as a 'good Methodist', although the way she theatrically mispronounced Methodist – as 'Meffadist' – suggested she was aware of both what it was to be a good Methodist and what it was to waive or loosen some of its obligations. Dad was a quiet and unrebellious Anglican. They received a visit from the Anglican minister. You were down at the front door instantly to greet him and lead him back up the stairs. But you slipped on the first stair. And as any three-year-old son of a good Meffadist might do, you sang out, 'Christ, I almost broke my bloody neck'. I need to emphasize that these were the words Mum *always* used in telling this story!

Neither did your interaction with the workmen end with the learning of new vocabulary. On pay days, the foreman, because he had envelopes of cash to distribute, would carry a revolver in his bag. You found it in one of your searches and began to wave it around. You might have been given the idea by one of the many Westerns which were on television at the time. Anyway, the image of workmen running for cover in various directions while you handled the gun provided Mum with a memory which, from the safety of passing years, only grew in its capacity to delight her.

You did not pursue an interest in guns but you were, nevertheless, able to achieve the same effect with your sense of humour. You could scatter a room with it. It was as if social norms were like bubble wrap and you could not resist popping them. We were at Adelaide Oval, having a day with Dad at the test cricket. At lunch you and I went downstairs to get something to eat. When, with food in hand, we got to the checkout and it was our turn to be served, the young woman asked, 'Are you together?' You answered, 'Yes, but we've been together for far too long'. I saw the momentary destabilization in her work-face and wanted to reassure her that the question had been entirely reasonable. But I thought better of it. How could I explain that you were just playing with bubble wrap?

You had an imperviousness to others' opinions which I never had. I am saying this in a good way, because for many years we did truly value each other's opinions on any number of issues. I am referring to your resilience in the face of others' expectations. When we were teenagers you were, as my older brother, very cool: in your taste of alternative music; in your choice of clothes and how you could wear them; and in hair length that I would never have contemplated. To extrapolate Crocodile Dundee, 'That's not long hair; this is long hair' – your hair was not shoulder length; it was waist length. Mum must have pointed at you one day, while saying to Dad, 'Go bond!' For you and Dad went on a road trip north from Sydney to Grafton, where Dad grew up. *Bond* may have been on her mind, I think, since this occurred not long after she had travelled 80km in to Sydney from Springwood one weekend, in order to bail you from Darlinghurst Police Station where you were sojourning, having been caught in possession of marihuana. In any case, Dad told Mum, who later told me, that on the first day of your trip you stopped for lunch at a pub in country Muswellbrook. The local patrons in the front bar in the early 70s were obviously not used to male youths whose hair brushed their waist belts. A sort of miracle of metaphysics took place: all eyes in the front bar were on you, but it was only Dad who felt the weight of stare.

Then you went away. You followed the overland (hippie) trail to Europe and were not seen, by us at least, for several years. You became the prodigal son in Mum's eyes. She would say, following a long period without hearing from you, 'He's out of the will again'. Eventually, you came home to Adelaide. There was an elder brother in the story of the prodigal son. He was resentful of the unambiguous welcome home his wayward brother received, having fulfilled *his* responsibilities at home for many years without apparent appreciation or love. You had an entirely different hermeneutic for the story. Your logic seemed to be, 'If I did a good job at being a prodigal son then I can *do* an even better elder son'. You made the transition as easily as stepping across a puddle. You became the good elder brother who supported Mum and Dad, faithfully and tenderly, as they aged. When Mum had bowel surgery you took Mum and Dad to the hospital and waited with Dad the whole day. I arrived in the early evening after work. Our sister Jane would come a little later on. Dad was saturated with fatigue and anxiety. You took the call from the surgeon. I watched you tell Dad the good news about the surgery, speaking to him with soft, reassuring words, as if you were sponging the anxiety from his face. Years later, when Dad had a massive stroke, it was you who was there to see him off in the ambulance, comfort Mum and mop Dad's blood from the kitchen floor where he had fallen.

Anne and I were working with the Red Cross in Afghanistan at the time of Dad's stroke. We returned home, as speedily as we could, within a few days. You asked if I wanted to accompany you to the hospital to formally identify Dad's body. I went with you. But when we got there I did not want to go in, saying that I would prefer my last memory of Dad to be the hug we had on our leaving for Afghanistan a few weeks earlier. You could have said, 'I have done everything so far. Can't you even help me with this one?' But you didn't. Instead you said, 'Here are some chairs. You wait here. I'll be just a few minutes'. There was no rancour or judgement. You *were* the good elder brother.

Unlike you, I was anything but the prodigal son in being away for a prolonged period. Some people thought we were foolish in going to Afghanistan. But on the whole, people had a view of us that lay somewhere between the adventurous and the admirable. Instead, it was in my coming home that I saw myself as prodigal, as though I was squandering the opportunity that had been given to me to do something important. And there was another thing. I felt like a stranger. In ways I could not articulate because I didn't understand, I was changed and 'other' than people expected me to be.

On our return from Kabul in May 1987 I was diagnosed with a bacterial infection of the stomach and put on a combination of antibiotic and acid-inhibiting medication. While ostensibly identifying and addressing the cause of my health problems, this diagnosis and medical management was neither a sufficient account of nor remedy for my ills. Although this conclusion would only unfold and make itself clear over the next few years.

The new physiotherapy school building was erected towards the end of 1988, the year after we left Kabul. Its construction was overseen by a retired Adelaide engineer, Tom Fowler, who, with his wife Betty, left for Kabul not long after we arrived home. We stayed in their house in the Adelaide Hills for a time while they were in Kabul. We were grateful but

PART TWO: ADELAIDE AND MEXICO 1987–2004

it was not the association with them which we had envisaged. We were meant to still be in Kabul, with them, not at home in their vacant house. Nevertheless, our families were glad to have us home. Our parents and siblings got to know and spend time with the children. The children came to know this suddenly widened family who loved them greatly.

Those closest to us had both wisdom and the time to allow any answers to the question 'What was it like in Afghanistan?' to be expressed gradually, and haphazardly, without any particular need for ordered sense or commentary. Answering this same question from those we knew less well was more difficult. How does one adequately translate the experience of being in a war zone? Do you even try to explain the paradoxes of life in Kabul with its juxtapositions of delight and horror? Or do you opt more for an 'imagination grabber' by reciting some terrible event as emblematic of the difficulty of life there, thereby saving yourself time and effort in explaining what was often a confusion of ideas?

We experienced a reverse culture shock on our return: a common enough experience for cross-cultural aid workers. For the uninitiated, culture shock can occur in leaving what is familiar and becoming immersed in the unfamiliar. It is a confrontation with the realities of another place which occurs after the excitement of the 'tourist' phase has passed: the sensory stimulation of the surrounding newness is replaced by a sort of disillusionment and the realization, for better or worse, that this is now *your* place to live for an extended period. Part of this culture shock for us was that we were eye witnesses of the war and what it did to people. The consequences of this witness role seeped into our lives slowly and surreptitiously like salt damp, with arguably the same corrosive results.

The reverse version of culture shock occurs in returning to your place of origin or your home. You know it is the same place but it feels different. You work your way around to acknowledging, 'Perhaps it is *me* who has changed and it is *me* who no longer feels confident of fitting into this place that *should* be home'. Ocie, these are the kinds of internal conversations we had. This reverse culture shock occurred on various levels. For example, traversing supermarket aisles full of choices for dog and cat food, presented and marketed as high cuisine. Such capacity for choice was unnerving coming from a place where people had little choice about or control over anything. More generally though, we found that the pressing issues of life were different. The challenges of getting a home loan and servicing a mortgage were realities for our peers but were foreign to us at that point. Our world of the previous four years was one where each day or week was, for ordinary people, spent striving to escape or evade violence and where they were immured in grief by the ongoing loss of family and friends. Afghanistan was known then as 'the forgotten war'. But not by us. It felt as if not mourning with our Afghan friends, workmates and students, or at least not continuing to hold the very fact of their world with us and before us, would constitute some manner of unfaithfulness. In other words, reassimilating into life in Australia too readily would be like some kind of betrayal. We were left with the experience of feeling caught between two seemingly unbridgeable worlds, while belonging to neither, at least temporarily.

Ocie, when you were small – you still are but you won't be by the time you read this – I remember how you would act when someone you didn't know would try to talk with you. You were still learning how *to be* with others in the world. I was on the other side of this uncertainty once. I was to meet your mum and dad and you down at the beach, early one morning, to go paddling on boards. I arrived first and waited. I had on a rashie top and bright-blue bathers. I was not in my usual attire. The three of you arrived. You saw me but kept your eyes lowered and fixed on your hands. You also held a shy smile, which was seemingly bestowed on your hands. I probably contributed to this moment because I have never been one to rush up and grab you. I like to give you space. Noticing all of this, your dad said, 'What's up, Ocean?' You still didn't look up. Eventually, I uttered my familiar catch-cry to you, 'Hey Ocie, it's your Pop, what loves ya!' You opened your arms and swung your body towards me to be picked up.

When we came back after four years in Afghanistan, there were times when, like you, I wasn't sure how to connect with others. We were used to being strangers in Afghanistan where we were obvious outsiders. In Afghanistan it was common to have to answer questions about oneself: it was a daily entrée into conversation. Not being understood by others and not understanding others, due to different levels of language ability and cultural knowledge, had become an accepted fact of life. Also, there was always the sense of this changing and improving over time. Mistakes or misunderstandings were often an occasion for humour: '*Chetor asti?*' wrongly pronounced '*Shutor asti?*' turned 'How are you?' into 'Are you a camel?' In 2007, in mispronouncing his name, I inadvertently called one of my physiotherapy colleagues from the International Committee of the Red Cross a snake. What, in another context, would have been a real insult was taken with good grace and humour. Now, at home, not being understood was starkly different and largely humourless. It might manifest in someone's impatience with our reluctance to talk of our experiences or, on one occasion, annoyance that we didn't appear sufficiently grateful to have left Afghanistan still intact and be safely ensconced once more at home. Feeling like a stranger in one's own place was an isolating experience.

The ambivalence, and fearfulness, of my attempts to bridge the two worlds was evident in the following diary entry:

September 7th, 1987

The visas have been applied for. Or, at least, Melbourne has been notified to initiate the business.

One thought occurred to me which helped the final decision. It could be considered as a negative argument. It was this. If we decided because of the effects of stress upon my health not to go back then it would be time to settle here. This would involve finding a new job, a place to live (and in all probability trying to buy it) and the general process of settling back into life here – a kind of re-acculturation. All this would be not so different in terms of stress than going back to Kabul. Again, by using a negative argument to help clarify the situation one could say that the consequences of making a mistake by going back would be hard to take. However, the consequences of making a mistake by not going back may be worse.

Not long after this was written, my unreadiness to return to Kabul became less escapable as a fact. We put off any return and turned our minds to resettling in Adelaide, at least for the foreseeable future. I was able to find work as a physiotherapist in a large hospital. However, once more the notion of feeling like a stranger loomed large, this time among colleagues and the workplace itself. This was, of course, largely a self-generated perception. But it was still real in its effects on me. My discomfort can best be described as a state of impostorship. With impostorship there is an acute unease, at being perceived by others as some sort of fraud who does not know what they are doing. This was highly ironic given the nature and scope of my workplace experience over the previous four years, not only in the kinds of unusual cases – children with polio, leprosy or tuberculosis – I had seen but with the responsibilities I had in the design of both a physiotherapy program curriculum and a school building. Even with all of that work experience, there remained a sense of terror at being on the wards, together with a misguided sense of being scrutinized by colleagues. One time I paid for a weekend refresher course in neurological physiotherapy, only to get to the door of the venue and turn around and come home. Anne was not impressed at the waste of this course fee when we were not financially well off – a small example of my prodigality. But again, I felt like a stranger, looking in on my own community of practice from the outside.

We were well looked after by our sending agency within the constraints and practices of the day. I was placed on anti-depressants for the first time in my life. A certain equilibrium had returned to our lives, including the birth of our third child. We purchased a house. I was able to move from the hospital and find a job working at a rehabilitation centre for injured workers not far from home. However, there was always a pull on an imaginary line connecting us to Kabul. Any news of Afghanistan was like a sensitive scar being touched or tugged at, resulting in peaks of distress in an overall emotional flatness. And then I developed back pain.

13

Sunday 29th October, 1989 and the night refused to settle. There were flashes of coloured light, like the incandescent red of tracer bullets. The streets were smoke filled, and the steady noise of traffic was punctuated by explosions. I was disorientated, wondering whether I had already arrived in Kabul on an active night. No, I was in Delhi, as I should be, and it was the festival of Diwali: panoplies of lights and fireworks launched by suburban Delhiites, mimicking war in an overly vigilant mind.

I was making a journey to Kabul to assess the situation first-hand in order to help Anne and I decide if we should return there with our children. There were now three – Bronnie had been born in December 1988. An original three-month leave of absence had so far turned into a two-year deferment of any return. In June 1989, two years after leaving Kabul, I received an Order of Australia Medal for my physiotherapy service in Afghanistan. This affirmation of my work was very welcome and went some way towards validating the four years we had spent in Kabul. But it also provoked another pull on the line and further thoughts of returning to the project in Kabul. These strong ties – more like fishing lines with hooks – had never left us, and the tension in the line, and our emotions, would move between periods of quiescence and bursts of active jagging.

There was no Afghan Embassy or consular service in Australia at the time and so it was necessary to pick up one's visa in Delhi or London. My visa was purportedly at the Afghan Embassy in Delhi but when I went to have it stamped in my passport, they would not acknowledge or issue it. The office in Kabul insisted it had been granted. I also had a back problem and whiled away significant blocks of this time in a horizontal position in my room in the guesthouse between visits to the Afghan Embassy. I spent seventeen days in Delhi trying to resolve the impasse. I gave up and returned to Adelaide.

The pull to return to Afghanistan was a strong one. I didn't seem to be able to go back to Kabul and I didn't seem to be able to live, contentedly, at least, at home in Adelaide. On my return from Delhi in 1989, I had some X-rays taken of my lumbar spine and consulted with the medical director at the rehabilitation centre where I now worked. Seeing me for this personal, non-work-related matter was a collegial and generous gesture on his part. On slapping the views he wanted onto the X-ray viewer, he said in his unguarded and frank manner, 'Shit, there's not much disc space at L5/S1'. [L5/S1 is an intervertebral segment in the low back.] There is a history that I attach to this bit of information. I first hurt my back playing rugby some eleven years previously. I was in possession of the ball trying to keep my feet while others above me were intent on heading earthwards. This injury had left me very sore and stiff for a week or two but I recovered okay and without any ongoing limitations in my life. I had experienced backache occasionally in the intervening time, including in Afghanistan, but usually dealt with this, quite easily and effectively, by some self-stretching and mobilizing of my lumbar spine. After all, I *was* a physio. More recently, I had experienced some back pain following the lifting of some moss rocks, together with my next-door neighbour, for placement in our respective gardens. This was prior to my trip to Delhi.

Hearing my boss's words about the narrow disc space at L5/S1 was a little like hearing about the engineer who chewed antacids in Iran – the one who died of a perforated duodenal ulcer. The information penetrated deeply and, regardless of the collegiality of the remarks – his other advice was to continue the exercise and fitness work I was doing – I learned unintentionally, and also unhelpfully, about the 'unreliable' and 'defective' structural intervertebral level in my low back. My thinking was now focussed on a particular structure of my back, and the compelling visual image of a narrowed disc space, as the source of my problem and my pain.

It would be at least another decade before the findings of pain science studies would make their way into clinical practice, having empirically demonstrated that pain is a processed *output* of the brain and not just the result of an *input* to it from damaged tissues. In other words, my ongoing pain was perpetuated, in large part, by the way in which I interpreted the level of threat presented by the symptoms rather than primarily arising from the lumbar intervertebral level about which I had so much concern. And being a physiotherapist who did not seem to be able to get this better did nothing to lessen this level of threat posed by my back.

Rehabilitating workers with ongoing back pain was my professional domain. I had the skills and clinical experience for managing others' back problems and, therefore, my overriding thought was, 'I ought to be able to fix this!' I was faithful to my professional work paradigm as a physiotherapist and took a very active, exercise-based approach to the problem, at least when I wasn't in temporary retreat from activities due to the onset of one symptom or other. There was a gym and a pool at my workplace which I could use before work and during lunch breaks. I swam a kilometre each lunchtime. I followed a regime of strengthening and flexibility exercises in the gym before work. I was otherwise very fit and not carrying excess weight. The assiduousness with which I exercised was only matched by my diligence in 'monitoring' my own symptoms. I was vigilant, overly so, and developed a phobia about sitting. I bought a myriad of different back supports for sitting. Going to new or unknown places always involved a kind of scouting of the types of chairs in a room: would they be supportive of my lumbar spine or would they make my problem worse? Where could I sit so that when I needed to stand I could do so discreetly? I missed the funeral of a close family member on my wife's side of the family because I did not think that I could cope with sitting for the duration of the two-hour car journey to a town south of Adelaide where the funeral was being held. This was not good: my problem had shifted from its origins as a musculoskeletal injury to become a more existential issue, shaping both how I saw myself and how I made significant life choices. It was more than a professional conundrum. I had failed to do what I had set out to do in Afghanistan and now I was failing here, both as a physiotherapist and a person, in the matter of getting on top of an ordinary back problem.

While I mostly insisted on managing this problem by myself, I did on occasion consult with physiotherapy colleagues. I would not have been an easy patient for them to make sense of what was perpetuating my symptoms, let alone how best to manage them. I recall their patience; patience perhaps tinged with a reluctance to say what they really wanted to about my back problem. It usually ended with me asking them to loosen or massage certain structures and their compliance with my requests.

After a year or so of exercising and following accepted postural and lifting guidelines, the measures which *ought* to have got me better had not done so. I heard about a new, relatively non-invasive method of treatment for bulging lumbar discs called chemonucleolysis. This involved the injection, under X-ray guidance, of chymopapain, an enzyme derived from papaya fruit, into the problematic disc. The theory was that chymopapain would desiccate the soft, bulging part of the disc, the nucleus pulposus, leading to the recession of the 'bulge' and, hopefully, a more stable intervertebral segment. A prominent orthopaedic surgeon was doing this procedure in Adelaide at this time and, following our consultation, was prepared to offer it to me. He did suggest that afterwards I might feel as though I had been kicked by a horse. He was right. For some time I wondered what on earth I had done in pursuing this course.

It was as if I had set in train a further escalation of existing hostilities, going from poorly judged diplomacy, in trying to subdue my back problem with a strict regime of exercise, to issuing orders for a precision air strike on the L5/S1 lumbar disc. Slowly, after around six weeks, the pain and stiffness began to settle once more and I resumed exercise but less aggressively. Peace was now called for. I finally accepted its terms and looked forward, perhaps for the first time in four years. We went on a family holiday to the west coast of South Australia, which is a wild and beautiful place. And I just didn't think so much about my back. It became less of a threat that always required something be done *about* it or *to* it. The modified biblical injunction 'Physio, heal thyself!', with its undertone of hostility, became a more hospitable 'Physio, go a bit easier on thyself!'

I have read that post-traumatic stress disorder (PTSD), often diagnosed in people returning from theatres of war, has been called 'the moral injury', in so much as it describes the challenge of recovering a good or worthy self in the face of the terrible things a person has seen or even perpetrated. It seems paradoxical for an aid worker, who was doing good works, to contemplate such a notion. But I searched fruitlessly for the settled self that had existed prior to Afghanistan. I was never given the diagnosis of PTSD. Nor have I ever appropriated this label for myself. 'Burnout' was the term I heard. I can say that for some years after leaving Afghanistan the sound of a helicopter, even one benevolently patrolling our local beach for sharks, would instantly evoke an unpleasant and visceral reaction. Regardless of the significance of this (or not), not being able to talk about Afghanistan, and the feeling of being a stranger, an outsider, in Adelaide, conspired with my recalcitrant back problem such that *it* became a proxy upon which to lay all that sadness and confusion.

14

Nothing about us without us.

DAVID WERNER

Sometime late in 1992 I came across a book called *Disabled Village Children* which spoke to many of my personal experiences as a physiotherapist and novice teacher in Afghanistan. These experiences had been confronting, even disturbing, but had remained largely unexpressed and unshared. In Adelaide, parents no longer brought their children for physiotherapy because of impairments resulting from leprosy, poliomyelitis and tuberculosis or, for that matter, as a consequence of paralysis caused by bullet wounds to the spine. In rural Mexico, as in Afghanistan, those without resources, which were the majority of ordinary people, did not have access to treatment or rehabilitation for their children. The insidiously disabling effects of these undertreated conditions therefore remained in the lives of many. Paralysis, deformity and stigma not only disabled these young people but excluded them from meaningful participation in the life of their communities. Reading this book was like having a conversation I had not been able to have since leaving Afghanistan.

Based on the experiences of a locally run community-based rehabilitation centre in the Mexican village of *Ajoya*, the book explained in simple, accessible terms the nature of particular conditions and also offered practical strategies to address the physical, psychological and social needs of the person. In short, it was a book written for use by village health workers and others without high levels of formal education for doing rehabilitation in contexts with few resources. This approach included instruction on how to use local materials to make exercise equipment, splints and aids for ambulation and mobilization. It was an approach to physiotherapy and rehabilitation where valuing and including the person's own understandings and aspirations called for a process of mutual learning and problem-solving. And it was this idea, rather than the uniqueness of locally made rehabilitation equipment, which captured my interest as a physiotherapist. A central message was that disability was not just the result of the physical impairments. Disability was experienced even more strongly by the person as a form of exclusion from the life of the community and society around them. The book named attitudes held by the wider society, and too often by health professionals, which perpetuated these various forms of exclusion.

With so few physiotherapists in rehabilitation-hungry Afghanistan, and with so much need, I could see that the valuing and harnessing of the existing knowledge and abilities of people were also needed there. I had to admit, even though some intuitive nod of agreement had been stirred within me, these ideas had not been explicitly part of my previous physiotherapy practice or teaching. In wanting to express something of this internal conversation, I took the unique step, for me at least, of writing to the author, David Werner, saying that I wished that I had access to this resource when I was in Afghanistan. To my surprise he wrote back, suggesting that we would be welcome to come and spend some time in *Ajoya* with the people and the project. It so happened that around that time Anne had an aunt, the one whose funeral I missed because of back pain, who had recently passed away and left her around $15,000. This was sufficient for airfares and accommodation for the five of us to financially cover a two-month period. After some discussion, primarily about how to use this money – we, too, had acquired a house mortgage by now – and after further correspondence with Project *Projimo* staff by

PART TWO: ADELAIDE AND MEXICO 1987–2004

letter, we arranged to spend time in *Ajoya*. Ocie, I am still in awe of your Ma's capacity to embrace uncertainty and adventure, and very grateful for it too.

From not perceiving myself able to travel two hours south of Adelaide to Goolwa by car, preparing to travel to rural Mexico represented quite a shift in my mindset. Anne and I knew that we were going with our three young children to an isolated village with few amenities, as well as to an unfamiliar rural Mexican culture. We prepared the children, Nick nine, Coby seven and Bronnie five, for this experience by reading them stories of the project and life in the village while we were still in Adelaide. We were able to do this from reading older issues of a publication called *Newsletter from the Sierra Madre*. We read 'Lupe the wildcat', which told of a feisty young girl who was accidentally shot in the spine by a ricocheting bullet resulting in paraplegia; a not uncommon cause of spinal injury in the Sierra Madre region. Lupe's story showed the many challenges in learning to live in an isolated rural community with paraplegia. Following her recovery from the acute stage of the injury, she had to relearn how to do everyday things such as washing and dressing herself and moving around in an environment not conducive to either crutches or wheelchair use. She also had to look after herself in new ways to prevent dangerous pressure sores around her tailbone and buttocks. But more than that, in her story we also learned of the obstacles that Lupe had to overcome in order to feel useful and wanted once more. 'Marcelo and Luis' was quite a different story about two friends. Luis was very limited in his physical abilities, with muscles in constant severe spasm (spasticity) preventing him from controlling his limbs for even simple movements. This caused Luis to feel very isolated, frustrated and lonely. Marcelo, on the other hand, was very strong and mobile but had problems with being able to think and express himself to others. Their friendship not only showed how each boy's acceptance of the other was a good and helpful thing but also how this friendship allowed each to make best use of their own abilities. Marcelo helped Luis get around and Luis helped Marcelo in his interactions with others. Our children enjoyed these stories which offered insights into village life and the ethos of the project to which we were going.

The village of *Ajoya* (pop. 750) appeared at the end of a winding track, an hour from the small town of San Ignacio, which was, in turn, a few hours east from the coastal city of *Mazatlan*. We arrived in early December 1993, to a village and project environment which had changed since the writing of the stories. *Ajoya* as a poor rural community was not quarantined from the joblessness, falling wages, crime and violence that were occurring throughout Mexico at that time. The village of *Ajoya*, as it turned out, was a strategically located exchange point for illegal drugs grown in the mountains and the drug traffickers making their way northwards, up the western coastal highway through Sinaloa towards the US. The early success of the project serving disabled children and their families had raised its profile in such a way that young adults with spinal injuries, who would otherwise face a dramatically shortened future due to infection, were now drawn to *Ajoya* and Project *Projimo* for rehabilitation and treatment of pressure sores. Many of the spinal injuries sustained by these young adults resulted from violence associated with their past involvement with alcohol and their using or trafficking drugs. Unfortunately, they brought these habits and this culture of violence to the project. This meant that families with disabled children felt less safe and those who were there already gradually began to leave, while others stopped coming to the project and the village. We arrived not long after a volunteer, by the name of Quique, who had high-level quadriplegia, had been asked to leave the project for these very reasons. The project team were demoralized both by the general direction of things and by the conflict caused by Quique having to leave. But they were hoping that a planned course in January 1994 for parents and their children with cerebral palsy would catalyse a renewed period of purpose and direction for the project.

Despite the candour of *Newsletter from the Sierra Madre* – after all, it was written in the same vein as *Disabled Village Children* – one can never know the true struggles of any family or community anywhere until you actually spend time with them. We were not aware of the extent to which these issues affected the lives of project members and villagers alike when we decided to bring our young family to *Ajoya*.

Upon our arrival the villagers were friendly enough and our hosts Lupe and Bella quickly showed themselves to be decent people and generous hosts. However, there was a harshness about life there that was immediately redolent of Afghanistan. Despite being in the countryside among mountains, there was nevertheless a constraint on our movements brought about by the isolation and the hazard of unpredictable violence. We were told early on which paths from the village into the surrounding countryside were safe for us to walk along and which weren't. As if to confirm the gravity of this advice there was a murder in the village, only three days after we arrived. One man shot another during an argument, leaving a widow and several children. My Spanish did not allow me to understand what the argument had been about. It was, nevertheless, immediately clear that in this small village violence and murder were not irregular events. We were told to stay inside and not unlock our doors that night. There would be a wake with young men drinking, with the potential for deteriorating behaviour. We followed the advice of our hosts as to where we should or shouldn't go on our excursions around and out from the village, but we soon fell into a conformity with the more natural habits and rhythms of the village. One of these was the alignment of life and work with the position of the sun. Darkness came early in these parts. The five of us would retire each night at about 8pm, finding ourselves alone – well, almost. We bunked down on a double bed and single bed pushed together in one room of the two-roomed adobe casa. We were separated from the other room by a thin curtain across the adjoining doorway where, in some sort of symmetry, our hosts Lupe and Bella slept with their two young sons (Victor and Antonio) and a third, even younger child, granddaughter Alicia.

Previously, I would have said, along with many others, that it was the cries of children, or their wakefulness, which mostly interrupted the sleep of parents. Here, at least initially, it was the sounds produced by our *sleeping* children which disturbed my attempted surrender to sleep. As I lay awake thinking in the complete darkness, I listened to the little catches of air pushed through small noses and, in the case of one of our daughters, an open mouth. The steady pulses of breathing, although at first an irritant, became after a while a source of comfort to me. What was most near was also most dear.

We had this much in common with the *campesinos* of this remote village: a responsibility to look after and provide for our children in both good and bad times. But for these villagers it was also the source of much heartache that the responsibility of nurturing their children had to be constantly carried out in a context of such indigence and violence. Project *Projimo* would, in a few years, need to uproot and leave *Ajoya* and move closer to the main highway. Kidnappings became a particular tactic in a larger pattern of sustained, indiscriminate violence, as *campesinos*, like ordinary Afghans, happened to find themselves in the way of others' conflicts. In *Ajoya* it was mostly to do with drugs, and disputes about money and loyalty.

15

Ajoya really was a small, rural Mexican village. There were no hotels, motels or restaurants. A government shop functioned as a general store. A few smaller shops, not marked in any way, sold an identical range of wares, mostly processed grocery items. Our children would come to indicate which shop they meant by the colour of its walls. They spoke of the yellow shop, the pink shop and the shop opposite the tortilla shop. There was one sign painted on a wall which advertised services relating to cattle. There was also a place to buy beer, an outlet rather than a cantina. Thankfully it was at the other end of the village since young men would impatiently, and sometimes noisily, hang around outside it. There were no street signs or street names, and *Ajoya* had no sealed roads.

Ajoya was a place which shared with Afghanistan, but in its own way, gaps in the sequence of development. It had been hooked up to electricity in the 1970s. Some, but not many, of the residents had large aerials and therefore televisions. Incredulously, there were satellite dishes to be seen on three roofs in the village. I say incredulously because there was no phone in the village and no official postal service. We learned that you could give the village bus driver your letters, either with stamps on them or with money to buy stamps, and he would post them in *Mazatlan*, the city on the coast. One bus serviced the village. It left between 5.30 and 6.00am each weekday morning and Saturdays, first doing a circuit of the village, horn blaring to encourage passengers to present themselves if they intended going to Saint Ignacio or *Mazatlan*. It returned at the end of the day.

There was no glass to be seen in the village, the exception being the windows of a few pickup trucks. These were just about the only vehicles one saw except for the village bus and an occasional truck. Even the school did not have glass or louvered windows. The climate seemed to predicate that the free flow of air was better all year round. Windows were rectangular openings in the wall with wrought iron bars (more or less decorated) across them. The adobe (mud brick) walls and roof tiles, supplemented with another layer of dried mud over thatches of bamboo, were very effective in keeping inside temperature constant in comparison with that outside. It was like the house design in Afghanistan in this respect, although the climate in Afghanistan was generally much colder.

There were no sporting fields or venues in *Ajoya*, save for one basketball ring which I did not ever see used. Towards the end of our time, I did witness an impromptu game of baseball played in the village square by a group of teenagers. To connect this lack of amenities with other issues in the village such as unemployment, drugs and violence, it was significant that there was no police station in *Ajoya*. The police would come as needed, which was fairly often, from San Ignacio an hour's drive away. When they did come it was dramatic. They would pull up in a pickup truck in the village square in a show of force; a half dozen police in the back, all wearing bulletproof vests and helmets. That is, they were in riot gear and armed with semi-automatic weapons. We witnessed this on more than one occasion and made sure to stay well out of the way.

A medical clinic existed staffed by a nurse. This did not provide any surgical or emergency services. Alejandro, the village dentist, was the only one who spoke English at the time of our arrival and for the first few days was our interpreter and informant. He told us that when someone was wounded, for whatever reason, and it was an emergency, they usually drove that person to *Mazatlan*. However, because *Mazatlan* was over three and a half hours away, and over rough roads, the injured person often died before they got there.

PART TWO: ADELAIDE AND MEXICO 1987–2004

Proyecto *Projimo* had achieved an accepted, even respected, place in the village for both its contribution to its economy and the rehabilitation services it offered, notwithstanding the recent controversy brought about by its own unwitting importation of violent behaviour. The project compound was at the northern end of the village, about 600 metres from Lupe and Bella's cottage, which sat on its southern edge. It consisted of a number of single-storey adobe buildings, not so different from others in the village except that they were arranged around a piece of land; clay so hard and well-trodden it was almost shiny. Confirming the long continuity of existence, the men digging foundations for a new *baño* (toilet block) uncovered broken stone axe heads that had been used and discarded centuries before. One part of this ancient ground had been turned into a playground. Given the spartan nature of village amenities, entering the compound and coming across this playground was a surprise. Adding to this, the swings in this playground were even more unusual in so much as they had back and arm rests for the seats. There were also two large tyres strung between wooden uprights and further stabilized with poles. Each of these tyres had a wooden handle protruding from it, simulating a saddled and waiting horse or burro which, to a physiotherapist's eye, was ready for 'riding' by those who had impairments in sitting balance or in arm or leg control. The playground was clearly a project aimed at including children with disabilities in the life of play and fun enjoyed by able-bodied children: even if able-bodied village children here had far less time for such play than children at home.

When we first saw the playground, there were no children in sight and it seemed somehow bereft and not merely vacant. The buildings also seemed uneasily quiet and devoid of activity. There was a longish, rectangular building consisting of a few adjacent single rooms with a shared veranda sheltering the entrance to each. This was used for accommodation by those engaged in rehabilitation. But they were empty.

There was also a clinic building where patients were assessed. Another nearby structure was subdivided into rooms for workshops. One of these was a woodwork shop for making mobility aids and wooden toys for sale and another was dedicated to working with leather. A garage housed a metalwork shop where wheelchairs, prostheses and callipers were made. Then, further towards the river, whose five-metre-high bank formed the eastern boundary of the property, was the physical therapy department, not much more than a small room with low plinths. The 'gym', with parallel bars, and by which physiotherapy departments are usually recognized, was outside in the yard. We were shown through the project compound by our host Lupe, who was employed as a general hand for the project. Mari, the person in charge of therapy and rehabilitation, was away, as was Conchita, the administrator.

On the wall of the main clinic building were two drawings which characterized what the project was about. The first was a stick-figure diagram of a boy high atop a horizontal bar, upturned and swinging by his outstretched arms. His spindly legs splayed skywards, as in a celebration of freedom and daring, and his crutches, temporarily discarded, rested against the uprights. The picture was completed by an explanatory text below it: *Fijese en mis dones no en mis defectos* (Look first at my strengths not my weaknesses). The other, unlabelled in any way but with a message nevertheless self-evident, was a picture of four hands, each grasping their neighbour's wrist to form an interlocking and strong bond. *Projimo* is an acronym of the Spanish version of Program of Rehabilitation Organized by Disabled Youth of Western Mexico. *Projimo* also means *neighbour*. This was rehabilitation for persons with disability by persons with disability. These things, the pictures and playground, all spoke the message of solidarity and inclusion. However, there was little evidence of anyone, children or otherwise, currently involved in rehabilitation.

The main activity just now appeared to be a building project. Several men were constructing a new *baño* (bathroom or toilet) prior to the January course. This course was to support and provide strategies for parents and carers of children with cerebral palsy as well as teach assessment and management skills to lay physical therapists. We were not invited to it. The *Projimo* team were expecting visitors, both teachers and participants, from interstate in Mexico as well as the US, Nicaragua and El Salvador. They were concerned to retain a balance in numbers between local lay health workers, such as the Central American guests, and the participating parents and children. It was about 'voice' too. Having too many professional visitors might inhibit the sharing of experiences of either the Mexican and Central American teachers or the participants themselves. We understood and had agreed to this condition prior to leaving Australia.

We had come to *Projimo* as observers and learners. No other particular role had been negotiated. The problem was that at this time there was not much in the way of community-based rehabilitation to observe. Meanwhile, in the temporary absence of Mari and Conchita, I offered to help the men preparing foundations for the new toilet block. They were interspersing work on this project with other tasks such as repairing equipment and putting new parallel bars in the ground outside near the playground. There were different-sized sets of parallel bars reminiscent of three well-known bears: a small child size, an adolescent middle size and an adult size set. My initial help consisted of wheeling barrows of dirt, before and after lunch, for which I received two home-made empanadas (pies) from the woman at the casa where we returned the wheelbarrow. *Mucho sabroso!* Very tasty! I learned some Spanish early on. On another day I would assist with some digging. My shovelling style didn't go unnoticed. The fact that digging was not a daily occupation of mine, combined with the now inbuilt protective strategies for bracing and protecting my back, undoubtedly contributed to the observation offered by one of the leaders of the *baño* construction. In a very loud and public way, he pronounced something about the way I was going about the work. The use of the word 'gringo' with its pejorative meanings and the laughter of those around me was sufficient for me to get the gist of his remark, even though my Spanish did not allow me to pick up exactly what had been said.

While we waited for the project to become active again, Anne and I began informal Spanish lessons with Cecelia, the partner of Ines, the lay physical therapist in the project. Given there were few English speakers in either the project or the village, this had an obvious functional benefit for us. To start with, we could talk more with our hosts Lupe and Bella, hearing their advice to us for living safely (and enjoyably) in the village and, equally important, begin to understand life from their perspective. Living in their cottage, in such close proximity, there were times when it was arguably better that we did not understand them nor they us.

Personal washing took place in an outside small room rather more like a shed. It had a sloping concrete slab. This slab was both raised and corrugated and stood at about waist level, enclosed by slightly raised edges which formed a trough. There was a hole at the lower end which allowed the water to escape into a kind of drain. The drain from this washstand went straight past the outside 'kitchen' of the house next door. The neighbour's pigs didn't mind that at all since they wallowed in it. Lupe and Bella had a good arrangement in that two 44-gallon drums were kept full of water by a hose that came from the front. From these drums one used a small dish which was kept there to scoop out water for washing in this concrete trough. We got used to the snuffling and grunting of pigs in close proximity while conducting our ablutions in this way. The pigs were both audible and visible, snouts muzzling in the gaps of the flimsy wooden fence as we, on our side, stood soaped up and naked, ready to rinse with our scooped water. These pig noises, along with the distinctive contributions of roosters and donkeys (burros), formed a daily soundtrack of village life, punctuating the day like town clocks. This was at its most notable in the early morning and evenings. Sometimes we were fooled by what we heard:

> **Friday 10th December**
>
> Anne almost dropped a bombshell the other night. Fortunately, she said what she said in English, not being able to say it in Spanish. The pigs move close to the house on various occasions and Anne, hearing Lupe burp, mistakenly said to the children, 'Children, listen to the pig'. It did sound remarkably similar.

Village life connected the chain of need and supply, in a sometimes grim way that we suburban city dwellers found hard to understand. One morning in January our next-door neighbour's pig, having been tethered over the previous few weeks and fattened by handfeeding, was slaughtered. It was an unnerving, even distressing, experience to hear its high-pitched, frantic squeals for survival, and because of this, just as unnerving to later address the plate of freshly prepared pork we had for lunch. In this event I came to learn the substance behind the expression 'squeal like a stuck pig'. My former colleague Joshua had once applied this expression to me and my complaints in Kabul. It was a pointed reminder of the intensity of our conflict.

Our Spanish lessons, haphazard but enjoyable, provided some income for our teacher Cecelia and the project. In contrast the children were remarkably at ease in getting along with Victor, Tony and Alicia and the neighbours' kids, Luis, Marcella and Maria Louise. They generally ran around together playing marbles, cards and looking at books. Our kids learned the skill of spinning tops. All of this occurred without the aid or crutch of language lessons. One afternoon, our youngest daughter, Bronnie, turned up with green paint all over her hands, not water soluble of course. Finding out *why* she had green paint all over her hands was less important than finding some petrol to clean them, not our first choice of solvent but the only option it seemed. Even this was not straightforward since the village had no gas station. However, one of the neighbours kindly produced some from somewhere.

Mari and Conchita returned and we had a further induction to the project and its ways when we were invited to observe a team meeting.

> **Friday 10th December**
>
> We sat through a two-hour community meeting. Fortunately Alexandro interpreted the discussion in a general way. They don't pull punches with each other. One person was upbraided for having developed a hard attitude with the patients who come. Another, our host, was declined holidays because of a break in service with the community ten months ago.

Even with Mari and Conchita back in the village the project was quiet. People started coming to see me for physiotherapy consultations. Initially there were people outside the project who sought an opinion. And then various members of the project began to approach me.

> **Friday 10th December**
>
> Less than a year and a half ago, Pedro was shot in the stomach. I counted three bullet wound scars. As a result of one bullet hitting the spine he is a paraplegic from lumbar vertebra 2 down. He was brought to me

to ask my opinion on bracing – 18 months down the track! I saw four people this morning for opinions and therapy.

There was a rule at *Projimo* – not so much explicitly stated but more as part of the ethos of the place – that visiting health workers should not treat patients unless this was done in the context of teaching and with a local counterpart present. Ines was the resident lay physical therapist. He was therefore the logical person to work with me. Like all the rehabilitation staff at *Projimo* he had a disability. He had incomplete paralysis of one leg, having had polio as a youngster. Ines had a nickname at the project, *Camaron*, meaning 'shrimp'. Perhaps it had been given, as some nicknames are, because the opposite was true: he was very strong. I jump ahead to a diary entry about a month after we arrived.

> **Monday 3rd January**
>
> I need to mention another of Camaron's (Ines) deeds today. Quite amazing. He was carrying logs and that is the term which should be used, such was the size and circumference of these lengths of wood. It was during the process of mending a fence. He would walk across the compound (remember that he is on elbow crutches with only one useful leg) and there he would somehow hoist a log weighing 100 plus kilos onto one shoulder, his right. He would balance this log on the shoulder and walk, with the log balanced and both hands on the elbow crutches, back across the compound. His gait was smooth enough, his strength great enough, and balance skilful enough to enable him to walk some 20–30 metres and then with a heave of the right shoulder throw the log off. It would hit the ground with much reverberation because of its weight. He did this several times.

At the time we arrived at the project Ines was mostly busy with the building of the new *baño* and other general repairs. He did accompany me early on with consultations but this changed. This may have been because he was too busy with the *baño* construction. It may also have been because he felt he had little to learn from me. Or, it may have had something to do with the fact that, when other project members gradually came to see me for opinions or advice, personal vulnerabilities were exposed which were too difficult to share with the others, and his staying away from such sessions was by mutual, if not tacit, agreement:

Wednesday 15th December

Today I was asked by the worker who works in leather (Huarache) about the pain in his stumps. He is a double above-knee amputee … His stumps have shrunk and his prostheses, which are excellent and made in *Projimo*, need to be redone. This will be done in January.

I was also asked … to examine Miguel. He works in the carpentry shop and is a paraplegic. His paraplegia is the result of gunshot wounds. He was shot seven times and yes it was drug related. He has a multiplicity of problems, including scabies, but in my opinion the most significant of his problems are his pressure sores – three of them over his coccyx and buttocks. One of them is about an inch from his anus. He has had this one for about nine months and I suspect (because I did not have anything sterile to probe it with) that there is a sinus tracking down and inwards towards the ischium. The chances of infection are high. The opinion I gave is that by now it probably needs surgery. The problems are that his own body care is so poor that surgery, even if arrangements were made now, would be six months away and even then there is no guarantee that the appropriate follow-up care would occur.

This was an example of how things had gone at the project. Even this member of the team was not doing the right thing by himself. Understandably, if not unwisely, since he needed support, Miguel did not want me to tell anyone about his problem. Having sat in on the team meeting, I could understand his not wanting to be excoriated by others in the team for having neglected his health in this way. Ironically, *Projimo*, in the past, had achieved an excellent record in 'curing' and healing pressure sores by use of gurneys and mixtures of honey in dressings for the sores. On the gurneys the patient could get around and do some work without prolonged sitting. They felt useful and employed. I held Miguel's secret for the time being.

Carlos was arguably the most vulnerable member of the *Projimo* community. He was a twelve-year-old boy who had sustained a traumatic head injury following an accident while working as a farm labourer a couple of years before. He came from the distant south-western state of Oxaca. Following his injury Carlos had been abandoned and somehow found his way, or more accurately, been brought by someone, from Oxaca to *Ajoya*. This traverse of distance alone spoke of *Projimo*'s reputation for care and rehabilitation. Carlos certainly needed care and was not a productive team member, at least in the sense of contributing to the rehabilitation work of the community. A middle-aged woman called Rosa, who did cooking and washing at the project, had taken on the job of looking after him and became his primary carer. She asked me to work with Carlos. He would spend most of his time wheeling himself about in his wheelchair, seeking companionship and attention, sometimes at inopportune moments from the point of view of those whose work or conversation he 'wheeled into'. He would be welcomed or teased depending on which person he encountered or interrupted, and this, in turn, could cause either delight or frustration for Carlos. If delighted, Carlos had a wholehearted laugh. If frustrated, he might respond by spitting or by shitting or pissing in his pants. While these could happen anyway, nevertheless such actions provided Carlos with a tangible form of protest.

Marcelo was a gifted artisan. One afternoon I watched him make an above-knee prosthesis for a visitor to the village. This visitor was a medical doctor from interstate who had bypassed the services of several larger centres for the quality of artificial limb that she knew she could obtain from Marcelo in a garage in this small village. Marcelo's own story had also been documented in the *Newsletter from the Sierra Madre*. Like the other members of *Projimo*, Marcelo had contracted polio as a child and lost the use of his legs. And like the great majority of *Projimo* rehabilitation workers, Marcelo had achieved primary school education but not graduated from secondary school. In his case, though, his intelligence and talent had been recognized and he had experienced a sort of apprenticeship at a prosthetics department in a hospital in *Mazatlan*. Marcelo's skills in action were a glimpse for me of what had taken place at *Projimo* – even though I had not seen much evidence of it so far – and what could be achieved by people when they were provided with even informal opportunities to learn.

Marcelo had made some callipers for Carlos's legs to support him in standing. However, Carlos was presently not able to use them since he did not have any shoes, having lost previous pairs. I bought Carlos a pair of shoes and began to work with him on the parallel bars (the middle-sized ones).

Wednesday 22nd December

Carlos likes his shoes and Rosa, who mostly looks after him, seemed genuinely pleased that he had some shoes. One problem is that Carlos is not very used to them and so he has taken the laces out and now they are lost. I have found some white twine which should serve just as well. For the time being the shoes can stay in the physio department and be used when he has walking practice. Today Carlos and I were singing together (to the tune of La Cucaracha / the cockroach):

> *Con aparato, con aparato,*
>
> *Carlos puede caminar* (repeat x3)

Translated:

> With his brace, with his brace,
>
> Carlos is able to walk!

Singing in physiotherapy sessions seemed quite a natural thing to do here. Music was always present in the village in one form or another. The house across the street from Lupe's and Bella's place was on one occasion filled with people singing to the backing of a lone guitar player. Everything about the song was simple but it produced a wonderfully relaxing atmosphere at the end of the day's work. In contrast to this 'live' performance, the village was not short on cassette players, which seemed to be always played at near to or full capacity. For example, Conchita next door would give hers a real wind up. I was by now familiar with a great deal of her collection. The music was more often than not in a waltz time and the Mexican equivalent of 'country music', which was not surprising since we were definitely rural here. Some of the music reminded me of Ry Cooder, with livewire piano accordion, pleasant vocal harmonies and a little hooting and hollering. And I enjoyed it. I think you might have too, Ocie.

16

We went to *Mazatlan* one day to do some banking and shopping, in that order. The five of us arose at 5.00am and walked through the village in the early morning darkness to catch the 5.30am bus. The driver must have known that the battery was flat as he appeared at his doorway at 5.35am with jumper leads in hand. The first vehicle they tried was a truck. This did not seem to be able to breathe life into the old bus. Next on the scene was a kind of ute. He reconnected the jumper leads, turned the key and we were on our way at 6 o'clock.

These bus journeys were somewhat personalized. The bus stopped to set down or pick up wherever the need existed. It also detoured. On one journey we left the main track and went down a side track for a kilometre or two, to a very small community not far from *Ajoya*. The bus's right rear wheel was very much on the driver's mind. He got out to check it on several occasions. Just outside San Ignacio the bus stopped by a cemetery and two ladies got off, one carrying a plastic container of water. The bus driver waited till they had watered the flowers on whoever's grave it was and the ladies had returned to the bus, and we were on our way again. On this occasion the route from *Ajoya* to *Mazatlan* was certainly a tortuous one and not the same way we went the first time we came.

On one return journey from *Mazatlan*, we were between San Ignacio and *Ajoya*, the slowest leg on an indifferent dirt track. A person was up the front talking to the driver. The 'ticket man' seemed to have gotten off in San Ignacio. This unknown person was drinking cans of Tecate (a brand of beer) with considerable athleticism. After a while this seemed to lose its challenge for him and he switched to something more substantial – whiskey. I must say to his credit, and to our relief, the driver was not involved in this sport. At one point along this narrow track we encountered a truck. The truck and the bus both occupied the full width of the track and so the truck reversed quite a distance to where it could pull over to one side and let the bus pass. The driver and his unknown companion seemed to think that this action merited some reward. So when the bus pulled up, abreast of the truck, the companion, with encouragement from the driver, handed the bottle of whisky across to the three occupants of the truck. They drank liberally from the bottle as each turn came. They then handed the bottle back to the companion and we were on our way.

The children survived the trip quite well, there and back to *Mazatlan* and the four hours in between. This was a twelve-hour day. As we hauled ourselves and our grocery-laden rucksacks back through the village streets towards Lupe's and Bella's house, people were watering the dirt road and yard in front of their houses, in much the same way that people in summer stand out the front and water shrubs at the end of the day at home. There is a reason for this, as there was in Afghanistan where it is similarly practised. It was to keep the dust down. Sometimes at the end of the day we were able to spend some time down at the river. The water freely rippled over stones and there was solitude and a wonderful vista of mountain scenery. The mountains near *Ajoya* had some very unusual rock formations. One had a summit with three finger-like projections, which up close must have been of a considerable size.

Christmas approached. Lupe and Bella packed to go on vacation for a week or so. In contrast to the decision of the team meeting we had attended, where his application had been denied, there must have been a change of heart somewhere. They were joining Bella's relatives, including her daughter, in *Culiacan*, a town in the northern part of *Sinaloa*. We were given instructions as to running the house and I daresay an implied trust in our being in their house while they were away. These instructions included looking after their dog and parakeet. The parakeet talked a little.

One of its favourite sayings, obviously taught by some sensitive soul, was 'Victor feo'. This means 'ugly Victor'. Poor Victor! This would be said a hundred times a day by the bird, which unfortunately taught our children to say it almost as much. The puppy, though cute, would be a little more troublesome, whimpering at night and coming into the house, against our wishes, in the day. Lupe's and Bella's going away meant that we could modify our diet within the constraints of what was available. This was a relief for Nick, who had early on decided to part ways with frijoles (beans). Frijoles together with tortilla (flat unleavened bread prepared on a hotplate fresh each day) were the staple foods in the village. Lupe had picked up on Nick's earlier decision and each evening would call to Nick, as though announcing some surprise he knew Nick would delight in (not): 'Hey Nick, frijoles!'

Wednesday 23rd December

The day got off to a good start today with Ines opening the department spontaneously for me. I think he must have lost the keys because he used a long pole which he poked through the window to unlatch one of the doors. The brief exchange between us was pleasant enough and that is encouraging. Later on he came to PT with a trolley and asked me to put a ¾ bag of cement onto it. It was heavy and I felt a certain strain in the back.

The children are growing more and more excited about Christmas. We have a dry branch without leaves and decorated with paper chains, made and coloured in by the children, standing in the porch as our Christmas tree. This year we have made Christmas presents for each other. For example, Coby made a word search puzzle for Nicholas and a maze on paper for Bronwyn. The others have done likewise. This will probably be the first Christmas which we celebrate without friends.

The following evening, Christmas Eve, there was a celebratory meal at the project. People didn't eat together as much as join momentarily and then leave. Many of the men didn't turn up at all. Cecelia, our language teacher, looked a picture of misery when she eventually turned up just as people were clearing things away. There was no sign of Ines. There did not seem much to celebrate.

Christmas day, however, was a unique day for us. Not just because we were away from family and not just because we were in a different culture – we had experienced Christmas in Afghanistan more than once – but more because Lupe and Bella were away and it was they whom we most regarded as our friends. Our simple Christmas had its own richness, paradoxically contributed to *and* eroded, at the same time, by our sense of remoteness and isolation.

Tuesday 28th December

Today Anne and I and the kids all gave therapy to Carlos. Rosa, from the project, took an interest as well in his walking and also his ability to write some letters and figures. She got Carlos to speak in his own dialect, which is quite different to Spanish. It had strong 'ch' sounds and was more guttural than Spanish. Carlos delighted in his therapy today and laughed and exclaimed heartily as we did different exercises.

Thursday 30th December

As I write I look through the window and see young Carlos in his chair, by himself, looking vacantly around him. He spends a lot of time in this way, occasionally tapping his left knee to produce clonus (the reflex rhythmical up and down movement of the ankle). This is a habit which seems to give him comfort and the leg, automatically as it were, bobs up and down for a minute or so before gradually extinguishing its own movement.

The Second-time Teacher

We came to the last day of the year. Lupe and Bella were still in *Culiacan*. Alejandro advised us not to venture out in the evening, suggesting that there would be drinking in the village that night to bring in the New Year. On occasions like this, he said, there was gunfire, mostly into the air, but sometimes less harmlessly and into people during fights. It proved to be so. The gun fights were not in *Ajoya* this time but in a village an hour north. Three people were killed and two injured. Just before Christmas we had taken our children to watch the local schoolchildren break open *piñatas* as part of the festival of Las Posadas (the Inns). Sadly, for these children and their parents there would only be an ever-growing violence in *Ajoya* over the next few years. In 1997 Proyecto *Projimo* would begin a move to a safer and larger village, *Coyotitan*, about forty miles from *Ajoya* at the junction of the main north–south highway. Some of the project team stayed in *Ajoya* and continued activities in the form of a skills training and work program for both disabled and able-bodied unemployed youth. Things seemed to go well for a while. However, on May 10th, 2002, Mother's Day in Mexico, there was a celebration in this same village square where we watched the young children break the *piñatas*. Later in the evening, as the villagers enjoyed the dancing and festivities, a gang of a dozen men, dressed as policemen and armed with M-16 rifles, arrived in the village and opened fire on both the existing police guard and the fleeing villagers. Twelve persons were killed and five injured. The youngest villager killed was a seven-year-old boy and the oldest a sixty-year-old woman. This massacre had its roots in rivalries which had escalated between local drug gangs but many of the so-called foot soldiers in this 'war' were unemployed and disillusioned local youths.

On the first day in January, in the evening, we were sitting in Lupe's and Bella's house. The children were in bed and we heard a voice at the front gate calling out to Lupe and Bella, who had not yet returned from *Culiacan*. It was David Werner, the author of *Disabled Village Children*.

He had arrived in *Ajoya* to participate in the upcoming course. David came in and we had a conversation that stretched over the recent history of the project and about life in *Ajoya*. I was also able to let him know, in good conscience and with some relief, about my concerns for Miguel's health since I had not felt able to tell anyone else in the project about this. This news was gratefully received and I was, in turn, gently admonished for doing physiotherapy without Ines present. I accepted this admonition and understood its basis, even if the way this situation had developed had not been of my choosing. I had drifted, unhelpfully, in the unresolved question of whether I was learner or teacher at the project.

On the following Monday there was a team meeting at 2pm under the big tree in the yard at the project. At this meeting our impending departure prior to the January course was on the agenda. I was asked to speak to the group, which, given the loud and uncompromising nature of these meetings, I did with some trepidation. I told the group about our involvement in developing physiotherapy in Afghanistan and how the approach to teaching and involving people in their rehabilitation which Proyecto *Projimo* had modelled was an approach which Afghan physiotherapists could benefit from learning. After this the project members voted on a motion to invite us to stay longer in *Ajoya* and participate in the January course. This motion was unanimously carried. We were warmed by this and the trust it imputed to us. I write 'us' since we would, as a family, all become participants in one way or another in this course. It was an extension of the hospitality we had received during the previous month. At the meeting I noticed that Miguel, who two weeks previously had enjoined me to tell no one about his pressure sores, was getting around on a gurney instead of sitting on those sores. Later that evening, Conchita produced some cassettes of Mexican music she had chosen and bought for me.

The Second-time Teacher

Over the next days, the visitors for the course, therapists, parents and children, began arriving in *Ajoya*. The whole village seemed to lift in anticipation. On the night before the course, Lupe's and Bella's house was jumping, alive with playing and talking kids and adults respectively. At different times three or more kids of our neighbours, Tony and Victor, and our own three all socialized in our room. Anne and I lay on the bed and talked while they shoaled around us. Eventually we scooted them out.

17

The course participants came from other parts of Mexico as well as from places like El Salvador and Nicaragua. To help lead this course there were two therapists who came from Nicaragua, Gladys, a PT, and Ligia, a social worker, and two visiting physical therapists from California, Ann and Susan, who had expertise in paediatric physical therapy. Ann and Susan had visited the project a number of times in the recent past and contributed to the content of *Disabled Village Children*.

Sunday 9th January

Today was a day of meeting people, of listening, and taking notes and, during lunch, giving some opinions on a few patients with Ann Hallum and David Werner.

Ann examined ten children with cerebral palsy today before the whole group, which comprises so far of three trained PTs, several lay therapists and mothers and fathers of children. I suppose at this stage there are some 35 people in attendance. I took notes on each examination for Ann which will hopefully help her to divide the large group into two tomorrow. She will lead one and Gladys (the PT from Nicaragua) will lead the other.

The running of the course took place outside. Along with the three sets of parallel bars, fixed in the ground out in the yard, wooden benches were set out there under the trees. At times the group was together and at other times there were two groups, one led by Ann and another by Gladys. The program for each day had to be reworked due to various factors. The timetable changed and sessions ran overtime. Gladys was not happy about the amount of time she had for input on day one. The mix of the group also took some accounting for, with the different levels of expertise and expectation. For example, parents mainly wanted to know how to treat *their* children. Lay therapists, however, needed to know how to apply principles of treatment to different children and different types of cerebral palsy.

Tuesday 11th January

In Ann's group bees kept disrupting the attention of participants. One lady got stung and there was general havoc for a time. Another time I looked up towards Gladys's group. On the fringe of the class, a couple of metres or so away from the seated members, a couple of young pigs were casually investigating the prospects for food and filth.

There was lots of noise and other distractions during the teaching; everything from crying babies, Carlos wheeling his way through a class, and boys from outside the project playing on bikes.

Our youngest daughter, Bronnie, became a model for PT Ann to demonstrate particular movements. A creche was operating now, which Anne, Nick and Coby helped supervise, so this made it easier to keep the noise levels down and concentration levels up. I moved between groups and helped out when asked. But mostly I watched and listened. Of the two Nicaraguan visitors to the course, Ligia had good skills as a group worker. She spent time with the course participants, mainly the parents, talking about the hardships and experiences and emotions of having a child with cerebral palsy in the family. In this part of the world there is little acceptance or integration of persons with disabilities into wider society. We heard the stories of several mothers in the group. One woman recounted how her husband had left her and now she had three jobs in order to survive. Her working day started at 5.30am and finished at 11.00pm. She had one other child apart from the child with cerebral palsy. Another talked of buses going straight past her and her disabled child rather than picking them up, as if they were invisible. Then there were the many outlandish 'cures' offered by different doctors and opportunists outside the medical system. One of the leaders at Proyecto *Projimo*, Conchita, had personal experience of this.

In Mexico, even more so than Nicaragua or El Salvador, there is still much shame and guilt about having a child with cerebral palsy. Some parents, including fathers, spoke of the belief – commonly held, and not contradicted by the folk Catholicism which was the local religion – that they had had children with these sorts of problems because they had done something wrong and this was God's judgment on them. It was hard enough living with the challenges of having a child with cerebral palsy in rural Mexico without having the added burden of believing that this was self-initiated. In short, these parents felt like outsiders in their own country. Our seven-year-old daughter Coby had asked me the day before whether all the children at this course had 'terrible palsy'. Despite her mishearing of the term, she had correctly picked up on the lived experience of these people.

David spoke to the group on fits and seizures in the child with cerebral palsy. He drew a link between the occurrence of the condition and its relationship with premature birth. He then talked about the causes of premature birth, one of which is poor nutrition. In this there were social and political considerations. One woman in the group called out, 'So we have to eat better with no money?' The night before, following dinner, Lupe had been telling us about poverty and unemployment in the village. Firstly, he said that there were many men who spent money on beer, with the result that there was less food for the children. In talking about unemployment, he said that there were many in the village who, not owning land, found occasional employment working in other people's fields, harvesting the maize crop in September and October. At other times these people were in real poverty.

The teaching in the course helped participants draw the lines between the various dots – blots – in their lives: between disabilities arising from physical conditions and impairments, such as cerebral palsy, and the added, some would say more real, disabilities which arose from the exclusion of these children (and their parents) from meaningful participation in their communities. Traditional notions of rehabilitation were subverted here. Instead of the aim of rehabilitation being to assist persons with disabilities to increase function and adapt, so that they might fit in with society around them, the *compañeros* at Proyecto *Projimo* were teaching an understanding of rehabilitation that also challenged the injustices in society – beliefs, attitudes and greed. It was a philosophy, I later learned, which had been adopted from the Brazilian educator Paulo Freire.

The grapevine was well and truly at work as *campesinos* now brought their children to *Ajoya* to be assessed.

Wednesday 12th January

Today a 17-year-old boy came in. He is a paraplegic of some two months and is from Mazatlan. The cause of his paraplegia is a common one around here – a ricocheting bullet. He was evaluated by Susan together with Ines in the presence of the family, David, me and other observers. The notion of privacy does exist here but it is a different notion than ours. Undressing etc is not something done easily for examination, as people get embarrassed. Listening in on people's situations, histories and problems seems to be fine. Everyone has a listen.

This young man would be taught most of his exercises by Alejandro, a young man who also had paraplegia. Initially, he would learn to spend more time upright, either sitting or in a standing frame. Such modelling incorporated powerful forms of teaching *and* empathy.

Later, we examined Lupito and his back. He was a sixteen-year-old boy who was born without a sacrum (tailbone). His legs were also congenitally deformed. It was his spine, however, which almost defied description. It had basically collapsed and the upper part of the spine was virtually parallel with the lower end with a sharp loop at one end. We considered ways of distributing weight away from a concentrated area which was currently taking all his weight when he sat. There were no easy solutions for this young fellow.

> **Thursday 13th January**
>
> Edgar … is a severely disabled young boy with cerebral palsy. Edgar, when seated, tends to wilt so that his head and shoulders fall forward towards his knees. This means that his spine is becoming increasingly stuck in flexion but it also means that in this position he does not see or take part in what is going on in the world. By placing a brick under the back of a wooden box which Edgar was sitting on he was immediately facilitated into a more upright sitting position such that he was looking around him at what was going on.

The reason this worked for Edgar was that this position took tension off contractured hamstrings which pulled his pelvis backwards causing him to otherwise 'curl forward' as he tried to sit up. Edgar was looked after by his ten-year-old brother during the week of the course; presumably his parents had to stay where they were and work. Even though he did a pretty good job, with the sense of responsibility which most Australian boys would not have or need to have, Edgar still got left to his own devices quite often. On these occasions he would begin to bang his head against the nearest object, be it a seat or wall, not in anger as in a tantrum. It was as if he was reminding himself that he was still alive; a bit like Carlos and his habit of tapping his knee to produce ankle clonus.

On the Thursday afternoon I was called out of a class to listen to Rosa singing with Carlos. He really came alive as he sang. Having previously sung with Carlos in physiotherapy, I had mentioned to others that music might not only be enjoyable for Carlos but that his cognitive and emotional capabilities might also lift with expression in music. One of the team members said that they would investigate the possibility of someone teaching Carlos an instrument, guitar for example, so that he might pursue it himself later, if he wished.

Thursday 13th January

Unfortunately 'the sprayers' are coming tomorrow, with their DDT, to do Lupe and Bella's house. What a pity. We'll have to get up at 6.00am and move stuff outside the house and then hope that by tomorrow night it will be okay to sleep in the house again. Susan is staying here now and is also looking forward to the exercise. Part of the reason she moved over here was that the house she was living in was sprayed and she had to sleep outside.

The DDT spraying was part of a government program to control the spread of malaria. We had no problem with the aim of the program, it was more the method which troubled us; our belongings and us being so exposed to this harmful insecticide. I wrote in my diary the following day:

Lunchtime took us home to the house of DDT. It did stink and we carefully rearranged our belongings. Following Lupe's lead we had cunningly taken most of our belongings and bedding material around the back of a neighbour's house which had already been sprayed. Apparently these guys who do the spraying like to spray everything in sight and, at least there, we were spared the experience of sleeping in DDT-impregnated sheets, pillows and blankets.

On Thursday night there was a farewell party for the participants, several of whom were leaving the next day. It was combined with a 'thank you' to the teachers.

> It was a pleasant well-controlled affair with no alcohol. Alejandro brought his guitar and a friend, who also brought his guitar. Together they sang songs while some of us danced. I was chosen as a dancing partner at one stage by Carina, a 13-year-old girl with athetosis. This is a type of cerebral palsy where the limbs move more or less uncontrollably. Our dance was watched by the whole group with applause. What an attitude she had! Carina heard the music and she was up and kicking dust (since that was what the dance floor was composed of). She's a hoot. Actually, Mexicans love to hoot during their music. She brought a few out of them.

The politics of the project became increasingly visible to me the longer we were in the village and as we understood more Spanish:

> **Friday 14th January**
>
> Apparently there is a person with an incomplete C4 quadriplegia coming in to the project for evaluation on Monday. This will really test the capacity of the team to cope with all that needs to be done in the care and treatment of such a person. It will also take the team or some members of it back to the time when some spinally injured young men, including a quadriplegic called Quique, were asked to leave the project because of their destructive influence on it through drug abuse and violence. At that time this decision split the team and the results of this are still somewhat evident in certain relationships, most notably between David and Mari. So the arrival of this young man will be an important time for them all. Quique died recently because of poor care at home. The story is more complicated than that but this death caused

grief to some. Statistically in the third world 50% of paraplegics die within two years of their injury and over 95% of quadriplegics. Which way will *Projimo* go?

I had come to Proyecto *Projimo* as a failed teacher. Well, this was my assessment of the role I had performed in Afghanistan. Being in *Ajoya* had provided me with an opportunity to watch others teach and others learn. And I had been at different times both teacher and learner. While it would take more time for me to process this experience overall, nevertheless I recognized a different way of teaching and learning than I had known before.

Saturday 15th January

We arose in darkness this morning to catch the 5.30am bus which leaves at 6am. You know the one. As we, along with others, awaited the appearance of the driver from his house, a figure appeared who was familiar to me. His name was Floro and, up until yesterday, I thought it had been Roberto.

Floro was the rough-mannered one who had so successfully and publicly put me down in the first week of our time in *Ajoya*. This was concerning my ability or rather inability to shovel and mix concrete and sand in the specific way in which they do it here. Yesterday Susan, who is liked here by just about everybody and who has been coming to *Ajoya* each year for some seven years, told me who he was and what he was like.

Floro is actually the elected 'headman' or mayor of the village and despite being a rough 'mountain man' who also likes his drink, he has achieved some good things for the village. For example, in the terrible floods last year he managed to get some truckloads of relief supplies brought to the village to help those most affected. Apparently, in times past these sorts of things would not have been forthcoming, not at

PART TWO: ADELAIDE AND MEXICO 1987–2004

least in 'end of the line' little *Ajoya*. But Floro achieved it. He is also a member of a national campesino (peasant) group which organizes and moves for social justice. The reason in fact that he was catching the bus today was as the first stage of a journey to Mexico City to meet with this group about the recent strife in the southern state of Chiappas.

The bus driver finally emerged from his house just before 6.00. Normally, the suitcases along with other more substantial luggage (such as engine parts etc) are stowed at the back of the bus. I was therefore waiting near the back of the bus in order to load them on. The back door of the bus was locked, however, and, with all the other passengers boarded and seated, I felt an uneasiness rise in me as the engine struck into life (this time without jumper leads) and the vehicle started to move off. However, in reality the bus was just moving under a street light. When I caught up, Floro was at the back door and took my suitcases as I lifted them and then positioned them. We then did the normal circuit of *Ajoya*, horn blaring, as late travellers ran to be picked up. Finally, we were on the road to San Ignacio.

At San Ignacio many folks got off to get other buses for other destinations. Some of those who got off were parents with their children who had been at the course. We said goodbye and they said to us Felize Viaje, which means 'Happy journey'.

Finally, a hand was thrust towards me and in awkward English a voice said, 'See you later'. I took the hand and looked up. It was Floro's.

I had spent the last six weeks not thinking well of Floro. Personal vulnerabilities again leading to personal hostilities both harboured and nurtured. To what end I still could not fully answer. I had not even got his name right. And yet, the offer of Floro's hand, together with finally knowing something of the facts of his life, helped disarm my suspicion of him. It was such a waste of time and emotion to have held these things against him, even if they had been concealed and restrained.

As we continued on our final journey from *Ajoya* to *Mazatlan*, I registered the many little white crosses, often adorned by flowers, which were periodically planted by the road. I saw them with new eyes. They were individual memorials, signifying sites where the bodies of murder victims had been found. But they were also vigils – even protests – maintained by families who refused to forget those they loved, now lost in the violence of various feuds, paybacks, 'examples being made of', or even for just being bystanders.

For all its problems there was still so much that was fundamentally good about *Projimo*. It reminded me that every place has its struggle and that wherever we are, or intend to be, our task is to act as creatively and constructively as we can in that struggle. For the *compañeros* at Project *Projimo*, this action was based on facilitating a person's analysis of their situation and using this new awareness to encourage the development of new capabilities and aspirations. That was what lay behind what the Brazilian educator Freire was suggesting when he said that when some individuals prevent others from engaging in the process of inquiry this is a form of violence. In this way, Project *Projimo* modelled a rough kind of hospitality, in an environment of violence, by providing a place of welcome and restoration for people like themselves who, because of disability, remained strangers or outsiders: 'outside' healthcare, 'outside' community acceptance and 'outside' fair economic treatment.

Anne and I, Nick, Coby and Bronwyn caught the bus to *Mazatlan*, the first leg in our long journey back to Australia. Again, as in Afghanistan, we had the freedom to leave difficult places and return to a safer, more prosperous world, unlike our hosts. We flew out to Los Angeles on Sunday January 16th. The next morning in our airport hotel we were awakened at around 4.30am, rudely and roughly, by a 6.7

magnitude earthquake. We knew immediately what was going on from our previous experience of an earthquake in Afghanistan. But our two rooms were on the eighth floor and being so far from the safety of the open ground outside was initially very worrying. We struggled to keep our feet, such was the strength of the quake as, having awakened the kids, we exited our rooms and found the nearest stairwell.

In this quake sixty people were killed and more than seven thousand people were injured, mostly in the San Fernando Valley. Several freeway overpasses went down and many buildings collapsed. We had largely been incommunicado in *Ajoya* because of its isolation and lack of facilities. Having confidently planned to ring our families in Australia when we got back to LA, we now found ourselves incommunicado again. Most telecommunications services were down, at least temporarily, at a time when our families were most seeking reassurance about our well-being.

Prior to leaving *Ajoya*, Anne and I had promised our children a trip to Disneyland. A promise we were eventually able to fulfil. However, even this had unwittingly emphasized a contrast, a separation of different worlds: *Ajoya* and Anaheim. It was as if the earthquake had intruded into this idea, reminding us of the false divisions and boundaries we allowed to be set between our world and that of others we had come to know.

18

Perhaps it was the urge to follow up on the *Ajoya* experience and work with those who were most disadvantaged in Adelaide which caused me to seek part-time work at a small medical clinic, affectionately known as 'the BBC'. I had also begun to undertake postgraduate study in physiotherapy. The Brian Burdekin Clinic was named after the Royal Commissioner who, in the early 1990s, first investigated the status of persons with mental health problems in Australia. There was a kind of mischievous pleasure in being able to refer to ourselves using the initials of such a well-promoted and universal presence in the world. *This* BBC stood for local, unpretentious, small-scale, personal contact and hospitality in healthcare. I worked for around six months in a volunteer capacity; there was no funding to remunerate me and no Medicare billing system for physiotherapists at that time. I was then remunerated for the next ten years, working up to two half days per week.

The desk in the physiotherapy room was not minimalist modern office furniture. It was ornate with an elegant wooden cover made of strips of varnished wood, joined in such a way that it could be pulled down over the desk and locked. And this was my error. In fiddling about with the key in the lock, the key snapped and I could not open the desk upon which I needed to write that morning as I saw patients. I let the receptionist know. Brigitte was a woman with an ever-present and generous laugh. She followed this particular chuckle with, 'I'll get one of the boys to come up and have a look'. My room was up a flight of stairs on the first floor. I had interpreted her remarks as implying that one of the male nurses employed at the clinic would come up with some tool or other from the clinic. Before very long, however, a young man, unknown to me, appeared and took from his pocket what looked like a set of oversized metal toothpicks. He began inserting various ones into the injured lock, carefully assessing the effectiveness of each towards unlocking the desk. He gave up after a few minutes and said he would ask someone else. A second unknown person then appeared, knocking politely at the door before conducting another appraisal. Shaking his head, he too disappeared downstairs with a convivial farewell. It only then occurred to me that Brigitte had recruited my helpers from those who were otherwise waiting for their nurse's or doctor's appointments.

This incident told me a lot about the BBC and the people it served. Our clients did not come from the 'big end' of town. Many of those who came had experienced combinations of the following: homelessness; mental health problems; substance abuse (the BBC was one of two private registered methadone providers in the state); chronic infections (hep B, C, HIV AIDS); and, as suggested by my helpers, 'run-ins' with the law. But they were all made to feel welcome at this clinic. People were addressed by their first name. They could go and make tea or coffee in the small kitchenette out the back. There was often fresh fruit which people could eat then or take with them. And there was always a stock of bus and train tickets to give to those who were caught short.

The waiting room at the BBC was fairly small and so there were chairs outside to accommodate the overflow. The patients waiting outside, sitting on variously arranged plastic chairs, could be quiet or noisy, depending on the topic of conversation, and who was there. Unlike other practices where I had either worked or, indeed, sat waiting myself for an appointment, the BBC patrons were patient and never seemed to complain about appointment times going over; which they inevitably did. Perhaps they had become inured to this, given that for many of them their other main source of healthcare took place at emergency departments of the large public hospitals, where long waits were the normal order. But they also knew that when their turn came they would get the time they needed to have their issues listened to and addressed. This image of people waiting but not constantly looking at their watches was redolent of the Afghans who used to wait for long periods for their turn. It seems the poor always have to wait.

One morning I asked Brigitte who was next on my list. 'Bobby,' she said. 'He's sitting outside.' I hadn't seen or met Bobby before. I went outside, called his name and, following his acknowledgment, greeted him with 'Hi Bobby, my name's Ian. I'm the physiotherapist'. Bobby's answer to my greeting was short: 'Big fuckin' deal!' I was startled but retained my equilibrium, even though this was not an auspicious beginning to the consultation. During the session, however, things went well. By the end of the treatment, his attitude towards me was positively warm and we parted on good terms.

It was an odd experience, being confronted with such aggression without previous contact and for no other discernible reason. And he had not been under the influence of alcohol or other drugs either, as far as I could tell. The experience rolled around my thinking for some time and I gradually came to understand what had happened. In the ten years I worked at the BBC I heard story after story of how patients were used to being dismissed by healthcare practitioners in a variety of ways and places; talked down to or not respected due to their appearance and behaviours. Some dealt with it passively, linking it to their own downward trajectory in life, even thinking, sadly enough, that in some ways it was deserved. Others felt the unfairness of it more acutely, and their method of defending their sense of self-dignity lay in aggression. And if you are chronically unwell and living a life that is mostly in some kind of transition or chaos, then being calm, articulate and even rational in explaining your experiences and needs to healthcare practitioners won't necessarily be one of your strengths.

Our patients, like the *campesinos* and their children with disabilities in *Ajoya*, were often outsiders, and therefore also felt like strangers in their communities. They were stigmatized by their 'difference', which included how they looked, where they lived and how they behaved. On the latter, those of us working at the BBC wondered whether *we* would always make the right choice or take the 'best' course of action in some of life's crises were it not for the benefits we each experienced in having a caring support network and community. And it was that care and support which our patients often lacked at crucial times in their lives. Much of the ethos behind how the BBC worked as a health unit was in practising a 'mutual recognition' between the staff and those who came seeking our care. That is, it was a project in recognizing each other fairly. At the BBC the obligation of hospitality was taken seriously.

I found that I had to adapt my approach to physiotherapy practice in various ways. For example, there is a method for palpating the shoulder region. It is not the only method but is usually effective in that it allows the therapist to make a comparison of even subtle differences of tissue thickness, swelling and tenderness of the structures between shoulders. It involves having the patient sit on a chair or lowered couch. The therapist stands behind the patient and reaches lightly around the neck, such that the therapist's hands can feel the contour and position of both sternoclavicular joints in the front of the chest (just below the throat). The palpating fingers then move laterally along the clavicles, right and left, towards each acromioclavicular joint, prior to the fingers 'dropping off' the acromium bone in order to feel the outer parts of the rotator cuff tendons of the shoulder.

One morning a young woman presented with shoulder pain. She was accompanied by an older female companion. Having asked her some questions about her pain and its history, I started the physical examination and arrived at the palpation process described above. I explained what I was about to do and asked if that was okay. Before I had gone very far, however, the companion said, 'I don't think what you are doing is a good idea'. Of course, I stopped and moved from my position behind her. I did not need to ask why.

Other elements of my physiotherapy practice changed as well. I first saw Novak because of pain he was experiencing in his thoracic region. Even before investigating this, the thing that impressed on seeing Novak for the first time was that he was big; not so much in stature, as he was not overly tall, but he had limbs of remarkable circumference. He told me that his body weight was somewhere in the high 180 kilos. I have to say that I would have looked at Novak, at some point in my earlier life as a physiotherapist, and come to certain conclusions about him: conclusions expressed in questions like, 'How can a person let themselves get into such a state? or 'Why doesn't he just do something about that weight?'

The pain seemed to bandage his chest like cling wrap. He was very tender at the sternal-chondral junctions at the front of the chest while at the same time stiff and sore in the joints of the thoracic spine at the back. I found out that he had an anxiety disorder. He wasn't able to travel, at least comfortably or reliably, on buses. He would have panic attacks and have to get off, leaving him, at the point of disembarkation, having to figure out a way either to get back home or to continue on to his intended destination or appointment. Mostly, it was a long walk that he then undertook.

But there was another dimension to Novak. He loved sport; and not just watching it. He told me he was currently playing Saturday afternoon cricket. 'When I bat I don't run much,' he ventured. 'I mostly go for fours and sixes.' My eyes were drawn to those massive forearms and shoulders, and I had no doubt that, when he hit a cricket ball, it not only stayed well and truly hit but was probably contused as well.

He added, 'In winter, I play soccer. But I can't get around the park like I did and so they put me in goal.'

We made a start in physiotherapy working on Novak's stiff thoracic spine and tender sternochondral junctions. However, Novak's physiotherapy with me became the management, over time, of a succession of sporting injuries – ankles, knees and shoulders as well as episodic low back pain. But this was not all bad. We were getting him ready and able to play for that Saturday or the next. And he was up for it; doing what *he* could in order to be right for the game. Each time I treated a strained a/c joint of the shoulder or medial ligament of the knee, which invariably placed a strain on our budget for sports tape, it also felt like I was helping remove a piece of some invisible cling wrap surrounding his life as a whole.

Novak's weight was the barrier to many, if not most, of his hopes for a better life. He was receiving psychological help for his anxiety disorder, and weight loss and nutritional support from a dietician. Unfortunately, at that time at least, he was not deemed suitable, due to his anxiety disorder, for bariatric or lap band surgery, and he did not have private health insurance. Part of the job of physiotherapy was to explore ways of exercising in order to burn calories and improve muscle function. He couldn't go on the exercise bike which I had purchased for the clinic: he was at a weight well beyond its warranty guidelines. However, in avoiding buses whenever he could, he took to riding his push bike to the city to get to his appointments. He also rode to a local gym where he used the pool to do low-impact exercising and the hydraulic gym equipment to build strength and endurance following a program developed in physiotherapy. On one occasion our clinic provided him with a small cash loan to have the spokes on the back wheel of his bike repaired so that he could continue to ride to his gym and pool program. Come winter and the soccer season, when goalkeeping and the throwing of his body around became too much, he took up 'goal umpiring' in a local footy competition.

I came to not just appreciate Novak's challenges but to admire his courage and willingness to adapt to circumstances. There were so many others who were pulled, this way and that, between their difficult pasts and their uncertain futures. Freya had a chronic pain condition. She had been sleeping on the couch in her living room for the past eight years. Her bedroom was vacant except for its memories. Marco had been sent to Australia from Italy by his father when he was fifteen years old. He worked in a fruit market with his uncle in Melbourne. He was supposed to have been sent to school but this did not happen. He was not well treated and, worst of all, he never saw any of his family in Italy again, including brothers or sisters. Marco carried his pain, musculoskeletal and otherwise, with him like an unwanted companion. He once threw a dinner for all of us at a well-known Italian restaurant in Adelaide to celebrate his birthday. It was a great night. We enjoyed the food and the wine but most of all we revelled in Marco's joy at being *our* host and welcoming us.

It was over fifteen years now since I completed undergraduate training as a physiotherapist. And I felt that it was time for a more fundamental development of my knowledge and skills than could be gained through weekend courses. I enrolled in a post-graduate study program in orthopaedics and musculoskeletal physiotherapy at the University of South Australia. The program contained a high number of international students from Europe, North America and the subcontinent. Most of these students were attracted by the expert teaching in joint assessment and mobilization but also to learn clinical reasoning. This was first developed as a discipline in order to teach medical students the thinking skills required for making a diagnosis. As physiotherapists became first contact providers – that is, able to see patents without medical referral – clinical reasoning became a relevant discipline and problem-solving skill for us. For example, when a person presents with pain or other impairment, physiotherapists can examine and make a diagnosis of what might be causing or contributing to the problem and, at the same time, decide whether it is a condition which lies in their purview or should be referred for medical evaluation.

The existing theoretical model of clinical reasoning in physiotherapy had been constructed and published by my lecturer, Mark Jones, who is an internationally recognized figure in our profession for his work and teaching. It was a model which emphasized the cognitive (thinking) activities of the physiotherapist practitioner. That is, they assessed the nature and extent of physical impairments, bodily function and performance by generating hypotheses about possible causes and contributing factors for these problems. These hypotheses were then 'tested' via further questions and various clinical tests, elevating or demoting each hypothesis according to the findings.

As a requirement for my very first course, we all had to do an essay on clinical reasoning. I sought and gained permission to consider clinical reasoning 'outside' of its application in Western, suburban physiotherapy clinics. I had patients in my mind such as the Afghan man who asked me whether he could eat watermelons, tomatoes and yoghurt and also Bonita, from *Ajoya*, whose hips and spine were severely twisted as a consequence of the lack of treatment she had following poliomyelitis as a child. Informed by what I learned from my activist friends with disability in *Ajoya*, I added another section to Mark's model. This addition illustrated the importance of taking into account the beliefs and experiences of the patient and how these might coalesce with or diverge from the physiotherapist's reasoning during the interview and examination. He liked the modification of his model so much that he adopted it in future publications and also incorporated it into his teaching of clinical reasoning. This was to be the beginning of a twenty-year collegial partnership in this area of physiotherapy teaching.

My interest in how we make decisions in physiotherapy practice, and what influences us in that process, led me to enrol in a PhD program with Mark as my supervisor. I submitted my PhD thesis for examination in September 2000, at around the same time as the Sydney Olympics was getting underway. The main finding of my research was to identify a number of areas of problem-solving in physiotherapy practice beyond diagnosis. These included the ways in which physiotherapists formed relationships with their patients, how they set goals with them, what forms of teaching the therapists used, how they answered questions about the patient's future, and how they recognized ethical issues.

Following this prolonged study, I returned to clinical practice as a physiotherapist. I worked part-time at the BBC and part-time at a rehabilitation unit near where we lived. In the middle of 2002, I applied for and gained a lecturer's position at the University of South Australia. Part of my motivation in applying for this job was a sense that in my present clinical work I was not using the research skills I had learned in my PhD training and I did not want them to evaporate through lack of use or application. I was officially a second-time teacher now. Paradoxically, even though my recent studies had bolstered my physiotherapy knowledge in a number of areas, I nevertheless had little more training on how to be a teacher than when I was given the PT training program in Afghanistan all those years before.

Unsurprisingly, given the area of my PhD, I taught clinical reasoning in various courses. As I mentioned earlier, the traditional focus for teaching clinical reasoning was in its important diagnostic role. This diagnostic orientation of clinical reasoning is normative in that it teaches clinicians to search in the patient examination for that which they *ought* to find. That is, to interpret the answer to a particular question or interpret the response to a clinical test so that a particular known clinical disorder or syndrome can be recognized. Grounded in areas such as anatomy, physiology, pathology, kinesiology and other clinically-based knowledge, this form of inquiry looks for what should be expected from a set of signs and symptoms. This process therefore leads clinicians to necessarily reduce often complex and diverse information regarding a patient down to a 'case' of something. While there is a necessity and point to this, so that diagnoses can be made and management plans formed, it also shapes and constrains thinking in certain ways. For example, I found that students doing clinical placement provided accounts of their difficulties with uncooperative or aggressive patients which had 'diagnostic' overtones. There was a tendency to apply diagnostic labels to people who responded to our overtures differently. The lexicon of rehabilitation had long included expressions like 'secondary gain' and 'functional overlay' and 'psychosomatic' – devised as pseudo diagnoses – to explain those patients with attitude who were judged as being unmotivated, non-compliant, rude, ungrateful or, just as importantly, recalcitrant to treatment. In my experience I had rarely met anyone who chose to be like any of these things as an intentional personal goal. Conversely, I had observed that such behaviours or attitudes were usually expressions of other less understood realities such as fear, frustration or anxiety.

To be different, in such terms above, seemed to be a cognitive irritant for the clinician. Moreover, I had personally learned on site in Mexico that it was precisely *difference*, and the lack of others' recognition of this, which was at the heart of many persons' struggles with health and disability. How did we teach students to understand difference? It was not that these intelligent young people weren't capable of this. But the method of the reasoning they learned pulled them in almost the opposite direction, away from difference, and mostly towards recognition of familiarity. Inquiry and reasoning to understand *difference* would prove to be my single most important task as a teacher. People wanted recognition of *who* they were and what they faced. At this point I had little idea that teaching clinical reasoning would be the means by which I would once more teach in Afghanistan.

19

In 2003, Anne and I were asked by an immigration agent to help settle a refugee Afghan family in Adelaide. We were happy to welcome the family and show them the ropes regarding life in the city and Australia. It was good to have the opportunity to reactivate language skills which had ebbed away since our return.

A few months after our initial introductions, I took some of the kids to Football Park and an AFL match between Port Adelaide and Collingwood. Coming from NSW originally, I remember my own first attendance at an AFL game and the realization of how much this is a sport filled with ritual. Prior to the commencement of the actual game, players run onto the ground through huge banners of paper mache (8 x 4 metres), put together during the previous week by faithful cheer squad members, and which carry messages of exhortation and worship. Squads of umpires practise bouncing oval-shaped balls or running backwards at high speed. Others loosen the shoulders in readiness for the lavish arm movements, closely followed by dramatic flag-waving routines, which they perform in order to signify a point or a goal. There are armies of water carriers and support staff populating the pitch. The murmurs of forty-something thousand people create a humming like the sound of electricity from high-voltage pylons. It is all quite tribal. I had taken Hassam and his two younger brothers to an AFL match between our team, Port Adelaide, and the big Victorian club, Collingwood. They watched the spectacle quietly in awe. Before the first bounce, there was the usual pushing and jostling between players, particularly among those who were in or around the centre square. The oldest boy, Hussein, seemed distressed. He turned to me, and with customary respect asked, 'Uncle, why are they doing this? These people are your guests.'

I was amused by the tangle of cultural sensitivities. He was an Afghan in Australia still under the obligations of hospitality. What he had just witnessed grated with everything he had ever been taught about hospitality to guests who had travelled from another place.

Eight years later, I was waiting for a flight in Herat airport. Herat is Afghanistan's westernmost city, near the border with Iran. I was in the country to run a number of courses, in various cities, as part of an upgrading process for Afghan physiotherapists. Airports are vulnerable places in Afghanistan. They are, on the one hand, bolstered by innumerable security checks, starting a kilometre or so from the actual airport, where cars are searched for bombs. The searches continue throughout the check-in process, finishing with a body search prior to entering the airplane cabin. Despite such security, airports remain strategic targets for attack. The day before we had flown to Herat, Kabul airport had been attacked by the Taliban, with the loss of several lives. You sit in an Afghan airport, therefore, with a level of vigilance and a suppressed anxiety quite different to the milder stress of negotiating airports and flights in Australia. These feelings were not helped by being separated as we waited: me in a male-only lounge, and Anne in an all-female lounge.

While I was waiting, a group of about twenty Afghan army personnel came into the lounge. Evidently, they were also catching the flight back to Kabul. I noticed after the first boarding call for the flight that these young men were becoming restless. It seemed that some of them weren't happy about being the last to board the flight. As far as I could tell they were unarmed. However, some pushing and shoving began between them and voices were raised, turning into shouts. Knowing how quickly things escalate in Afghanistan, and how no one is ever that far away from violence, I quickly became alarmed by the *'argy bargy'* between the young men. Thankfully, things seemed to settle with the appearance of a more senior officer. Anne and I were reunited, boarded our flight and flew uneventfully back to Kabul.

Eventually, I got to thinking once more about Hussein becoming upset at the sight of young men jostling each other at the beginning of the Port–Collingwood game. I now understood the darker element to Hussein's perspective. As I got to know the family better, I learned that Hussein's brother had been shot and killed by the Taliban. He and his family knew what it was to live under threat. I wished that I could retract that benevolent but condescending smile I had offered him at Football Park.

Part Three
Afghanistan
2005–2011

Host

Honour the guest, O son. Even though he is an infidel, open the door

Afghan proverb

20

In the latter part of 2004 I heard about a community gathering which took place each Friday night at Murray Bridge, a town about 80km from Adelaide. This involved a group of Afghan men, most of whom worked at the abattoir just out of town. These men were on temporary protection visas. The catalyst for this community gathering was the suicide of one of these men on hearing that he was to be sent back to Afghanistan by the Australian government. The despair of this man was communicated not only by the manner but also by the place of his death. He had hung himself from an electricity pylon. It was the visible death of an invisible person. Many in the town decided that some kind of local response was required.

Communal meals were offered at the community health service in the grounds of the Murray Bridge hospital. A group of senior citizens with the support of the health service cooked the meals, with the men sometimes taking a turn to cook Afghan food. Some of the men also had swimming lessons in the pool that was adjacent to the centre. These Afghan men were mostly Hazara. They were universally lonely and fretted about the uncertainty of their futures. However, they really appreciated these Friday night gatherings. I started going and enjoyed the opportunity to 'drag out' my Dari language ability. I wrote to my friend and past colleague in Kabul, Tom Little, and asked him to send me a Dari learning book (I had lost mine) so that I could oil my knowledge of verb tenses and replenish my reservoir of Dari vocabulary.

Greetings are always an important and ritualistic opening to any conversation between Afghans. Much like the ritual with shopkeepers described earlier, the exchange which follows 'Salaam, how are you?' is multiple and involves a series of questions about the welfare of one's health and family, both persons usually asking and answering these questions almost simultaneously. Sometimes I surprised even myself with unexpected language recall. One night, during the greeting ritual, I was asked how I was by one of the men. I replied, without knowing where the words came from, given it must have been more than a decade since I had uttered them, '*Dam ghanimat ast*'. This is a very colloquial expression used in Kabul and it certainly wasn't in the book Tom sent me. Literally, this expression translates as 'the breath (or air) passes', meaning that I am 'surviving'. Upon hearing this my Afghan partner in conversation exploded in laughter, obviously dumbfounded and delighted at once to hear this familiar, homely slang from such an unlikely source. Its equivalent, as a colloquialism, would have been if, in my asking him how he was, he had responded with, 'I'm flat out like a lizard drinking'. I was glad that my spontaneous recall of this Dari expression had provided him with some joy. These conversations, following the long greeting, usually went on to discuss their place of origin in Afghanistan and the last time they had heard from their families, and, of course, the status of their applications for a permanent visa.

There was a main coordinator of these evenings. She was a woman in her late sixties named Lina. Lina offered encouragement to these Afghan men by writing to politicians; inviting them and, on occasions, *getting* them to come and meet the men; arranging English and computer lessons; and organizing volunteers to accompany the men to their interviews with the Department of Immigration. The men adored her. They respectfully called her 'grandmother' and would hug her. Having spent so much time in Afghanistan I could observe this with something of a unique perspective. What might seem to others a friendly and grateful but otherwise unremarkable gesture on their part was to me much more remarkable, knowing the social and cultural milieu which produced these men. I knew that they came from a place where publicly hugging a female was an enormously strong taboo, let alone hugging someone not of your own family. These men in their gratitude at this friendship and hospitality had transcended these cultural rules.

Ocie, I was deeply impressed with this. But I was just as taken aback, and equally impressed, to learn that Lina was a member of the Liberal Party (the party that boasted about 'stopping the boats' and refugees from reaching Australia). And not only that, she was a member of their electoral college and had a hand in choosing candidates. It seems that love has a way of going beyond particular categories of thinking and acting. Perhaps that is the point: we are never fully produced or finished by our cultures or anything else. There is always some new response we can learn and make.

Ocie, this is a story that still causes us to scratch our heads in bewilderment. If the community meals with the Afghan men on Friday nights at Murray Bridge represented the welcoming of the stranger and the 'unguarding of hearts' (to borrow Richard Flanagan's phrase), then this story is just the opposite. It is about your great-grandfather and his mother – your great-great-grandmother. Since your great-grandfather was my Dad, that's how I will speak of him. But I hope that you can still feel a connection with him and your great-grandmother, Ruth, from whom you receive your middle name. They loved your mum and Nick and Bronnie well. We do our best to love you well too.

I mentioned before that Dad was a pharmacist. In the summer of 1979–80 he was invited to join a team going to Cambodia to provide much-needed medical care following the fall of the Pol Pot regime. But he did not have a passport. To get one of these he had to supply a birth certificate. It seemed that Dad never had cause in his life, up until this point, to actually produce a birth certificate for anyone or anything. He sent away to the NSW Registrar for Births, Deaths and Marriages for it. A response to his application didn't arrive.

Aunty Teddy (her real name was Rita) used to come over to Adelaide from Sydney, where our family originally lived, to spend a few weeks each summer with the family. She was Dad's older sister. Teddy, often contracted to Ted, had a wonderful sense of humour. Wodehousian-like expressions such as 'I feel as full as a poison pup', 'You can put that where the monkey put the rusty sixpence', 'You slobbered a bibful there, brother' and 'You're worth your weight in tin tacks' used to fly around our conversations. We welcomed the ones we knew like old friends and delighted in the ones we had not heard before, rolling them around our tongues afterwards, like wine tasters, so as to not forget them or their flavour. At the same time, Ted had a temper, and a turn of the tongue which, when unleashed, could scald, as opposed to merely scold.

I was no longer living with my parents during what turned out to be her last visit to Adelaide. As Mum was getting ready to take her to the airport, Ted produced the letter from the Registrar, which she had intercepted from the postman. When handing Mum the letter (Dad was at work) and prior to Mum having read its contents, she said, 'Tell Alan I always loved him'. The birth certificate recorded *her* as Dad's mother. Mum and Dad were gobsmacked. Dad was in his late fifties and had throughout his whole life been led to think of her as his elder sister. According to Mum, from that day on until she died seven years later, those few words, that declaration of love, was all Teddy would ever say about the matter. She had learned over a lifetime not to say anything and so it remained. And Mum, *our* Mum, who got on so well with Ted, and who never allowed any issue to remain unspoken or silently damage a relationship, tried to talk with her about it. Mum and Dad tried to tell her 'It's okay. This is good news for all of us'. For Ted, though, this revelation was a new shame laid over a very old one, and the laying of it was to be done silently, like placing a wreath. There was no Ted talk here.

The unravelling of Teddy's long-held secret began to explain many things for Dad. He had always been puzzled at the distance he felt existed between him and his parents, who it now turned out were his grandparents. He once confided that he knew they loved him but that there was never that close, physical affection or careless play that he saw elsewhere. He thought it was because they were that much older and he was their youngest by so many years. Dad's father on the birth certificate was Teddy's late husband Chas. Thankfully, we had known Chas as young children, likewise thinking of him as our uncle. He was an especially gentle and kind man, like his son.

Teddy and Chas had conceived Dad 'out of wedlock'. In the decades since, people in similar situations, together with their families, suffered embarrassment but often got married anyway and the whispers eventually floated away in the thin social air. For Chas and Rita, in the early 1920s in rural Grafton, northern New South Wales, it was just too socially embarrassing to allow things to proceed in that way. There was also the matter of Chas being from a Catholic family while Teddy's family was Anglican. Perhaps this was just as significant a barrier to their marriage: the Protestant–Catholic division stood like an invisible Berlin Wall.

We don't know the circumstances of how Teddy's confinement for her pregnancy was managed. But when Dad was born he was left with Teddy's parents, his grandparents, and brought up as their own. He was treated well.

The paradox of this story is that Teddy and Chas eventually did marry. Enigmatically, under some form of ongoing constraint, they were still not allowed to, or chose not to, claim Alan as their son. They loved him, just as Ted told Mum. Mum said, more than once, how hard it must have been for Teddy and Chas during the Second World War when Dad, who was a fighter pilot, was shot down over Italy. They could not even show their worry or grief as his real parents. When Mum and Dad were first married they even lived with Teddy and Chas for a period. And later, as young children, we were always visiting them and they us.

Teddy and Chas also had a daughter. Instead of a cousin, Dad had a sister, Bev. After *the revelation* she and Dad celebrated their new relationship over subsequent years. Even so, Bev remained both angry and sad that she had, for the greater part of her life, been deprived of her elder brother; of having an elder brother rather than an uncle. Dad's distance from the household, with its heavy secret, may have sheltered him from some of its worst effects. He reacted quite differently. Dad was also a big believer in the idea of grace: accepting himself and others. We regard this as his generous legacy to us.

Dad did not have his mother's temper. Similarly, we never knew Chas to excoriate anyone, with the possible exception of himself. But Teddy had not fared so well. Her anger used to flare unexpectedly, as though it had bitten through an unseen leash, seizing on some issue or remark that seemed insignificant to the rest of us. There were times in Afghanistan I had cause to wonder whether, in some epigenetic operation, the genes for anger and hostility could jump a generation and still be passed on.

We are now clearer in our understanding of why she was so angry. She had been forced, or chosen, for reasons we will never know, to perform an unfair and unnecessary charade for the greater part of her life. She was forever looking in on her son's life through an outside window; able to see what he was doing but not able to fully participate in his life as his mum. Ocie, I believe that my Mum and Dad did their best to open the door to Teddy and invite her to come inside. But she felt that she had no choice but to remain an outsider. That, perhaps, is the saddest thing of all.

21

Anne and I were on a flight from Kuala Lumpur to Amsterdam in early March 2005. I had been invited to speak at the Congress of the Dutch Association for Manual Therapy in Veldhoven, a town south towards the border with Belgium. We were going to take this opportunity to visit friends in The Netherlands and England afterwards; friends we had worked with in Afghanistan years before. It was the middle of the night, as it always seems to be on thirteen-hour flights, and I was awake and looking at the screen in front of me. An innovation called 'flight path' provided a map which included, among other things, details of our altitude, aircraft speed and distance to our destination. We were flying over Afghanistan. The westernmost city of Herat was depicted as being 10km distant. I presume the 10km meant straight down. It was the closest I had been to Afghanistan in many years and I nostalgically wondered whether I would ever set foot in the country again. Four months later all five of us, the whole family, were on the ground in Kabul.

This was quick by any standard of planning for a trip to Afghanistan. I had earlier received a request to conduct an official review of what was now called the Physical Therapy Institute (PTI) in Kabul. Somewhere along the line there had been a shift from the British/European term *physiotherapy* to the North American *physical therapy*. While definitely receptive to the invitation to be an external reviewer of PTI, and how it was functioning, the timeframe within which they needed this to be carried out could not be accommodated with my own teaching schedule. Nevertheless, the project administrator asked if I would like to come and do some teaching anyway. Since the month of July was the hiatus between semesters at our university, I suggested this time. And it came to be.

The Second-time Teacher

Upon hearing about this invitation to teach at PTI, the rest of the family announced that they were coming too. Nick was twenty-one, Coby nineteen and Bronnie would turn seventeen later in the year. Nick had spent his first few years in Afghanistan and Coby had been there as a baby. They were adamant that they wanted to go back and see the place where they had spent the early part of their lives. As it turned out, this would prove helpful to them in visualizing our situation when Anne and I made further trips to an even more unstable Afghanistan in 2007, 2008 and 2011. We had learned that there was a significant difference between forming a view of a place via television and other media and actually being there. Witnessing how people went about the ordinary activities of everyday life, getting about the place to work or buy food or visit friends, lent a different understanding of the country and its people from news footage which focussed mostly on violent acts and their victims.

Adding to our small entourage, a young colleague from the University of South Australia had expressed interest in teaching physiotherapy in Afghanistan. I planned a weeklong teaching program with Rebekah and her husband, Debashish, who was also a physiotherapist. After this week of teaching, Nick and Coby would return with Rebekah and Debashish to Delhi and then meet up with a friend to explore the south of India. Anne, Bronnie and I would have another week in Afghanistan. On our way to Afghanistan, we stayed at Debashish's parents' place in Delhi. Prior to our departure for Kabul, there was, however, a complication with Debashish's documentation, related to the fact that he was an Indian national. He and Rebekah were unable to depart Delhi at the same time as we did. They would make it to Kabul at the end of the week. The five of us flew to Kabul without them. I rapidly revised the teaching program in light of this unforeseen change in arrangements. Even this change in plans seemed reminiscent of being back in Kabul, like some kind of induction. Eighteen years had elapsed since we were last there.

PART THREE: AFGHANISTAN 2005–2011

As we approached Kabul and our landing, the machinery of war was visible. Helicopter gunships were clustered just off the runway, dozens of them. This time they belonged to another set of countries. The splay of multiple rotors side by side looked like a horizontal windfarm, only khaki instead of white. Armed soldiers were posted everywhere, and the overriding sense of things was military. We were back in a war zone.

We entered the terminal and waited in a line that was rapidly forming for immigration and visa checks. Two young Frenchmen were ahead of us and lit cigarettes to while away the time. Quickly and officiously, a man in green uniform appeared and communicated the unacceptability of this by vigorously waving his index finger at them, while intermittently redeploying the same finger in order to point to a 'No smoking' sign up on the wall. The two young men were quite cooperative and immediately extinguished their cigarettes. Some minutes later I smelled smoke once more and thought to myself, 'Whoever is responsible for this will be in trouble – surely it isn't the same guys?' The answer to my question came shortly afterwards as 'the green-uniformed, index-finger-waving, no-smoking official' walked past us, puffing luxuriously on a cigarette. We stood passively in line pondering the impenetrable relationship between 'what ought to' and 'what actually' happens in life.

Kabul was now a city of unbridled traffic. Where few civilians had owned cars here in the early 1980s, now many people did. Aspiring to better flow patterns for the surging volumes of traffic, the authorities had made various city streets one-way thoroughfares. A series of concrete canyons had been created by fifteen-foot concrete blast walls, which provided government ministries and major buildings some protection from suicide bombers using cars and other attacks. The traffic moved through the city centre like funnelled stormwater. Adjoining streets were side eddies where both cars and pedestrians became stuck and stationary, entrapped by the bigger torrent of traffic passing in front of them until, at some point, they would be swept up and carried away.

Last time we were here there had been around two million people living in Kabul. That figure had represented a rapid increase from a population of around 900,000 just a few years previously before the Russian invasion, and start of the war. Back then, I had driven across town without thought or concern. Now, Kabul was a city of almost three million people and, in the two weeks we spent there, despite numerous crossings of the city, I did not see any working traffic lights. Even if they *had* been in order, compliance with them, like the no smoking policy at the airport, may have been another question entirely.

Even the military convoys looked different. I remembered the Russian convoys travelling through town twenty years before. Now, as we watched the NATO-led International Security Assistance Force (ISAF) convoys moving through Kabul, it was an entirely different experience. The time of the suicide bomber had come. Driving into a diplomatic or military convoy, prior to detonating an explosive-laden vehicle, was not uncommon. In 2007 and 2008 I was working for the International Committee of the Red Cross (ICRC) and even with our clearly marked vehicles, we had to follow ICRC policy, which meant pulling over to the side of the road and stopping when an ISAF convoy passed. This was because the final vehicle in the convoy had a machine-gunner standing ready to fire at any vehicle that came too close. I saw close up the nervousness of an American Marine at his station. His face was severe with concentration and uncompromising intention. It seemed a long way from our sharing a game of basketball with Marines in the park in *Shah re Nao* all those years ago.

We stayed in *KArte Seh*, the suburb across town from PTI, where we had lived in the 1980s. We were accommodated in a house provided

PART THREE: AFGHANISTAN 2005–2011

for us by our friends Tom and Libby Little. Tom had sent me the Dari textbook in the previous year. Twenty years before, on a Friday autumn afternoon in 1985, Tom had announced that he was going for a walk up *Sher DarwAza*, following the ancient wall up the mountain that divides Kabul, and he asked if anyone wanted to go with him. Well, most of us thought that if Tom considered it reasonable to climb a mountain in a war zone then who were we to be concerned. A crew of several adults and around ten children drove around the *Chilsitoon* road, parked our cars beside the Kabul River and began the climb upwards. In its colour at least, the wall was not unlike the many simple dwellings in Kabul which now clung to the higher reaches of the nearby mountains. Tom knew to stop our ascent well before we got to the top of *Sher DarwAza*, where armed military personnel kept vigil in checkposts. We looked down on *Jadi Maiwand* far below. It was the main avenue of the old city of Kabul: its alleyways penetrated a maze of small mudbrick houses, so close together that they seemed interwoven, like some kind of patterned fabric.

The house we stayed in was only a few minutes' walk from Tom's and Libby's place and we were able to share most meals with them. Tom's and Libby's youngest daughter was doing a medical placement at a local hospital and was staying with them. There was also a young New Zealand man who had accompanied Tom, as part of a medical healthcare team, on a trip to *Nuristan* earlier that year. This was ideal as far as our young adult kids were concerned: people around their age to hang out with!

Our accommodation was familiar enough. It was large with white stucco walls and had a spacious yard (*aoli*) surrounded by ten-foot-high walls – pretty much like every house in *KArte Seh*. There was a laminated notice on the wall in the kitchen which was less familiar and somewhat sobering. It was entitled 'Quick Review Security Levels Action'. There were three security levels, green through red. Level one (green) was like going bushwalking. It read: 'Always inform someone where you go and when you expect to be back' and 'Keep a radio or mobile phone with you'. Level two (orange) introduced an unfamiliar note: 'Change travel time to home and work by at least an hour two times a week and change the route at least twice a week' and 'Make sure that you have a two-week stock of food and water'. Level three (red) got more serious. It had three further levels:

(1) No movement to and from home / work. Prepare an evacuation bag
(2) Follow evacuation guidelines
(3) Lie low – there is no opportunity to evacuate.

Regime change had seemingly ushered in other opportunities. One house where we used to live in *KArte Seh* had been demolished and in its place there was a massive and garish building with ostentatious pillars in the colour of operating theatre green. It was not just that such a building had been inflicted on the neighbourhood, we were sad because the place contained memories for us. It once had a large yard with a swing I had made for the children out of local wood bought across the river in *Chilsitoon*. Two of our kids learned to walk and play in that yard.

These new kinds of buildings were constructed with *opulence* as their guiding architectural principle. They did not derive from Afghan architecture but instead reflected foreign, some said Pakistani, influence. They were referred to by the expat community as 'narco palaces'. The term referred to the dubious sources of funding which enabled these extravagant houses to be built. While such houses had sprung up here and there, the streets outside remained in very poor condition, often potholed and close to impassable. On certain corners people dumped their rubbish where it lay and it rotted in the sun. This wasn't new and neither would it improve with time. Years later Anne and I would be in Herat and asking Heratis about their beautiful and green public parks. They would reply that they had community spirit in Herat whereas life in Kabul was 'dog eat dog'. The image was not inaccurate. Large packs of dogs did roam *KArte Seh* looking for food, enjoying what was on offer in the rubbish piles. And while they had been conditioned to be afraid of humans, courtesy of the penchant for stone throwing by Afghan boys, it could be dangerous to be out and about alone after dark.

Since the West had arrived back in 2001, there had been a flood of other new wealth arising from aid money given to the regime by various supportive governments. However, there were several 'filters' and levels of government through which this money had to pass before it was translated into beneficial projects on the ground for the average Afghan. Ironically, in the context of these demonstrations of new wealth, we also noticed many more beggars on the streets than we had in the past. We used to only see begging by persons with demonstrable physical disabilities.

At this time there happened to be a project underway in *KArte Seh*. A water supply was being dug with Turkish aid money to pipe water to the area from *Band e Kharga* (*Kharga* Lake). Previously there were only wells, and not deep ones at that. Since the water from these wells lay in a water table shared by contaminants from human waste, this was a real problem for everybody's health.

The PTI was on the other side of the city from *KArte Seh*. I would get there each day by first walking from our house a few blocks out to *Darulaman*, which was the main road linking the city from the exiled king's palace south of the city. I would wait by the side of the road and flag down a taxi, as I had done in past years. I enjoyed doing this. Speaking with taxi drivers was not only good language practice; drivers are also barometers of what the general populace are thinking. On subsequent visits, security policies would prohibit this as a method of getting around, and especially just hailing a taxi down on the street. We would be restricted to using specific drivers or booking vehicles and drivers belonging to our own organization.

The purpose of my teaching was to further introduce and teach the notion of clinical reasoning to local physiotherapy teachers. There was an implication which required consideration in teaching clinical reasoning to physical therapists in Afghanistan. It had to do with the dominant learning culture and style, which was largely authoritarian and hierarchical. This was not unique to Afghanistan. This same learning culture existed in India. What this meant was that a student did not easily question a teacher or more senior colleague. But clinical reasoning requires reflection and an ability to identify and declare the assumptions underlying one's reasoning. Clinicians in this environment therefore learned *not* to intentionally reflect on their own potential errors of reasoning and how this might play out in subsequent clinical actions. Clinical reasoning was in this context subversive to the prevailing educational culture and therefore a challenge to teach. I had personally experienced the value of critical questioning in *Ajoya*, Mexico. This was why I had become interested in clinical reasoning in the first place.

It had been helpful that in late 2004 I had practised some conversational Dari once more. PTI had hosted many physiotherapy clinicians over the years who had taught various assessment methods and treatment approaches for particular conditions. This had been done didactically: in other words, 'This is how you do it. Now show me'. This was something different: teaching reasoning skills, and the relevance of these skills, so that practitioners could make various decisions together *with* their patients. It was teaching skills beyond just the performance of techniques or rehearsed protocols. Curriculum development was now a necessity. Afghan physical therapy was isolated from the global physical therapy community and the knowledge exchange of conferences, journals and published research. Afghan physical therapists were highly disadvantaged by all these things mostly being in English. I had noticed an increase in spoken English since I had last been there but accessing, let alone understanding, journal articles, and being able to draw upon research evidence and emerging approaches in physiotherapy, was for Afghan physical therapists still a distant shore.

After class, early in the week, one of the PT teachers accompanied me to the hospital gates and said that he would help me find a taxi back to *KArte Seh*. Beyond the hospital gate was a single service road, a branch off from the main airport road, which services three adjacent hospitals: *Wazir Akbar Khan*, the children's or paediatric hospital and the *Char Sad o Bestar* military hospital. This arrangement was unchanged since the 1980s except that there was now more traffic; a sort of raised blood pressure uncomfortably pulsing this small artery. The road was lined by small shops, mostly carts on wheels that were pushed in by their vendors each day to sell food and other convenience goods to hospital staff and the many other visitors who were entering and leaving the three hospitals. There was high competition for taxis. My colleague spotted one and taking my arm drew me up to the side window. The driver seeing that I was a foreigner, and knowing that he could exact a higher fare, nodded for me to get in. As I did so, I became aware of a ruckus at the opposite window. I had just sat in the back seat and now the door on the opposite side opened and a group of men were gathered there. One voice in particular was telling me to get out. Its owner was extremely agitated. Hazel eyes bulged in a face reddened by elevating anger, while a Nuristani cap did not entirely conceal his near auburn-coloured hair, another instance of the cultural melting pot that was Afghanistan. The meltdown hadn't finished with his eye and hair colour. Amid a torrent of expletives, I heard the word *AmrikAI* (American) used pejoratively in much the same way that the word *RusAwi* (Russian) had been spat out when we were there last. My PT colleague rapidly opened my side door and called me to get out, in his direction not theirs. He apologized if we had inadvertently jumped in on 'their taxi' and drew me away, back towards the hospital gates. The men climbed in and were driven off. We waited some minutes inside the hospital grounds and then he found me another taxi. In the four years we lived in Kabul in the 1980s I had never personally experienced hostility like this. Then I had been more aware of my own.

The week moved to its conclusion. I enjoyed the experience. The work of others, both expatriate and Afghan, in consolidating and developing the school and its Afghan leadership over the previous eighteen years was quite evident, and impressive. They had initiated an arrangement with the medical school at Kabul University such that medical students attended PTI in order to learn about physical therapy and, importantly, also about disability. My octogenarian orthopaedic colleague Gerald Golden would have been pleased to hear this news. He had died some years before, having gained assent from his children to stay in Afghanistan until the end and be buried in Kabul.

22

Rebekah and Debashish had arrived from Delhi at the end of the week. For the weekend, Tom arranged for two four-wheel-drive vehicles and a driver from NOOR (Tom drove the other) to take us all to *Istalef* the following day. *Istalef* is a small town at the northernmost point of Kabul province, some thirty kilometres north of the city. We paid for the use of the vehicles and the driver's time. There were nine of us. Men were in one vehicle and women were in the other; that is, apart from the NOOR driver. We left the city, driving northwards through suburbs such as *Khair Khana* which had only ever been names to me before.

When we began learning the Dari language not long after our arrival in Afghanistan in 1983, our teachers would eulogize over *Istalef*'s many qualities. It was a place of shady trees and orchards, set on a hillside overlooking a large and fertile valley. It was also a well of creativity and was known for its artists and pottery makers. It seemed that whenever we practised sentences which contained *maghbUI* (beautiful) or *khUb* (good) or *pAk* (clean) or *tAza* (fresh) we would frequently be constructing a sentence with *Istalef* as the subject. Unfortunately, at the very time we were practising these sentences about *Istalef* and its beauty, it was being bombed into submission and ruin.

Apart from our early visits to *Band e Kharga*, this was for Anne and me our first ever foray outside the city of Kabul and a chance to see a different Afghanistan: a rural Afghanistan. In the four years we had lived here in the 1980s we were never allowed to venture out into the countryside. It was too dangerous. Escaping the intensity of the imperatives pressing us in on us from work and life in the city was not that easy. We used to leave our house in *KArte Seh* and walk down some seventy metres to the river where, through the gap in the houses, we had an uninterrupted view of the mountains to the west. There we would sit on the stone wall beside the river, which could be rushing in the spring due to melting snow or slowing to an almost stagnant trickle in late summer, clogged by the rubbish carelessly thrown in. The majesty of the mountains, however, could not be undermined by either bombs or human carelessness. They were both imposing and beautiful, capped by snow for all but a couple of months of the year. This view became our means of imagining a country outside of Kabul. It was our wider Afghanistan, apart from the silent topography offered from an aircraft window, pictures in books or, using other senses, stories from workmates and patients. The space where we used to sit and look at the sun setting over the *Paghman* range was occupied in 2005 by a continuous line of containers, providing premises and storage space for various businesses, mainly offering building supplies. Further along, in line of sight of the mountains, there were now small shops on *Pul e Surkh* (the Red Bridge), not just completing the obstruction of the view but further constricting the opening through which traffic and pedestrians could pass. Later the bridge would be cleared of shops once more in the interests of traffic flow, one of the very few examples of things reverting to a previous time.

 Once we were out of the city, we were reminded that it was Friday and that others had decided to take a leisurely drive out to the countryside for a picnic. Afghans love picnics. The road north was like some kind of exodus with a capital 'E'. I was sitting in the back seat and turned to look at the traffic behind us. What I saw was overtakers overtaking overtakers. Although each lane was of a generous size, the road was essentially a two-lane highway. That is, one lane for each direction of traffic. At one point four cars, like charging Hussars, collectively occupied the whole road *and* the verges on either side, while attempting to overtake each other. Afghans often used expressions such as *qAnun e jangal* (law of the jungle) or *bE qAnun ast* (there is no rule) when explaining daily life in Afghanistan. Despite there being an absence of *qAnun* on the road that day, I relaxed in the knowledge that Tom was *besyAr balat* (very accustomed to this). He did not seem at all fazed.

When we arrived at *Istalef* it was crowded like any place of pilgrimage. We walked from our vehicles between picnicking Afghan families sitting on carpets under pine trees. They grouped around table cloths that were weighted down by plates of food. We came to a building that, at face value, had not suffered too much bomb damage. We were ushered to a spot outside under a tree where we took off our shoes and sat down on carpets. These were a deep red colour with an overlaid design on them known as *fil pAi* (elephant foot). Bowls of white mulberries called *Shah tut* (king mulberries) and trays of freshly cut watermelon were laid before us. We drank glasses of cold *doogh*, a yoghurt-based drink garnished with mint and cucumber and chilled by crushed ice.

After this sojourn, we drove further on, following the river back up its course through the foothills and towards the higher mountain range beyond. We were on tracks where two vehicles could not pass at the same time. Occasionally we did meet another vehicle. Where it was too difficult for one vehicle to back up and return to the last 'pull over', then negotiation and even impromptu road-making was required. Vehicles would be manoeuvred carefully and very slowly by each other with only a few centimetres between them. On one occasion this cooperation had to be supported by placing some extra stones on the valley side of the road in order that our wheel had *terra firma* beneath it during the passing manoeuvre. What was most remarkable was the way in which this was all conducted in a good-humoured and social manner: a kind of mutual problem-solving that, when it worked, gave everyone some sort of satisfaction. After reaching a point where the track became less a track for vehicles and more a walking path, we sat beside a clear stream which, now that we were further up the valley, was falling rapidly over and between large glistening rocks. Boys looking after a small herd of fat-tailed sheep came over to talk to us. This was the old Afghanistan, or a historical snapshot of it, a village-oriented life of animals and orchards.

On Saturday Nick, Coby, Rebekah and Debashish left. The first work trip of the week was to *Charikar*, a town 70km north of Kabul. I accompanied Tom, who was investigating an expansion of the ophthalmic service at the local hospital. We sat in the office of the *rais* (president) of the hospital and drank tea. At some point after Tom introduced me, and the words 'physical therapist' were processed, the *rais* asked if we would follow him. He led us to another part of the compound and into another *shOba* (department). He pointed to a large couch-like piece of furniture. 'What is this?' he asked. It had been donated but they did not know what it was for and it had them baffled. I saw that it was an electronic lumbar traction unit. Part of its 'electronics' included a massage contraption, built into the padding, at the point where the lumbar spine would be positioned during traction. There was a touch screen display to control it all, which in itself was no bad thing but it was not able to be fixed by anyone locally, should it break down, as it inevitably would. It was an example of goodwill not attuned to the real issues and needs of a local situation.

We passed *Bagram*, the large ISAF airbase and prison, on our way to Kabul. Along the way tracts of land were marked out by red flags, and specialized bulldozers moved carefully across the terrain. This was landmine clearing and was generally a sign of the aftermath of war. When we arrived at the *Wazir* hospital compound, Tom invited me into the old garage sheds that NOOR now used. It was an irony that NOOR, which once had its own substantial and modern hospital, had its administration and storage in these old garages which we had used all that time ago, while just up the way the PTI now had its own purpose-built premises.

Part Three: Afghanistan 2005–2011

It didn't seem to bother Tom at all. As we entered a number of people approached him. 'Mester Tom,' they would begin, as they brought one or more issues to his attention regarding NOOR. 'I'll see how many of these I can sweep under the carpet,' he said wryly. They were not the words of someone uncaring or lackadaisical. 'Dealing with one or two problems at any one time is enough,' he explained.

Tom said that he was going to *Chaki Wardak*, a province south-west of Kabul, and invited Anne, Bronnie and me to go along. The purpose of this visit was to discuss a request for an ophthalmic nurse at a small rural hospital. This hospital was quite a way off the main Kabul–*Ghazni* road. It took some careful navigation once we had passed *Maidan Shah*, and asking several persons along the way, to establish the location of the turn-off. There was no sign. When we did turn off the main *Ghazni* road, we travelled further for over an hour along a potholed dirt track, not unlike the *Ajoya* track, in order to reach the village. We were in a NOOR project four-wheel drive and Tom and a NOOR driver took turns to manoeuvre carefully around flocks of sheep and goats and, at other times, through flowing river crossings and fords. We reached the village to find abandoned tanks and field guns, rusting and derelict but somehow still standing sentry-like in the streets. The hospital was run by a German woman in her sixties who had been very able in soliciting funds from various donor agencies to keep the hospital afloat. The discussion revolved around the living situation of the ophthalmic nurse and whether it would satisfy the demands of her family for propriety, safety and the capacity for her to regularly come back to Kabul to see them.

After lunch, we were shown around the hospital at length. We came to a tent full of people lying on makeshift beds; an obvious overflow of patients in need and waiting for attention. Tom, in an aside to me, said, 'It's like this everywhere you go in Afghanistan: people suffering, and the poor always wait'. On an earlier occasion, when we had been living in Kabul, he had once said, 'Love never needs justification'. This stayed in my mind. Over time, Ocie, my interpretation of what he said is that caring for others is not a means to some other end. It has its own justification simply in the doing of it. Mind you, the *doing* of it is still hard enough.

As we drove out of the village, heading back towards Kabul, Tom said that the place was well run with one important caveat: what would happen when this wonderful, committed German woman got too old or the political situation became too volatile and unsafe for her to stay? How would the operation of the hospital be sustained? There was no real method of indigenizing this service and work. It was like her empire. Although benevolent and providing much-needed health services for the poor, it would most likely fall whenever she left, which, like all of us, she must inevitably do. Of course, another way of *leaving* was to die here, like Gerald Golden. And we would see this come to pass, too, in ways less peaceful than Gerald's passing.

On the last Friday of our second week, the day before our departure, Tom and Libby took us on another picnic, this time following the Kabul River south. We walked beside a fast-flowing river, clean before it reaches Kabul, and irrigating a valley green with orchards. On either side of us were mountains that appeared close and misleadingly climbable.

23

The following year in June 2006, Aziz, the director of PTI, visited Australia. He was sponsored by the Australian Physiotherapy Association (APA). I assisted in arranging this visit as part of the lead-up work to an application of the AAPT for membership of the WCPT. He spoke at the APA conference in Melbourne about the challenges facing Afghan physiotherapists and the enormous need for rehabilitation services for the Afghan people. We returned to Adelaide together. He stayed with us and undertook a program of visits to local hospitals and rehabilitation units and discussions with various physiotherapy teachers at our university.

Aziz and I took a day off together and drove south through the Adelaide Hills to the coastal towns of *Goolwa* and *Victor Harbor*. Where he was from it was the mountains that were dry and rocky and the valleys which were green. Here, at least at this time of the year, it was the hills which were green. He was mesmerised by this reversal of landscape.

In June of the following year, Aziz and I met up in Vancouver at the WCPT conference. I was a speaker. He was there to formally accept membership to the WCPT on behalf of the AAPT. It was an important step in overcoming the longstanding sense of isolation of the Afghan physiotherapists and cause for great celebration.

Physical therapy education in Afghanistan had become a joint enterprise between several foreign NGOs. The work of the PTI, which had been long supported by International Assistance Mission, was supplemented by other organizations who also trained PTs. The reason for this was that PTI could not, by itself, train enough of them. These organizations included the ICRC, the Swedish Committee for Afghanistan, Handicap International and the Sandy Gall Foundation.

The Second-time Teacher

Four of these groups employed Afghan physical therapists to work in hospitals and health posts around Afghanistan. These organizations had, by and large, worked extremely well together by encouraging their own PT staff to attend joint educational courses.

Earlier in 2007 an Italian physiotherapist had expressed interest in doing the Masters course in Advanced Clinical Physiotherapy in Adelaide at our school. She had been working with the ICRC in Kabul and asked whether any of the teachers in our program would be interested in teaching a course in Kabul. I had been very grateful for the opportunity to return and teach in 2005 but had not given much active thought to any further trips. This inquiry activated such thought.

In Vancouver at the WCPT conference I met with the director of the orthopaedic ICRC hospital in Kabul. I said to him that I was willing to come and teach the thirty-four physical therapists working with the ICRC but that I was not skilled to teach them about physical therapy in the management of, for example, persons with spinal cord injuries or amputations. He said, 'No, that's okay. Teach them clinical reasoning'. And even though the teaching of clinical reasoning occurred in a context of assessing and managing musculoskeletal conditions (about which I also had knowledge and skills), I would never have predicted that it would be clinical reasoning which would open the door for continuing my involvement in Afghan physical therapy.

For this teaching visit to happen, two other things required negotiation. With respect to the ICRC, Afghanistan was classified as a non-family/no spouse posting due to the security issues. This meant for Anne to come she would have to obtain her own posting. With the support of the ICRC leadership, Anne was able to contact a Finnish colleague, Seija, we knew from our earlier time with IAM in the 1980s. I had worked with Seija's American partner, Dan, who had supported disabled persons to make children's elbow crutches for the physiotherapy school in 1985. Seija was senior nurse at the American-funded CURE hospital. She welcomed Anne's offer to work in the neonatal intensive care unit at CURE. The second 'irregularity' to be worked out was that, after my work and contract with the ICRC was completed, I wanted to then teach at PTI as a volunteer. The ICRC proved to be very flexible and generous in allowing us to remain in ICRC accommodation for the duration of our teaching work in Kabul.

In November 2007 we flew into Kabul on a small, turbo-prop ICRC plane from Peshawar, Pakistan. The ICRC staff were accommodated in the suburb of *Wazir Akbar Khan*, which was also the diplomatic area in Kabul. *Wazir* had its own particular streetscape. An assortment of private security companies patrolled different sections of this precinct, looking after the *nafar e kalAnA*, 'important people' who had contracted them. These security employees were kitted out with various distinctive military-looking uniforms and were armed to the teeth with automatic rifles. The houses stood like small prisons. Each had one or more of these 'prison officers' at the gates, which in turn were buttressed by concrete bulwarks. Razor wire adorned the tops of the walls. Speed humps, like small hills, had been put in place on the adjacent roads where, because of their extreme height, they caused even four-wheel-drive vehicles to cross them with particular care. Police also circulated, driving green-coloured utes with machine guns mounted on the back. A third layer of security existed in the squads of the Afghan National Army, which also patrolled the main street in the next block. It had the largest vehicles and most potent firepower. Everyone was armed except us and all the other civilians, who were of apparently less consequence than those who lived permanently in *Wazir*.

On our very first day of work, we were in a Red Cross vehicle with other staff heading across town to the ICRC orthopaedic hospital. We had just exited *Wazir* onto the main road which connects the city centre with Kabul airport. There was a loud explosion. The radio traffic surged as various personnel asked for intelligence about what had just happened. A suicide bomber had rammed a diplomatic convoy just down the road about 400m from our house. Even from that distance, we found out later, the blast was strong enough to blow the windows out of the houses. The force even caused the metal catches on the windows to burst through the timber window frames of the house where we were staying. If our experience of Kabul had always been as a war zone, this incident made explicit to us that *this* Kabul was different to the one we had known. That evening there was an ICRC meeting at which staff were given permission to withdraw from their postings if they felt uncomfortable with the current level of threat.

The physical therapy course proceeded. Participants came from various parts of the country, where they worked in ICRC orthopaedic centres. I was running an eight-day course, which would then be repeated, each time for a group of seventeen physical therapists. The classroom was arranged as for other classes and gatherings in Afghanistan: men sat on one side and women on the other. There were a couple of ICRC therapists who could speak English very well and they took turns in translating my lectures and practical demonstrations.

Practical classes were conducted in two different rooms. When it came time to practise assessment or handling techniques, the women would retire behind closed doors. However, I was welcome, with appropriate notice, to enter and from there would simply ask my female PT colleagues, on each occasion, what they were comfortable with regarding my demonstration on them and my observation of their handling with each other. Given that this took place in a group setting, they were quite clear in letting me know what was okay or not. This was extended when they were seeing patients and I was supervising their clinical work. One time, I found myself teaching through a door. The patient was a woman who had come from a remote village. As she was assessed and treated I could not go into the room. I asked questions of my colleague and heard her answers through the keyhole.

A kind of democracy evolved in the teaching sessions such that the women in the class could call out answers or critique a male colleague's assertion, including my own, with a freedom which was much less visible outside the classroom. My own language skills began to strengthen again and I got to the point where I could hear the Dari version of what I had just said and correct it if I thought the meaning of what I said had not been rightly conveyed.

Following the completion of the second course I accompanied the team leader of a home care program on his rounds. It was a program which monitored the welfare and progress following rehabilitation of some 700 spinally injured people in and around Kabul. Our visits took us to some areas of Kabul that I had never been to before. These were villages on the south-eastern outskirts of Kabul, which were now like outer suburbs – Kabul had grown to a population of some 4.5 million people. In these locations the effluent from houses exited from a hole in the wall and joined an open 'stream' dividing the main thoroughfare which everyone had to use. These walkways were already difficult to negotiate and there was mud aplenty. For a person with a disability, isolation and being confined to the house was almost an inevitability.

One house we visited was freezing but the fuel the family had needed to be saved for cooking alone. Life for some was just subsistence. Food rations were provided to the poorest of those we visited. However, I also witnessed people with spinal injury leading confident and participatory lives instead of succumbing to what was often the alternative: death through infection of pressure areas. One man was running a small business selling fuel, having participated in a microcredit scheme as part of this program. Another woman revelled in her independence in a range of activities.

Anne and I were invited by Seija to have lunch one Friday afternoon with her and Dan. It had been twenty years since I had seen them. Dan was like Tom in that he was immensely experienced concerning life in Afghanistan and how to live there. Unlike Tom, Dan found it hard to work within the timeframes and reporting constraints of NGOs, which they instituted in order to meet their obligations to both government ministries and the external donors who kept projects afloat. That is not to say that Dan lacked either integrity or insight. It was more that, having lived most of his life in India and Afghanistan, he was not culturally or organizationally conditioned to value such things as KPIs (key performance indicators) or strategic timeframes. But he knew his way around and could talk to anyone almost anywhere in Afghanistan. His current interest was in understanding the factors that caused young men in villages outside of Kabul to be radicalized. It took him to dangerous places. He was never armed and he confided, 'I realize that I may get my throat cut one day'.

Following the second ICRC course, I taught at the PTI. It was a teachers' course and four of the ICRC PTs participated. This was after the *Eid Adha* holiday. The year was nearing its end and our thoughts were turning towards our trip home.

Peshawar was already a hostile place for Westerners to visit. However, in the few days before we left Kabul, things in the North West Province became more volatile due to the assassination in Rawalpindi of prime ministerial hopeful Benazir Bhutto. We landed in Peshawar late one afternoon. We were picked up by a Red Cross driver and taken directly to an ICRC guesthouse. In the thirty-six hours prior to our departure for Abu Dhabi, we were confined to the compound.

PART THREE: AFGHANISTAN 2005–2011

At Peshawar airport, a month earlier, we had been ignored at customs and immigration as we stood in a line marked 'Foreign passport holders'. A fellow passenger, a local, kindly let us know we would not be attended to there and should join the 'Pakistan nationals' line in order to be processed by the staff. It was very different on the way out. When we presented our passports, I was asked to step behind the counter and into an office. I wondered if I was in any kind of trouble. Instead I was asked to carry an envelope back to Australia. It was a strange predicament being asked by the authorities, whose mandate was to prevent the illegal transfer of goods, to break the law for them. I was not sure what choice I had. I did say that I would need to see what was in the envelope. The officer assured me that it was a personal letter to a relative in Australia and that he was giving it to me because their mail was being read. In a complete reversal of roles, I inspected the envelope and scanned the letter he handed me. It was written in English. We took the letter and posted it in Melbourne.

24

We were invited back to work for the ICRC in Kabul the following year. We did not want to fly into Kabul from Peshawar. Dubai was our choice. The process of leaving one world (Australia) and entering another quite different one (Afghanistan) in the space of hours is always cause for reflection. If only as a means of getting oneself psychologically ready for leaving the airplane once you have landed in Kabul. Going from Terminal 1 at Dubai International Airport to Terminal 2 was a visible stepping point between these two worlds. It was a point at which you can say, 'Here is where it all changes'. At Terminal 2 the departures board had the following destinations: Islamabad, Baghdad Int'l, Isfahan, Mosul, Kabul and Kish. I was not sure about Kish. It is in fact a small island off the Iranian mainland. The other place names were familiar, but only from TV news. I had not seen them on other airport destination boards.

Tuesday 11th November (diary notes)

In Terminal 2 the smooth efficiency of Terminal 1 gives way to a kind of good-natured chaos. The PA system and gate signs aren't working and so employees walk through the crowd, announcing flight departures without amplification, pleading for late passengers to report to their gates, their voices reaching just above the volume of the collective conversation in the terminal. Passengers in ad hoc groups have stacked ridiculous volumes of carry-on baggage in readiness for the dash to their boarding gate. I witness a chance conversation between a young African American in civvies and a middle-aged Afghan man. They pass the time, affably, before their respective flights. The American hears his boarding call and moves to board his flight to Baghdad. He smiles

PART THREE: AFGHANISTAN 2005–2011

bemusedly but also graciously as the Afghan man exhorts him to be careful. I enjoy this simple exchange for its incongruity and humanity.

Anne and I have been informed a couple of hours earlier that the UN humanitarian services flight on which we were booked is cancelled due to a technical problem. We are pointed in the direction of Safi Air, one of Afghanistan's new airlines. Having very few options seems to facilitate decision-making quite well. We line up and wait for the harassed and solitary staff person behind the counter at Safi to do her bit on our behalf. We get on only to find out later that this is not an ICRC-approved carrier. The ash trays in the arm rests indicate that, although the airline is new, its fleet is not and has been constituted with aircraft which others no longer want. I can't think how long it has been since I last saw an ashtray on a commercial jet. Closing the overhead lockers requires a strength and aggression which other airlines do not require of their stewards, as luggage volume and locker storage capacity do not easily approximate. At 29,000 feet over the mountains of *Waziristan* it isn't helpful to speculate on the aircraft maintenance standards in relation to all these other observations. But the food is okay and the landing at Kabul is performed with skill. We taxi past a wind farm of military helicopters, secured for the night like livestock, and we prepare ourselves for the unwelcoming air of an autumn Kabul night.

Things had deteriorated in the space of a year by several measures. Gayle Williams, a Briton working with disabled children, was gunned down a few weeks earlier while walking to work in *KArte Seh*. Two months before that, in August, three aid workers, all women employed by the International Rescue Committee, were ambushed and shot near *Pul-I-Alam*, some fifty kilometres south of Kabul. They were travelling back to the capital in clearly marked vehicles. Violence against foreigners had increased and security levels kept rising to meet the challenge. The previous year we were able to visit Dan and Seija on the other side of town. Now we were no longer able to leave *Wazir Akbar Khan* on such social expeditions. So, this was what it was like to live in a gated community.

On the first night in our ICRC house we were shown to our room. It was on the ground floor, with two large windows facing the *aoli* (yard). Floodlights filled the *aoli* with visibility. Our curtains did little to reduce the blazing light. I placed a pair of underpants (clean) over my head in order to sleep. Anne shook her head, and went to sleep. The following day I spoke to the *chaukidar* and asked for one particular light, the one nearest our bed, to be extinguished at night. He said that he couldn't do this but showed me where the switch was. Good enough.

The first morning of work found me in the ICRC compound in *Shah re Nao*. I met Sanguin, an ICRC physiotherapist I taught the previous year. He welcomed me with a kiss. The Afghans have a saying: '*Yag rOz didi dost; dega rOz didi, Beradar.*' (We meet one day as friends; the next time we meet it is as brothers). This kiss on the cheek is a sign of affection and respect and goes beyond the usual politeness of shaking hands or even brushing cheeks. I welcomed it and looked forward to the start of class.

During the teaching one day there was a demonstration outside the ICRC hospital by Kabul University students on the issue of language (Pashtu versus Dari-Persian). The students were protesting over the attempted ban of the word *dAneshgAh*, which is the Persian word for university. The clash is really a proxy for a larger and ongoing conflict between Pashtu and non-Pashtu influence, cultural and political, in Afghanistan. I looked at the machine guns on the back of police vehicles and had a momentary vision of things going very badly. Caution is needed even as a spectator. We stayed behind the hospital fence.

As part of its obligations as a new member of the WCPT, the AAPT was required to develop, disseminate and oversee the implementation of a professional code of conduct which conformed with the WCPT Code of Conduct. This was more of a challenge than it might seem.

At the 2008 General Assembly of the AAPT, I helped lead a workshop to allow our Afghan colleagues to share the kinds of ethical issues they face in their clinical practices. A senior physical therapist from the ICRC got to his feet and asked the room, 'Should we therapists tell our patients the truth?' I heard this question knowing that in Afghan culture the giving of bad news is not generally considered to be helpful. I had heard several instances of Afghans who were away from home, in or out of the country, and were sent 'salaams' by one family member on behalf of another family member who had in fact passed away. The rationale was that the person who was away from home could not do anything about the situation and it was best not to upset them. It was a cultural practice which flowed through to healthcare, and over many years I had heard doctors say to patients, regardless of prognosis, '*KhUb mEsha*' (It will be fine).

My colleague went on to tell a story of a mother presenting to the ICRC hospital with an infant girl who had hydrocephalus. This is a condition in which cerebrospinal fluid accumulates in the brain, which can in turn create tissue-damaging pressure. The mother had asked my colleague what lay ahead for both the child and the family: how disabled was the child likely to be in the future? My ICRC colleague related his response to the group. His explanation to the mother sounded, in my opinion, well balanced and informative. He had been realistic, but not overly bleak or pessimistic, offering hope for a life which, while constrained in certain ways, described a child who could still be an active and loving part of the family. Early the next day the baby was found by staff. She had been abandoned at the gates of the hospital. He repeated his question to the group, 'So should I still tell the truth in the future?'

This story evoked other stories from therapists in the group describing the dilemmas they had experienced. Many of these focused on balancing the ethical obligation to provide equal and fair access to patients for physical therapy, as stated in the WCPT code, with living in a communitarian society such as Afghanistan, where the rights of the individual are subordinate to the demands of family and clan. In Western societies the needs and rights of the individual are pre-eminent. This is expressed in healthcare ethics, where principles such as respect for patient autonomy underpin codes of conduct.

The ethics workshop brought to light the different demands of the WCPT Code of Conduct and those of culture and context in determining how Afghan physical therapists perceived and responded to ethical issues. The term *waseta* describes how things often get done in a tribal-based society like Afghanistan. Friends, relatives and *watandArs* (people from the same village, clan or even province) have an obligation to meet each other's needs. If a *watandAr* has a need, health or political or monetary, then that person has a claim on your resources and time as a health professional which cannot easily be relegated by a derivative of justice such as 'wait your turn'. *Waseta* operates in spider-web-like reciprocity. But it is also governed by who has influence. The problem with this is that it leaves the poorest and the most vulnerable (in other words, those without influence or connections) out in the cold, and they often get the scraps of resources and services which are left over after *waseta* has been fulfilled.

There is an Afghan proverb, *Du tarbuz da yag dest grefta namesha*, which translates as 'You can't pick up two watermelons with one hand'. This captures something of the difficulty in developing a code of ethical conduct which conforms with that of the WCPT but, at the same time, acknowledges the realities of practice in Afghanistan. But it was not just the cultural influences which made ethical healthcare practice so challenging. It was the war, always the war, causing the further degradation of services and security, worsening the existing poverty and increasing people's desperation. Picking up two watermelons is not easy when one hand is tied behind your back.

I admired my colleagues' thirst for their willingness to share publicly of such difficulties. Three years after this workshop, in 2011 on another teaching trip to Afghanistan, I had an opportunity to further reflect on how I had laughed at various healthcare practices I witnessed there all those years ago. Like an unwanted gift, a memory came to me. I didn't really want to open it. I posted my recollection of it in a blog I was writing. Like the memory itself, for so long my diary writing had been a private and personal account of my observations and feelings. Now my diary was public. And this was not a bad thing, Ocie.

The young girl and the splint

Posted on April 14th, 2011

A young girl was brought to physiotherapy because her hand was severely curled up, her clenched fingers now digging relentlessly into the palm of her hand. The background to this problem was that she had a form of cerebral palsy which resulted in excessive muscle tone. In her case the problems were manifested primarily in one side of her body (hemiplegia) and this meant that the flexor muscles of her right arm were 'out of control' so to speak. Part of the management for this girl would be to make a resting splint, to be used at night in particular, and on other occasions and times, so that the fingers and wrist could be supported in a more neutral and less damaging position for the rest of hand. As the physiotherapist, I gave directions to the splint maker, and the girl, living distantly, was given an appointment for follow-up some weeks later.

She returned later as appointed. The splint (which I had designed) had been too flat. The inexorable pull of her muscles had allowed the tendons in her fingers to 'slip their moorings' (the attachments and sheaths which keep them in place), resulting in these tendons now bypassing the finger joints in their contractile 'effort' to create the shortest distance between their origins and insertions. This resulted in the formation of new deformities of the finger joints, so-called 'swan neck' deformities; where the base of each finger is bent and pulled into flexion, the middle joint of each finger is effectively bypassed by the tendons such that it is extended (bent in the opposite direction to the other joints), and the final joint at the end of each finger is bent and pulled into flexion. If this girl had a problem with her hand in the first place (and she did), then I had finished this process off, well and truly. She now had an even worse disability and one which would only be improved through skilled surgery, something she was not likely to get in Kabul for a number of reasons; money to pay for it and the finding of a skilled hand surgeon being the two primary ones.

Of course, there are a number of contextual factors which explain, in part, why a young, inexperienced (in that field at least) and isolated physiotherapist in an under-resourced situation perpetrates such a mistake. However, the end result is unchanged by any of that.

Some tests we fail, Ocie, and there is no getting away from that. If I hadn't already changed my way of looking around me while I was working in Afghanistan then this memory made me – emphatically so – less quick to judge any of my colleagues and their practices.

It was only a couple of days after this AAPT workshop that I received news that my father had died suddenly. Some three years later in 2011, teaching again in Afghanistan, the safety of distance allowed me to reflect on this horrible time.

My father and the Afghan man with painful knees

Posted on May 29th, 2011

It was in November 2008 that I spent some time in the physiotherapy assessment area of the International Committee of the Red Cross (ICRC) orthopaedic hospital in Kabul. I was working with a physiotherapy colleague, Sanguin, in a department which received and then assessed all those who came to the hospital for help. These included parents with children who had cerebral palsy, persons with spinal injuries, persons with 'cold', untreated fractures, children with contractures from previous burns, and persons in pain from a variety of causes. Here they would be assessed and referred to the appropriate department in the hospital – a kind of triage system.

An old man came in. He had white hair, thinned and wispy as hair seems to go in advanced age. A single remnant tooth populated his mouth (at least as far as I could tell). It was an incisor, top right. The muscles in the arms, legs and face were wasted, producing a haggardness beyond any fatigue which might have been brought on by travelling here. The skin on his legs was friable: it seemed like it would tear as easily as paper, a suspicion heightened further by unhealed sores down each shin. He was not from Kabul but from a province to the east and was complaining of bilateral knee pain. That's what had brought him to seek attention. On examination his knobbly old knees were all the more prominent for the relative lack of muscle in his thighs. I looked upon him with sympathy, imagining the harsh existence he must have endured over the long years and the vagaries of life he had confronted.

It was very close to that time, within a few days of doing this particular physiotherapy clinic, that my own father passed away. I remember the phone call and how shocked I was: he had had a massive stroke and was gone. The distance and the separation compounded the shock. One of the foundations of my 54-year existence had suddenly been taken away. Even during the times our lives had not intersected on a day-to-day or even a week-to-week basis, there was always the secure knowledge that our relationship was there and intact; the kind of love, support and acceptance which exist, at best it seems, in just a few fortunate relationships in our lives, and which are seemingly impervious to erosion of any kind. With this news the 'house' suddenly lurched, as it were, and there was a loss of equilibrium. I could not speak, more than a trembling word or two, that day or the next. My emotions seemed to have locked themselves in my larynx. At least I could cry.

I have a last memory of seeing my Dad alive. He and Mum used to come for tea to our house most Sunday evenings. On getting out of their car, laden with a quiche, an apricot pie and sometimes a bottle of red, they would make their way around the back. At the back corner of our house, Dad would always scan the yard for sight of our dog, before bending down to gather him up with warm greetings and mutual gladness. Our dog, a cross between a Jack Russell and Silky Terrier, was a self-appointed chaukidar who decided, entirely unilaterally and not based on any criteria that we could ever work out, which visitors were welcome and which visitors weren't. In his view Dad and Mum were always welcome. It was a Sunday evening, two days before Anne and I were due to fly out for Kabul. Dad appeared around the corner. He was wearing braces. And even if it was not the first time he had worn them, it was certainly the first time I had really taken notice of them. As I took him in, it was as if, now at 86, a mantle of frailty had descended upon him. The stoop had been evident for a while but lately he had lost weight in a surreptitious, pathological manner rather than due to any dietary effort, and his clothes now hung upon him voluminously.

While always a quietly spoken and self-effacing man, the volume of Dad's speech had also diminished in latter times. And it was an effort for him to make himself heard when there was any extraneous noise surrounding a conversation. The warmth of his gaze and smile were still there but, in short, my dear, gracious Dad had indeed become old.

Sanguin had sat down following his examination of the old man with the aching knees in order to write his notes. The examination had been conducted in Pashtu. I asked Sanguin in Dari how old this man was. The man heard me and answered himself. I knew immediately that he had understood the import of my question and I was suddenly embarrassed by it. 'I am 55. I am old before my time,' was what he said, almost guiltily, in a gesture of resignation. I was sorry to have turned my thoughtless question into this public commentary on his life. Beyond my contrition, however, was utter amazement that this man was only one year older than I was. It had only been a few weeks since I had last seen my father and surely it was to this age group that this man belonged?

Women do not generally know their age in Afghanistan; usually referring to a nearest multiple of five years – 15, 20, 25 and so on until the older they get the less certain they are, even to the nearest five or ten years. Men usually have a better idea. It is an indictment on this society and the situation and value of women here. There was no hesitation from this man. He was 55 years old. Thinking generationally, I was the same as him. And yet, he was the same as my father. It was an extremely disorientating observation.

It was not so much that this man's life had been cut short by illness or accident: it had more been 'ground' short by a lifetime of deprivation and lack of opportunity; having to use his muscle every day of his life in order to survive. And yet, his life story is one among many …

having a similar trajectory; including the millions of 'ageless' women in Afghanistan.

When Dad died my Afghan colleagues were solemn in the offering of their condolences and surprisingly gentle in their acknowledgment of my grief. My colleague Aziz, having told me how sorry he was, added something like, 'This is a hard thing. It is something we have as part of our lives'. Gratefully, I realised that he did not put the stress on *our* as in comparing what I was experiencing with the ubiquitousness of loss and grief suffered on such a regular basis by Afghans. He would have been justified in doing so. Instead, he was including me in a general observation about our shared condition as human beings. And, even in that time, when I did not seek or want philosophical or even theological explanations, I found this simple observation somehow comforting, probably because I could appreciate the tenderness of the motive behind it.

Two and a half years later, I see waves of suffering continue to break over these people; ocean-like swells in their seeming endlessness. I can describe it (well, almost maybe), but I still do not comprehend it. And I am still unable to reconcile the life of my father with the life of the Afghan man with painful knees.

25

It was early 2009 and not so long after our return from Afghanistan. I was in the kitchen and had a fistful of letters, just retrieved from the morning's post. They were mostly appeals for support (monetary, of course) for a range of projects in overseas countries. The names and logos of various NGOs flashed into view as I shuffled the stack of strategically designed and coloured envelopes to see what else might be in the post. Even though I knew each NGO was supporting worthwhile projects in needy communities, I complained about the number of extended hands wanting my money. Our youngest daughter, Bronnie, who was living at home at the time, heard my carry-on. Her response was rapier-like: 'Dad, not everyone can save the world by going to Afghanistan!' It was as if I had suddenly been pinned and then attached to the fridge like an oversized reminder of something. I remember how much you enjoyed hearing about this, Paulo. You opined on how well you thought Bronnie's point had been put – not so much to me as through me.

Bronnie's rebuke did, however, become a catalyst for answering the question – even of myself – of why we kept returning to Afghanistan. Firstly, I don't think that I ever really embarked on any 'saving the world' enterprise or, for that matter, considered myself an agent for such a mission. The question as to whether going to Afghanistan was saving *me* was a more valid one. Had I felt, after the first four years, and the unsuccessful conclusion to them, that I needed redemption? Maybe, but it was no longer the kind of redemption that was characterized by the gritting of teeth or the adoption of a mindset like 'this is something I must do'. I think that my failed trip to Kabul in 1989, when I was temporarily stranded in Delhi, was like that, as though I was fulfilling some self-imposed duty. Now, going to Afghanistan to teach felt much more like a gift: something to be grateful for. I enjoyed the teaching immensely. There was such passion in the classroom. I admired my Afghan colleagues' persistence and hunger for learning in often very difficult contexts. I was sure that there was a contribution I could still make in supporting them to further develop their physiotherapy skills, for themselves as well as the Afghan people.

In early 2010 Anne and I began preparations for long service leave and a return to Afghanistan for the first six months of 2011. Returning this time under the auspices of IAM would be like joining the ends of a large circle. We corresponded with Tom and Libby and the IAM leadership and undertook the necessary procedural steps. These included psychological interview and testing. But our psychologies and emotions would soon be tested from another quarter.

In early August 2010 we got the news that Tom and Dan had been murdered on their way from a medical camp in remote *Badakhshan*, together with nine other healthcare workers. They had been conducting eye, maternal health and paediatric clinics in the village of *Eshtiwi* in the valley of *Parun* in remote *Nuristan*. We had been following this journey from late July, via emails from Libby who, in turn, was receiving two half-minute satellite phone calls from Tom each day. The idea was that we would keep them all in our thoughts and prayers: which we did.

The team had worked long days in the village providing medical and eye care to both the villagers and others who made the difficult journey from surrounding areas. These clinics lasted six days. The hike in to reach the valley had also taken six days. And so would the hike out. They had to walk over a 16,000-foot pass. There were atrocious weather conditions high on the pass, with rain and snow of such severity that there were catastrophic floods in Pakistan from the run-off. But they managed to find shelter in a shepherd's hut. They got back, exhausted but okay. It was just after they had reached the vehicles, crossed a rising river and started the two-day drive back to Kabul that they were ambushed and shot. No group ever claimed responsibility.

If I hadn't realized this before, it became clearer to me that prayer is not just entreaty: Lord, please do this or please do that – no matter how altruistic or unselfish the request. It is the necessary cry of anguish, even protest, at the state of things, where argument and understanding are left far behind and words fail. With many others, we were shocked and very sad.

We were encouraged by IAM to not change our plans to go to Afghanistan. We arrived in the third week of March 2011 just a few days before the Afghan New Year, 1390. We posted regularly to our blog.

Nao ROz 1390

Posted on March 21st, 2011

We are in a suburb of Kabul called KArte Seh. It is south-west of the city and quite a distance from the diplomatic area. And while there are clear security guidelines which we must follow, including where we can and can't walk or venture, we generally move around this area freely and without much tension. We can walk to the local bazaar and buy what we need as well. You just have to get used to walking past men with guns; in the back of utes, in pillboxes and on the street generally.

Yesterday we were called for lunch and found ourselves sitting around the dining room table sharing soup, nan, fruit and tea with the chaukidar and the cleaner. It might not seem significant that we should sit down to lunch with our chaukidar and cleaner at this guesthouse but let me say that it is; it really is. Having travelled (and lived) in this part of the world over the course of three decades we had not come across this before. We had certainly seen (and tried ourselves) to treat such employees with respect and dignity but had never witnessed, or ourselves, sat down to meal with them in the course of a regular daily schedule (we have been to many Afghan homes for meals in the past but that is different). So, here we were together, obviously the result of a simple decision on the part of the person in charge of the place. And what struck us was that the conversation between the four of us was not characterized by either over-deference or excessive effusiveness. It was just a pleasant meal and exchange. I doubt that I have adequately explained how unusual this was and perhaps cannot do so without providing much more background on class and caste in this part of the world. But simple things such as this seem quite profound and gratifying as well.

The welcome has been very warm and we therefore feel very encouraged about the worthwhileness of what we can contribute in the relatively small amount of time (three months) that we will be here. We have been out to dinner over the last two nights to other team members' places. We now find ourselves in the 'senior' demographic. The two families, one Finnish and the other English, we visited each had bright-eyed, playful children between the ages of 6 months and 10 years; the parents being some 20+ years younger than us. Both lots of people were so very likeable and capable. It brought memories back to us of being here at that age and with young children.

We found a team still in grief. It was only six months after the murders. Security was increased and the awareness of threat it produced each day was like an unwanted companion. Getting across to the PTI was not so simple these days. We weren't allowed to use just any taxi. They had to be drivers known to IAM. There was also the chaotic and time-consuming drive over there.

Part Three: Afghanistan 2005–2011

Physical Therapy Institute, Kabul

Posted on March 24th, 2011

It is something over 10km from KArte Seh to Wazir Akbar Khan where the training institute is. It can take anywhere between 55 minutes and two hours to do this journey.

We arrive. I walk up through the grounds, shared by several institutions including a large public hospital, and see changes to the PTI building. There is now a long, impressive ramp sweeping upwards and to the right which then connects with a new extension, a later inspected new classroom. So, there is now access to the first storey for wheelchair users; a visible sign of progress and change. I enter. Recognition, greetings, hugs, cheek-to-cheek brushes and handshakes: I am back.

Later after a morning of planning for the course in Mazar, we have lunch; men in one room and women in the other. There is nan of course, a vegetable stew, green tea and fruit. I always like these work lunches. I speak enough Dari to encourage my colleagues to do the same. In other words, not to use their recreational time in the effort of speaking English. The noise level rises, the number of conversations multiply. Cricket is a new passion in this country. Even to you non-cricket-lovers (and I know there are some among our family and friends), there can be no doubt that there is at least some unifying effect in the following of the national team in a country that has traditionally been a mix of quite different and separate geographical and ethnic groups. My colleagues favour India to beat Australia today. Other conversations proceed in rapid Dari. Although I am working up to some functionality in my language, now I 'rest'. My comprehension of the conversations rises and fades like reception of an old short-wave radio. Kabir looks across at me and smiles. He knows where I am and his smile translates as a warm welcome.

After lunch, I meet a female colleague in the hallway. She is a woman of mature age and president of the Afghan Association for Physical Therapy. She has been committed to the development of the profession for a long, long time and will also be coming to the World Confederation for Physical Therapy Conference in Amsterdam in late June. And it is excellent news.

Meanwhile Anne was at work on the other side of Kabul.

Dashti Barchi refugee camp

Posted on March 25th, 2011

Today I went to a district outside Kabul called Dashti Barchi. I accompanied two midwives, one foreigner and one Afghan, as well as a clerical worker. There are four clinics in this large district of approximately one million people.

These clinics are held in houses as an outreach of the Afshar hospital. Most of the houses are very small mud brick and the people are very poor. One in four children die before the age of five in Afghanistan and the maternal mortality is one of the highest in the world. The purpose of these clinics is to find the women with high-risk pregnancies that need extra care and to refer them on to the hospital as well to educate the women about their conditions.

The house we went to today belongs to a poor family who offer it free to be used as a clinic once a week. The woman whose name I was unable to get is passionate about helping her community. She also hosts a self-help group in her house weekly. Each woman coming to the clinic is charged about 20 Afs, which is about 40 cents. And this money is given to assist the self-help group.

Today we saw five pregnant women, one postnatal woman who had pre-eclampsia, and her baby who is 10 days old. Usually more people come but because it was the week of Nao rOz there were not so many today. We checked blood pressures, haemoglobins, abdominal heights, fetal hearts and two U/S scans were done to check the baby size and position of the placenta. We also did a full baby check on a newborn. Using these scans today, we were able to identify a serious condition called placenta previa. This is when the placenta covers the opening of the uterus and so when the woman goes into labour she will bleed. And so, a Caesarean section is needed to avoid this. Iron tablets were distributed for the women with low haemoglobin.

The Afghan midwife used three poster-sized pictures to explain to the women when it was necessary for them to seek medical advice and the best way to get to the hospital. And if they are delivering their baby at home it is explained how the equipment (e.g. scissors, clean material ties, nailbrush for clean fingernails, plastic for the woman to lie on when delivering etc) needs to be kept clean for a safe delivery.

Unlike the challenges Ian faces in travelling across town through extreme traffic and changing roadblocks, the challenges of travelling to Dashti Barchi are quite different. Here the roads are mud and more mud and very narrow. In the wet weather they are impassable and you have to walk.

Another week in suburban Kabul

Posted on March 31st, 2011

We have been in our own place for just over a week now. Upstairs are a Finnish family with three small and delightful children aged 8, 4 and 18 months. Some afternoons we are able to play games together. We have a kind of two-bedroom unit below which is split on two levels; partly ground floor and partly basement. We tend to cook in the basement part and spend the rest of our time on the ground floor section where the sun is able to find its way in …

I went to PTI across the city for the first time in a week this morning. This week I was not able to travel across town because of security alerts. There are several security assessments carried out and pooled for the benefit of aid and development organizations (NGOs). We are then informed by email directly or via our office … this morning I got a local taxi across town. We left early, before the peak hour(s), zigzagging our way down the main Darulaman road towards the city in order to avoid, where possible, its deep potholes, and which are in part the result of the effect of heavy military traffic. On the positive side such manoeuvring slows the traffic down. On the less positive side the roads become the scene of a massive 'square dance'. Further diversions created by concrete blocks or other devices necessitate many changes in direction which are further orchestrated by personnel in variegated uniforms: cars, hand-pushed carts and pedestrians, 'dosey do', 'allemande left', and 'sashay' in improvised groups and clusters to the self-provided music of an impromptu horn section. Depending on your outlook this 'dance' can either be intriguing or intimidating.

My driver was excellent, both skilled and careful, and so I was freed to cast my attention elsewhere. Some 25km to the west of Kabul, the morning sun was catching the snow-laden flanks of Paghman, a mountain range some 4,500 metres high. And this sight today, as in past years, has never failed to engender a sense of awe; a reminder of the intrinsic beauty of this country. We passed on. It took us only 25 minutes to make the journey. This place can always surprise. Like my discovery that food can these days be ordered in. Sounds unremarkable perhaps; except to say that the streets, many of them, have no names and the houses no numbers, not in any visible form at least. It tends to go like this, 'Go to the sixth street after the bridge and turn left and then go to the house with the blue door with the razor wire on the wall'. Most houses have razor wire and so that characteristic doesn't distinguish one house from another too much.

Tomorrow we leave for Mazar-I-Sharif, which is the capital city of the ancient province of Balkh in northern Afghanistan; some 300km by air and 370km by road from Kabul. We are flying there. Ian will co-teach, with an Afghan colleague, a physiotherapy course on assessing and managing shoulder instabilities and impingements. The notion of co-teaching is a significant one and I am glad to have had the opportunity to both prepare for this with my colleague and to share this teaching experience. We are hoping that it will be an encouraging and equipping experience for the 36 physiotherapists from northern Afghanistan who will be attending.

26

We landed in Mazar on the first day of April. It was a Friday, for Muslims the day of assembly and prayers at the mosque. We had been told prior to our departure, 'You will enjoy being in Mazar. Lately, it has been more stable and peaceful than Kabul'. Things changed. After our disembarkation following our flight from Kabul, the murmurs about something having happened in the city began while we were gathered around a high-sided, steel-meshed trailer from which people, not airport employees but those brave enough to climb atop, were finding and extricating their luggage. While we were standing there, I got a phone call from the regional team leader, who happened, ironically, to be in Kabul for meetings at the time: 'There's been an incident in the city. A taxi driver we know and trust is waiting for you at the airport. Go straight to the team house and on no account set foot outside it. Okay? Don't go anywhere!'

We walked with our luggage several hundred metres down the dirt road; a security measure effecting a no man's land between the airport terminal and the external car park to thwart suicide bombers in vehicles. There we met the driver who was waiting for us. We learned, as we were driven towards the city, about how the compound of the UN had been overrun, with the loss of both expatriate and Afghan lives, during a riot following Friday prayers in central *Mazar*. This eruption of anger towards foreigners and infidels had followed the recent public burning of the Qur'an in the US state of Florida.

We got to the guesthouse. The mood was sombre and uncertain. We posted again that night, taking advantage of a brief window of internet connectivity.

Mazar

Posted on April 1st, 2011

Hi everyone. Obviously not a good day to arrive in Mazar. However, we are safe in an IAM team house and will not be venturing anywhere tomorrow (Saturday). We have internet access and will keep you informed. Ian and Anne

Due to the previous day's events, the course did not begin on the Saturday 2nd April as planned. There was uncertainty on the part of the staff of the physiotherapy department of the hospital, where the course was to be conducted, regarding the wisdom of having a foreigner in the department at this time. A number of family members and friends of the dead and wounded Afghan rioters had gathered at the hospital gates and around the various *shObas* (hospital departments), waiting for news of their loved ones' conditions. Whatever hostility they had felt towards infidels prior to the riots was now supplemented by further anger at the extent of casualties suffered in the ensuing gunfight.

Waiting in Mazar

Posted on April 2nd, 2011

Thanks for your concern. We thought that we would write an update so that those of you in Australia at least might be reassured before going to bed.

We are still waiting, having a very quiet day in the team house here in Mazar. It is not clear if the course will start tomorrow or indeed at all. We have investigated the possibility of moving the venue from the public hospital to either the compound of the International Committee for the Red Cross or even to the team house here. So far both of these options are problematic. Meanwhile physiotherapists have travelled from far and wide in northern Afghanistan to be here and are expending their resources in accommodation, food and time while we work it out. I feel sorry for them at this point that we can't get underway.

We listen to the noise of the street outside and feel very separated from the world on that side. This morning we heard a donkey, also unhappy with the world, bray and bray loudly. We used to see boys riding donkeys in Kabul, even in KArte Seh, but that seems to be a thing of the past for that area. So to hear a donkey bray again evoked another time. Waiting with a sense of indeterminacy is not always a bad experience. It slows one down and facilitates reflection.

We spent a similar day behind a compound wall in Peshawar in December 2007 some four days after Benazir Bhutto was assassinated in a similar atmosphere of unrest and uncertainty. Perhaps we are recalcitrant but we don't think so. Anyway, this is not the time to try and justify why and what we are doing here. The whole experience does, however, give us a vicarious taste of what people in such places go through on a regular basis: just like the physios that came here with expectation and displaying an amazing commitment to develop their capabilities but are just as likely to be frustrated once more.

We took some photos of the team house and garden for you but it simply takes too long to load them and as the Afghans say, 'Na mesha' – it won't happen.

We hope to receive advice either late tonight our time or early tomorrow morning about what we will do. Meanwhile, we wait behind the walls, listening to life go on in Mazar on the other side.

Paul, you got through to me by phone. The news of the storming of the UN compound had gone around the world as a headline. You interpreted the news for Mum and reassured her. You told me, 'Mum is okay. She is not worried. But I am! I'm really concerned. Are you safe?' It was good to hear your voice.

PART THREE: AFGHANISTAN 2005–2011

Things return to normal in Mazar

Posted on April 3rd, 2011

This morning following good advice and organization by a number of people, we were able to start the physical therapy course in the Institute of Health at Mazar e Sharif. The acting regional team leader for the IAM works in this same institution. Returning to work herself this morning following yesterday's lockdown – a security response to the tragic events of Friday afternoon, she 'scoped' the place and gave the okay to come. Parallel to this my Afghan colleague and co-teacher liaised with the local PT staff, gauging their feelings about having a foreigner come to their department at this volatile time. The various perspectives intersected favourably such that I was able to be driven in to the hospital, well inside the main gates (past waiting family and friends of the dead and injured), where I was met by the head of the PT department. From there it was a short distance to a welcoming and warm class environment populated by 37 PTs, several of whom had travelled more than 300km to attend.

The day went well. It is exhausting, however, even when you have an interpreter, to teach across cultures and language. The meanings of words and intentions have to be negotiated quite frequently. Today was also about co-teaching with my Afghan colleague Aziz and we had spent a lot of time preparing together. His lecture presentation was so impressive, both authoritative in delivery and yet engaging of his audience. This was gratifying. We shared the thought today that we are here co-teaching in northern Afghanistan in April and in a little over two months' time (In'shallah) we will be involved together in a joint presentation for a workshop in Amsterdam.

This afternoon, returning to the IAM team house after work, we passed the famous Blue Mosque (only some 500 metres from the hospital) where Friday's events all began. It looked innocuous; people going about their business and others just strolling in conversation. What happened was like a flash flood; deadly but passing quickly. This analogy is only partly right. There do remain deep resentments here. Mostly they are contained and rationalized but sometimes circumstances catalyse these underlying emotions in unpredictable and deadly ways. And yet, I remain convinced that most, the great majority of, people here are very decent …

The team house came alive today as various people appeared: there is a language school here. Anne was this afternoon a subject for a group of Afghans learning English. She was even asked what she thought of Friday's events here in Mazar. She replied that we can hardly understand the way a single action [*the public burning of copies of the Qur'an in Florida*] can ripple throughout the world and have consequences beyond our own comprehension. Sadly, a young 27-year-old Swedish man lost his life on Friday, along with a Norwegian, [*also a Romanian*], four Nepalis and several Afghans [*5 Afghans were killed and 20 wounded*]. If we turn this idea around, we can also take some heart from the notion that simple positive and constructive actions on each of our parts can have really helpful consequences in places and in ways which we would not have dreamed of.

In Class

Posted on April 7th, 2011

Najiba is participating in one of six groups, each working on a clinical patient scenario. She is smiling, engaged and collaborative. This may seem an unremarkable observation. However, this is a somewhat different Najiba than I remember. I first met Najiba in Kabul in 2008 during the teaching of another course. At that time she had the reputation among her peers and supervisors of being a testy and difficult person to work with. Indeed she remains by nature, it seems, an intense person with a well-developed sense of gravitas. After every lecture, she is the first, notebook and pen in hand, to approach me for clarification of a term or construct and pursues the issue, whatever it is, until she is completely satisfied. Najiba's story has its own sadness. She contracted polio as an infant which left her with a semi-paralysed leg. At some stage as a girl she had surgery on the leg (I am not sure what that was) and not only did the surgery fail but it left her with an ongoing pain, so-called neuropathic pain. Neuropathic pain is a nasty, complicated pain which is perpetuated in part by a dysfunction of the pain-related nervous system itself. And so, it is not amenable to treatments which approach it as a problem with its basis in the tissues which appear to hurt. To that end it can be enormously frustrating for patients who experience it and clinicians who treat it alike. As a person with a disability it has been hard for Najiba to find a husband. One of her sadnesses was that she had met someone but her parents, at that time, did not approve and so this marriage never occurred.

The course in 2008 at which I met Najiba was a course on understanding and managing these kinds of chronic pain. Basically, the course outlines how such pain is an output of the brain (the central nervous system) and not just an input to it (as touching a hotplate on a stove might suggest). In this understanding, it can be explained how various factors influence and modulate this pain providing an account of how one's experiences and interpretations of the pain, and the events surrounding it, all become active factors in the generation and perpetuation of the pain. It can actually be a liberating message in so much that it helps explain to sufferers why their symptoms appear so unreasonable and irrational, occurring as they do at odd times and in inexplicable ways. The corollary is that the person can see that this ongoing, recalcitrant pain is not necessarily their 'fault', the outcome of some neurotic bent or weakness. And so it proved to be for Najiba. After class one day she approached me to say that this lecture was 'just for her' and that it explained so many things for her and about her. She even went and told her boss about it. Of course, this was gratifying but one learns, in both teaching and clinical work, not to get too self-congratulatory because there are always situations and persons whose needs remain challenging or unmet.

This week I decided to ask Najiba how she was going over these last couple of years. She replied that it was now over a year since she had experienced 'psychological problems' (as she described them). She was very happy about this. So now I watch her in class as she works in the group: leading discussion, offering suggestions to others and listening in turn to them. I am neither naïve nor arrogant enough to ascribe what I see to a simple cause and effect such as a lecture. I know there are many other factors and people in her story who have helped her to this point. It is enough for me that she felt able to confide both her situation and her relief. Apart from that, the one certainty is that she will be approaching me with a question following my next class.

We flew back to Kabul and arrived from *Mazar* just in time to get home before a fresh 'lockdown': IAM terminology for 'you are not allowed to leave your house'. This lockdown was from 11am until 6pm today (at which time a meeting for reviewing security takes place). It was put in place because today, being Friday, there was significant potential for further demonstrations against the burning of the Qur'an. It was one of these that got out of control and led to the tragic events in *Mazar* on this day last week.

We were welcomed home from *Mazar* with a present of fresh bread, fruit and warming soup by our Finnish neighbours. We spent a large part of this afternoon playing with the children. We have found, to our delight, that we are surrogate grandparents to some of the children in the team.

During each teaching visit to Afghanistan we have found that the levels of hostility towards Westerners has continued to grow, particularly if you are from one of the countries contributing to the NATO-led ISAF. Thankfully, this hostility is not universal: our colleagues and patients certainly welcome us warmly and with gratitude. However, our security, as we move around the capital Kabul or travel around the country to other cities, is increasingly less certain. It is quite a different thing to be a foreigner in Afghanistan in 2011 than it is to be a foreigner in Afghanistan in 1983.

27

Getting to and from PTI, through the city, was expensive if I had to always get a taxi. Thankfully, I was often able to get a lift with Salim, who was an administrator at PTI. It was not just him and me in the car. There was a group of young men in their twenties who were studying accountancy and who would have these lessons at 5.30am before going to work afterwards. In fact, the business of the day starts at around 4.30am with the muezzin of the local mosque giving his vocal cords a stretch with the call to prayer. It is all done these days with amplification and speakers. It can be an aesthetically pleasing experience; some have excellent voices and the call fills the neighbourhood, reaching the houses of rich and poor alike, finding its way into the public and private spaces of everyday lives and routines. And the notion of a reminder to turn one's thoughts to God and a set of priorities greater than oneself is, after all, not a bad one.

When he arrived this particular morning, Salim told me that we were going a different way as there was a particular celebration taking place at a city mosque and it would be crowded and the traffic too slow. I was happy as it meant that we would go via the old city and *JAdi Maiwand*. We left *KArte Seh* for the PTI at about 7am. On this journey, I soon discovered a new kind of vulnerability: me in a car of young Afghan men at a US checkpoint. The Marines weren't casual; the threats to them were too ubiquitous and real for that. But I, too, was nervous as we slowly drove through the checkpoint lest anyone, them or us, inadvertently precipitated some kind of calamitous action.

PART THREE: AFGHANISTAN 2005–2011

Images of commerce

Posted on April 25th, 2011

We enter JAdi Maiwand and pass several four-storey buildings of which only the ground floor is used. This is because these buildings were rocketed in the 1990s and were never rebuilt. They are just incomplete walls and glassless window frames in all the upper storeys. On the ground floor are shops which have these three storeys of ruins above them as high ornate roofs. ... Driving on, in the bedlam of city traffic, we pass a man in a wheelchair, the kind which is propelled by a hand-turned cog connected to the wheels by a chain. Persons with disabilities are very much among the poorest of the poor here. What catches my attention in particular is the advertising sign on the back of his wheelchair: 'Looking for property? We can help. Afghan Property Management', complete with email address and phone number. The sign, about two thirds by half a metre, is newly painted, clean and unencumbered by any other article such as clothing or bags. It is obviously a commercial arrangement for all its incongruity. I suppose Afghan Property Management is, in its own way, helping this man and his daily challenge to sustain the presence of food and housing in his life.

As we neared *Wazir*, not far from PTI, we passed by the supermarket that we often used when we stayed there previously. The building was now a blackened shell, blown out by a bomb.

That night we went to Seija's house for dinner. She was still working in Afghanistan for the time being, training nurses. The other person at the table was Jerry, a paediatrician Seija and Anne worked with at the CURE hospital. We talked about Dan, and how Seija was going. She was pragmatic: 'He wouldn't have settled back in America anyway.' Tom and Dan were such different people but each was well loved by their Afghan work colleagues. They both lie in the Kabul cemetery rather than being expatriated – now part of Afghan soil.

For my first journey across town to PTI in 2011, I was able to get a lift with the new NOOR director. NOOR's 'offices' were in our old garages just down from the 'new' PTI. He talked a lot about Tom. Not long after his arrival Tom had advised him, in the context of adjusting to life in Afghanistan, that once you got used to the idea that you may die here then 'you're fine'.

Ocie, I remember just a few months ago lifting you out of the bath. We had looked after you that day. Your mum and dad were on their way over to our house for dinner. We decided to give you a wash before they came. When the washing, and your play in the water, was done, I lifted you and stood you on the tiled floor while reaching for a towel. Your feet went instantly from underneath you and you fell backwards at high velocity. I somehow managed to get a foot under your head just before it hit the tiles. You were disorientated by the fall but not hurt. I wrapped you in the towel and picked you up. You did not cry but I could have, such was the relief that your head did not smack onto those tiles. I can think of so many moments in our lives when different possibilities come into close proximity, and one thing happens when another easily could have.

Preparing for Herat

Posted on April 28th, 2011

Tomorrow morning (Friday) we travel to Herat, the main city of western Afghanistan. It is about 640km from Kabul and 100km from the Iranian border. It is a place which is, in general, more stable and peaceful than Kabul. And by all reports its infrastructure, including roads, buildings and historical monuments, are all in better order than those in Kabul. It will be hotter. And this coincides with the unfortunate reality that Anne must wear more conservative dress while there; both in colour and length.

I feel somewhat restless, identifying an underlying tension in my gut. Travelling does increase one's vulnerability, there is no doubt about that. Public places such as airports are part of this pattern of exposure. There was a shootout at Kabul airport yesterday resulting in nine deaths, albeit in the military rather than the civilian area.

Of course one's fears of what might happen and what actually happens mostly do not coalesce. Here it seems that one carries a more imminent sense of the possibility of what one fears actually coming to pass, and this is part of the hard thinking, decision-making and psychological preparation before coming here. Our lives proceed here within the context of teams (NGOs, places of work and neighbourhoods), as a process of risk management: on the one hand – following protocols and guidelines regarding safe(r) behaviour and movements – and, on the other hand, conviction and faith – realizing that what we do here is mostly worthwhile and there is no way to absolutely quarantine oneself from danger. It is more in my DNA that I worry and less so in Anne's.

Jane and I were with you one night at the hospice, Paul: three siblings sharing their thoughts and feelings. You would not die in the hospice. You were just there to get your pain medication reviewed and adjusted. You would die at home, three weeks later, on the same day a nurse was first scheduled to come and look after you through the night. This was not something you welcomed despite earlier agreeing to it as part of dying at home – the very idea of a stranger in your room watching you sleep!

On that final day you insisted in sitting out in the lounge room before retiring later that afternoon for a rest: one from which you never awoke.

Your partner Carol suggested that this was your final word on the matter of a night nurse. And we think she was right.

Three weeks earlier it was you, me and Janey at the hospice. It was quiet in your room. You sat up, as always, but needed to periodically lean forward and rest on the tray table in front of you while we talked. You told us how fearful and uncertain you were about what lay ahead. We told you how we were inspired by your courage and your concern for all of us throughout this period of your own suffering. It was an ineffably beautiful time that we three were given that evening.

Dear Ocie, life has a way of getting us to think in binary terms as if we are either good or bad, happy or sad, competent or incompetent. But it's not like that. We can be different things in the same breath: afraid and courageous; sad and yet grateful; flawed but still marvellous. If nothing else, it reminds me to be less certain or rigid in my assessment of 'who' someone is and what their motives are.

28

In Herat we were received at the guesthouse by a fellow IAMer, Kaija liisa. Part of her job was to run the guesthouse and she lived in a section of it. That afternoon she invited us in to share an early dinner and watch the wedding of William and Kate.

On a fine day in Herat

Posted on May 6th, 2011

On Wednesday night it rained and rained heavily. Thursday morning was perfect. The greenness of Herat was again impressed upon us. The blossoms of both fruit trees and the many flowers of *aolis* (compounds/backyards), together with the verdant public parks and spaces around the city, engendered a feeling of relaxation and restfulness we had not experienced in the last seven weeks.

When we arrived in Herat we were told by a local that Heratis take as much pride and care of their public areas as they do of their private houses and belongings, whereas in Kabul the public spaces are neglected and contested and people retreat to their privacy. We have found this to be true. In some ways Herat is a vision of what 'could be' in Afghanistan. While this remains a city in a country at war, a war which has been conducted in one form or another for some 30 years, there is, nevertheless, some evidence of community life and spirit here which is almost impossible to discern in Kabul.

It has been a busy week, rising at 5.15am and tumbling into bed, exhausted, at around 9.30 each night. The course for some 30 physical therapists went well. Anne was able to have a week as a 'tourist', notwithstanding the 'lockdown' in the middle of the week due to events in Pakistan, spending time with two other Australian women having a break from their work in Kabul. Both of us have things to share, from the humorous to the heartrending. We return to Kabul tomorrow morning. I will begin to work with a new co-teacher for the next course.

The next course which was due to be held in Jalalabad (a city towards the Pakistan border in the east of the country) has been shifted to Kabul. One of my Herat physiotherapist colleagues, tongue in cheek, looked at it this way, offering his own understanding of correlation: 'Teacher, when you went to Mazar the UN compound was attacked; when you came here, Osama Bin Laden was killed [*In Abbottabad in Pakistan*]. What might happen if you go to Jalalabad? I don't think they can take that chance.' I could see his point.

Those who wait…

Posted on May 8th, 2011

I am dropped off just inside the Herat regional hospital gate by my taxi. The rehabilitation centre where the physical therapy course is being held is located some 400 metres away, towards the far corner of the hospital grounds. To walk through these grounds, past the various *shObas* (or departments) is to observe, in microcosm, the vulnerability and pain of ordinary Afghans.

A line extends from the emergency department, spilling out onto the internal hospital road. People are waiting to be seen. Waiting is a way of life here. People always wait. And they wait in different ways and in various states of expectancy, urgency or resignation. A woman sitting on the pathway comforts a crying baby. Even 'closed off' to the outside world by her charderi (burka) she has a posture of fatigue, and her low, repetitive consolation to the child confirms it. Family groups sit around on blankets, the ones on which they have just spent the night, sharing what food they have for breakfast. Further off women squat together in a group, covered totally by their cornflower-blue charderis. They resemble an abandoned campsite from this distance. A man lies prostrate on the footpath, not even his lungi (turban) is used or bundled up as a pillow. It is as if he reached this spot and just lay down, unable, because of illness or exhaustion or both, to move any further. He is not far from the entrance and, he is relatively lucky, he has at least reached hospital and will be seen at some stage. But everyone waits.

Flying over the mountainous regions between Kabul and Herat provides one with a telling panorama of Afghanistan. In this panorama, innumerable and immense dry, treeless and saw-toothed mountain ranges are demarcated by narrow, tortuous valleys and mud-coloured rivers, their sources being the melting snow. At points along the valleys are green oases; places where the possibility of existence amidst the surrounding geographical hostility is confirmed by crops, trees and villages. From these villages dirt tracks can be traced. But where are these going? It seems just to other desperately isolated villages and maybe … hopefully, eventually some kind of main road. Poverty, isolation and distance are the conclusions that I am led to and they seem to explain much about the 'lot' of people here.

Nearing my *shOba*, where the course is held, I hear wailing. There is a family squatting around a blanket-covered body on a stretcher. Their waiting is over. I have no choice but to pass closely. I do not look. It does not seem right to observe such pain. And, in not looking, it is the sounds that capture my attention. The cries come from as deep and as primitive a place within a human being as one would think possible. The sounds are guttural and involuntary, like dry retching. This confronting 'language' needs no translation. Grief spares none but, if nothing else, it at least reminds me, uncomfortably, of our shared humanity. When I go back out at lunchtime the family is gone; the living must go on.

Inside is the physiotherapy training: training to further equip my colleagues to address the needs of their fellow Afghans. But, in several conversations, which spontaneously and individually take place in the gaps of the course during the week – that is, during breaks and before and after class – I hear the heartfelt cries of my dispirited Afghan colleagues. It is not uncommon that, on a physiotherapy course, colleagues approach you in order to ask questions about their own physical problems (or the problems of a family member). However, when in the process of doing this they are also able to show you the scars of bullet wounds or their prostheses it becomes more particularly Afghan. Those who work in the health system serving the poor above are also in pain. They are also waiting: waiting for a time when there is reason to hope that things will get better in Afghanistan. They feel beset from within Afghanistan and from without. They are young, educated and largely thoughtful people who want to provide hope and a future for their children. One colleague expressed the options for the future this way: 'We have two options. One is with those in power who just look after themselves … The other is to go back to the 13th century.' It is very hard for ordinary people to get things done without either participating in or perpetuating further corruption. To get electricity supply to your house; to get your child into university; to obtain licences, permits and permissions for various functions or actions in daily life are enterprises all characterized by *zer e mEza* (under the table) money transactions. It keeps many people desperately poor and a certain number rich. It makes everyone cynical.

From without, people feel the disdain and judgement of the rest of the world: 'If I am on Facebook, when they find out that I am from Afghanistan, they do not want to continue talking to me. They think I am a terrorist.' They also feel that the one certainty in their life, the one incorruptible 'good thing', their faith in God and Islam, has also been misrepresented. There is little to feel good about and little to feel proud of. During the week, I saw a byline in 'The Australian' (our national newspaper) which reported that 'Afghanistan is the worst place in the world to be a mother'. And so it goes. In a real sense, Afghans wait, in their minds and their hearts, for something to change. And many, despite the challenges, continue to work for change. However, after 30 years of war, there is no optimism that real change will happen anytime soon.

A funny Pathan and an unlikely reconciliation

Posted on May 20th, 2011

He swept into the classroom accompanied by two others. For some reason they seemed more like his entourage rather than fellow course participants. He was big; a good half to three quarters of a head taller than me, with a luxuriant black beard. The lungi (turban) and traditional dress of *peran o tamban* (flowing long shirt and billowing pants) while not out of place in the previous courses I had taken, nevertheless amplified the perception that he had somehow wandered in by chance from the bazaar. But no, he was a physiotherapist and here for the course; not on the list of participants for this course, but here nevertheless. He was from Kandahar, and a Pashtu speaker. And it was in this matter that some of the difficulties that were to follow could be explained. Mahmoud had originally been down for the Jalalabad course; a course which would be oriented to the needs of Pashtu speakers by virtue of the choice of co-teacher and translator who would have language skills in this area. For some reason, which had to do with his not being able to travel to Jalalabad from Kandahar by car (as far as we could tell), attendance at the Jalalabad course was no longer an option for Mahmoud and so it was to Herat he came. Adaptability and flexibility are two core skills for working here and so they were rapidly applied in this case and we got going with the teaching.

Being from Kandahar, Mahmoud was a Pathan. Pathans have a reputation for being intimidating people. They are often, generally speaking, physically larger than other Afghans and their appearance and demeanour, accentuated in part by their large beards and traditional head wear, can be severe. Their language, Pashtu, is almost impenetrable to outsiders and is universally regarded as an extremely challenging language to learn compared to the other main language of Afghanistan, Dari. It is worth noting in case you do not know that the Taliban are by and large Pashtu-speaking Pathans. By virtue of his size Mahmoud was indeed intimidating. However, he was not by nature, it seemed, the archetypal reserved, taciturn Pathan that one is led to believe is the norm for Pathans. He was a funny Pathan. And even early on, the rest of the class began to appreciate his non-physiotherapy-related contributions with some enthusiasm.

It soon became apparent that if Mahmoud had something on his mind then he felt it only right that the rest of the class know about it and know about it without delay. If Mahmoud didn't have a handout for a particular lecture, then it didn't matter if we were 15 minutes into that lecture; he felt the class should be apprised of his dilemma: 'Is there a handout for this lecture? I don't have one.' This was not helpful for continuity of teaching purposes.

Translation is a real issue in these courses. Many Afghan colleagues have achieved a functional level of English (some with similar English to my level of Dari and several with better English than my Dari). But this level of English does not usually equip them to read technical papers or notes in English. They therefore have very few useable resources unless they have been translated into Dari script. And this is a very time-consuming exercise. For example, several months prior to leaving Australia, I sent (electronically of course) two large wads of notes for translation. And this was done. However, unless the person translating has almost constant access to the author then such translations tend to be punctuated with errors: there are all sorts of linguistic challenges to be overcome. As a consequence of all this, participants are provided with some background notes which have been translated but which still contain errors due to the lack of opportunity for author and translator to work together beforehand. And no one is to blame for this. It is an issue of time and resources. And people (all of us) do our best in the circumstances. For each lecture, PowerPoint handouts are given which are in English (for similar reasons of paucity of time and resources) and the translation then occurs in class by means of a translator. Of course, the quality of this translation in class also relies on the translator's knowledge of the material (concepts and expressions) and their English ability. And we found out over the three courses that these two factors can vary considerably, impacting significantly on the scope and depth of material which can be covered during the week of the course. Further to this, it was decided that in these courses there would be a process of 'co-teaching': an excellent decision with a view to further developing teaching skills. To this end, a promising teacher was selected for each course to work with me. Preparation involved several sessions together, going through both theoretical and practical material prior to each course. Each Afghan co-teacher was also allocated two lectures and prepared these in collaboration with me, as well as practising various assessment and management techniques.

Mahmoud was quick to pick up on the issue of translation on the first day of the course. Being a native Pashtu speaker (Dari was at best his second language), Mahmoud announced to the class, pointing in turn, firstly at me, and then at Ayub, my co-teacher and translator, 'I can't understand him, and I can't understand him'. Mahmoud definitely had a sense of timing in his delivery and the class appreciated this. I must admit it was funny. However, when a pilot is flying a plane in bad weather and there are alarm signals going off in the cockpit then, even if he/she is generally appreciative of humour and the odd joke, he/she is probably not amenable at that particular time to hearing the one about 'the two Irish pilots, Pat and Mick, lost in fog at JFK airport'. And so it was with me. As the teacher responsible for the week's teaching aims and objectives, I could appreciate Mahmoud's gift for humour but not his current repertoire. Nevertheless, overall order in class was maintained. With my visiting status and experience and seniority, I felt that I had no problem with sustaining class interest and attention while I was teaching, including surprisingly, to a certain extent, Mahmoud. However, with the teaching of my young and relatively inexperienced co-teacher, Ayub, it was a different matter.

It was on the second day, while Ayub was giving a lecture, that things began to get difficult. Unfortunately, Ayub's grandfather had died just a few days before the course and Ayub, although still willing and able (and enthusiastic), had not been able to put in the amount of preparation which he afterwards debriefed he would have liked to have done. As he taught that day, questions began to flow from the floor. This is an area in teaching here (as everywhere) which is both valid and important: namely, that people can have points clarified along the way. Here in Afghanistan, though, one needs care and confidence in deciding when this process has moved from individual inquiry to communitarian conflict. This is because one question tends to invite other questions, questions which fellow classmates seem to feel that they have strong opinions on or, alternatively, solutions for. Anyway, it is another core teaching skill for this context that one is able to make clear decisions as to when to move on once more with the lecture or teaching task at hand. In many ways, I personally find it like the experience of being in Afghan traffic (which I described in an earlier blog – Another week in suburban Kabul), it can be very intimidating or intriguing, depending on your point of view. Being experienced and generally confident in the degree of respect in which I am held here (age helps too!), I find the teaching experience in this environment fascinating. Ayub, on the other hand, was finding it very, very intimidating. Mahmoud seemed to have come to a similar conclusion and was plying Ayub with question after question, on the one hand taking some delight in the discomfort which was manifested in this process, and on the other hand feigning indignation that the lecture was taking so long and 'when were we going to get to the treatment side of things?' Ayub only had to glance at me and his pleading eyes were able to communicate the word 'Help!'

I got to my feet and announced to the class that we were coming to the treatment section very shortly, and lining up Mahmoud said that if he stopped asking inane questions we would get there a lot quicker. I was able to do this in Dari and, pointing to Mahmoud for some effect, exclaimed, 'See I can understand Pashtu!' The class quite enjoyed this, indicating so with a loud burst of laughter. However, the current score line in the jokes-enjoyed-by-the-class stakes stood at: Teacher 3 (I had cracked a couple of non-Mahmoud-related jokes), Mahmoud 15 (or so it seemed), and Ayub 0.

Ayub vainly tried to struggle on but, in terms of this particular lesson, he was mortally wounded, and so he asked if I could continue. So I did. Some minutes later, just as we were indeed beginning to talk about 'treatment', Mahmoud got to his feet and walked across in front of me in order to leave the classroom. I stopped and asked him, 'Where are you going?' I decided to follow this up with a rapid, second strategy, one which I had every confidence would be a trump card: 'This is highly disrespectful.' The effect was both immediate and dramatic. Mahmoud stopped as if I had pulled out a gun and sat down in the nearest chair and did not say a thing. I had finally spoken his language; not his native Pashtu, but his cultural language. This was an understanding relating both to one's obligations to a more senior colleague and to a guest. In this case, it was a twofold responsibility which was thoroughly ingrained in his cultural and social upbringing. To assert that he was being disrespectful to an elder as well as a guest caused a jolt and brought about a response which was as automatic and reflexive as any physiological body reflex. I was gratified by the result of my intervention. But as on so many other occasions in life, the immediate pleasure (or perhaps it was relief) gave way to further deliberation. I had made him lose face in front of his peers and this was no small matter: had I alienated him entirely and, thinking selfishly, would there be possible reprisals, in or outside the classroom? My other Afghan colleagues assured me, as we broke for lunch, that he had been in the wrong and that what I had done was perfectly in order. Although, I must admit, there was one dissenter from this position who pronounced that Mahmoud was a big figure in Kandahar (obviously a metaphorical dimension additional to his physical presence) and knew several commanders (what he meant was Taliban commanders). I went to lunch still unbowed by my actions but, nevertheless, somewhat sobered by them.

Generally, on these courses, having eaten with 'the lads' (men and women always eat separately), I try and take a short walk outside, just to be quiet and restful for a while, before teaching resumes once again. It was while I was outside enjoying some quiet and sunshine that I saw Mahmoud from a distance. He was without an entourage on this occasion and waved to me. I noticed that he was also coming across to speak to me. I stood and wondered. He was with me shortly and took my hand in both of his, saying that he was very sorry about what took place inside before lunch and was very sorry to have upset me. I was shocked to say the least. Afghan culture in general, and Pathan culture in particular, is not infused with notions of confession, apology, forgiveness and reconciliation. It is much more a case of 'an eye for an eye, a tooth for a tooth', and has been so since ancient times. And this seems to characterize much of what keeps Afghanistan in a state of war.

The other aspect of this apology which took me by surprise was that Mahmoud was not 'performing' in front of anyone as he talked. It was just him and me. I was quick to ensure that I responded graciously to his apology. I did not have time to reflect either on his motives or my own but, intuitively, it seemed both a right and wise course of action to fully embrace his apology with my own gesture of conciliation. So, I apologized if I had caused him any sadness (shorthand for loss of face) by my remarks. He went on to tell me, in his second language Dari, about three failed lumbar surgeries which he had had in Pakistan and how he was in constant pain and could not sit for very long. As he spoke, I was suddenly on very familiar ground and could empathize readily with his situation. He would later in the week lift his *peran* (shirt) and show me not only these scars, but also some higher up which were scars caused by bullet wounds, a first for me in terms of consultations with fellow physiotherapists on a course.

And the rest of the week went very well. Mahmoud was more restrained in class; being very polite and warm in his relations with me, even if not convincingly engaged with the material. Whether the motivations for our reconciliation were due to self-interest, his related fear of not being able to pass the module or mine in relation to the trouble which he could potentially cause in or out of class is hard to say. It didn't matter in the end. And, on reflection, I think that our underlying motives for doing most things in life are rarely pure. It was significant that he decided, by some internal trigger or other, to apologize to me so genuinely and wholeheartedly and that I could embrace this gesture. I also followed this up by ensuring that I shook his hand publicly every morning before class, something that I do with every male participant (the women receive a 'Salaam Alekum' with the right hand held momentarily over the heart).

This episode makes me wonder about the larger possibilities for a culture of confession, forgiveness and reconciliation in Afghanistan (just as there was in South Africa in the time after Apartheid as evidenced in the Truth and Reconciliation Commission chaired by Archbishop Desmond Tutu) instead of one which is always intent on reprisal and repayment in kind. Mahmoud was certainly a product of his culture and yet, to me, still seemed able, albeit perhaps in just a small way, to transcend it. I wouldn't have predicted this at all and for me it is also therefore a small sign of hope, just a trace, in a land of apparently fixed and rigid social rules and responses.

As a postscript, Ayub recovered his equilibrium and seemed to enjoy the rest of the course as co-teacher, even registering a score on the unofficial jokes-enjoyed-by-the-class scoreboard (Ayub 1).

On the last morning of the course, a group of participants took me out to a lunchtime meal in a restaurant just out of Herat where we sat, ate kebabs and looked out over the city. They then drove me around Herat, where we walked around the ancient towers, the Musalla minarets constructed in the fifteenth century, the Herat Citadel also known as the Citadel of Alexander, and the *Jami Masjid*, the Great Mosque of Herat. It was wonderful to be a tourist for those few hours. Later that afternoon, on our last day in the city, Kaija Lisa generously took Anne and me shopping to the carpet bazaar.

29

Time out

Posted on May 15th, 2011

We are having a quiet day. Anne and I caught a bug from our neighbours, in particular the lovely coughing, spluttering kids from upstairs. This is nothing too serious. And, on balance, for the joy that playing and making friends with them has brought us, we would say this is but a small inconvenience. However, I started a new course for some 40 physical therapists yesterday and as the day went on my voice gave out. This morning I woke with not much more to offer than a 'croak'. So, today there is nothing for it but to take a day off and rest the voice. This is disappointing for all concerned. The PTs travel long distances for these courses. However, we lost a day in Mazar, due to the violence perpetrated on the UN compound, and so hopefully we can do the same in this case, resume tomorrow and still realize a useful time.

Yesterday at morning tea, one of the physical therapists from Jalalabad (where the course was due to be held until the events in Pakistan two weeks ago caused the UN to close operations) spoke with me and his words were very moving. He said something like, 'You know this is such a golden opportunity for us. We can't afford to miss these chances to learn more'. Such innocuous words, in this context, almost bring me to tears. I cannot but think that this is what draws us back. It is such a gift to us that it is in our hands to provide encouragement in this way. When I spoke to my co-teacher colleague by phone this morning, he asked whether it would be okay if the group got together and practised the assessment techniques which we covered yesterday. So, I am hoping to be in voice tomorrow.

I began the next day with an explanation – and a plea – to the class regarding the fragility of my voice. Even though I was using an interpreter, we needed to maximize each verbal transaction so that I did not have to repeat anything unnecessarily or over background noise. The sustained quietness that morning, in a room containing forty enthusiastic colleagues, was an incredible mark of respect and affection. There were always surprises. In the conversation earlier that week with a PT from Jalalabad, not only did he express how much he valued education for himself, but he reiterated its importance for his children. Smiling he said, 'All my children go to school. The girls are doing better than the boys!'

On Sunday, after the final course, we had the opportunity to charter a small aircraft (a Kodiak six-seater) and fly with some colleagues to *Bamiyan*, a valley in the centre of Afghanistan. This is the place which has always been known for the large Buddhas carved into the cliffs around the sixth century. The pilot firstly did a low pass of the landing strip to alert villagers and livestock to vacate the area – it was, for them, a pedestrian corridor. After landing, we walked across the valley to the foot of the Buddhas and were even able to climb stairs, carved in the rock, to inspect the restoration work. On the way back to Kabul we flew low over the famed *Band e Amir* lakes. The water was the colour of lapis lazuli, Afghanistan's precious stone. I was conscious that you had once swum here, Paulo. I had managed a fly-over.

I remember your last swim. Well, it wasn't actually a swim. We drove down onto the beach at Aldinga. With your arms around our shoulders, like trainers assisting an injured player off the field, one of the boys and

I helped you across the sand to the gentle shorebreak. It was a clear and sunny Sunday afternoon in late spring. The water swelled around your ankles and then receded with a washing sound, rhythmically, like phrases in a piece of music. You turned your head to look southwards over the water to the red cliffs above Myponga Beach: a view you loved. When we got back to the car, you sat once more and via the open window said to me, 'Am I just allowing this to happen? Am I somehow talking myself into it?' I am still not sure whether you were wanting a reply or not. But I gave you one anyway: 'No, I don't think you are. I just think you are on the final leg of your journey, mate.' Cliched maybe – it was what I had at the time. But you did not seem to take it as such – you would have told me not to talk bullshit. Instead you looked southwards once more, across the water to the cliffs, and the straw-coloured hills rising beyond them to the open blue sky: that scantiest of membranes between earth and eternity. You would be gone before the next Sunday.

30

An ordinary week in Kabul

Posted on May 26th, 2011

Yesterday we were playing a game with the children from upstairs. It involved two teams of two persons each trying to 'rescue' flags from the opposing team. Anne had 4-year-old, athletically gifted Noa on her team. I had 8-year-old Mea. It is actually more correct to say that we were on their teams. Mea is deadly at cards but is perhaps less gifted in the tactics for rescuing flags. Nevertheless, we were 'holding our own' as they say. 'Rescuing the flags' is perhaps a little like 'storm the lantern' if you are familiar with that game. Anyway it was a lot of fun. We were one game all and at a pivotal moment in the third. As it turned out, I had just rescued the flag and was making a bolt for freedom, having easily dodged past 4-year-old Noa (no, there are no qualms about pursuing victory at the cost of a little boy's feelings – Noa is competitive and wins most games we play by his own arbitration). Evading Noa, I had almost outrun Anne when my right calf muscle decided, on the spur of the moment, to tear. Needless to say, I was cut down and unable to complete the restoration of our flag to its rightful place. One could say that Noa had the last laugh but he was, even as a 4-year-old, more gracious than that.

I am using a plastic chair for a walking aid today. Those in the aid worker fraternity call this 'appropriate technology'. In fact one member of that very same fraternity, an Australian physiotherapist, currently working for another agency here, made a comment to me this morning about 'war wounds', and in doing so gave an idea for a potential title for this blog: 'Wounded and unable to walk'. However, on reflection, I decided that even though I will normally go to great lengths to evoke a response from my jokes (usually settling for any kind of response – my children will testify to that), it did not seem fair to create unnecessary worry (even for an instant) among family and friends on seeing such a heading on 'arriving' at the blog. We seem to be able to do that already without resort to such devices …

It is the juxtaposition of tragedy and danger with 'the commonplace and everyday' which adds uncertainty to a lack of hope (and at times despair). The Char Sad o Bestar hospital was bombed by an *EntehAri* (suicide bomber) at the beginning of this week. Among the dead and injured were medical students. These were sons and daughters of ordinary families whose lives were irrevocably changed in an instant on one Saturday morning going about their study and work.

The Physical Therapy Institute (PTI) is right next door to this hospital. I did not go to PTI last Saturday as I had just finished a week-long course in another place and was working at home, winding down a bit, and doing some marking. Speaking to my colleagues at PTI, I asked how it had been. They said that the explosion had been enormous. One person, Salim (the young administrator who often gives me a lift from KArte Seh across town to PTI) said that he had initially thought it was a rocket and had thrown himself under his desk. Another teacher, a female teacher, had also hidden under some furniture too, quite frightened and distressed. The street to the PTI section was closed and people were not able to leave work at the normal time as Afghan police and army secured the situation. They were kept at their workplace till early evening, not able to get either to other places of work or back to their families at home. While not an everyday event for these colleagues, nevertheless, getting to and from work every day always places these ordinary Afghans at risk; risks which are unpredictable and tragic when they are realised.

One of my physiotherapy colleagues, the one who co-taught in Mazar with me, is a speaker at a large international physiotherapy conference in Amsterdam in June. Together with two other colleagues we have written a paper on the challenges of teaching ethics to Afghan physiotherapy students in a professional practice environment of uncertainty (and at times danger). It is about this that he will speak at the conference. He has been in Delhi, India, for a week now. He had to go there to apply to the Dutch Embassy in order to get a visa for The Netherlands. In leaving Afghanistan and going to India he has had to: a/ find the costs for airfares and accommodation for this trip; b/ leave his responsible and demanding job as project leader for the Physical Therapy Institute; and c/ leave his wife and five young children at home in Kabul. He has an interview as part of this process tomorrow. Following this interview, there is a further ten-day wait in this process in order, if successful, to receive his visa. Delhi at this time of the year is not an easy place to be. The heat is quite oppressive. I did not mention that his first 'port of call' in Delhi was to report to the police and receive a kind of foreigner's registration card for Afghans from them.

I am also going to the conference in Amsterdam. Aziz and I are sort of partners in the presentation. In contrast to Aziz, I will receive my visa when I step off the plane and go through Dutch immigration. We all know, in this time of terrorism and terrorist acts, that governments have the right and responsibility to check out those entering their country. What I want to point out here is another kind of so-called 'collateral damage'; namely the imposed hardship on those hard-working, ordinary citizens who are trying to work for change and further develop the capacities of this country and, in the process of doing so, are faced with these inordinate extra challenges, on the top of those everyday challenges in life of working and raising a family.

Finally, we are aware of the sad news of the death of another Aussie digger this week and the suffering that his family and friends are now experiencing. We operate in different spheres obviously and endeavour to communicate perspectives which won't necessarily make the news at home. However, this war hurts just about everybody in some way or other.

A funny thing happened in the bazaar…

Posted on June 12th, 2011

We were shopping in our local bazaar of Pul e Surkh (meaning Red Bridge) a month or so ago. We heard someone call out: 'John, John …' We hadn't seen any other foreigners and not sounding like 'Rahim', 'Abdul', 'Rafiq' or any other Afghan name, 'John' naturally caught our attention. 'John, John …' said the voice coming from a man now approaching us with a young girl beside him. 'Do you remember me?' 'My name's not John,' I replied. The man look puzzled: 'But didn't you live in KArte ChAr (a suburb just across the bridge) all those years ago? Second street on the right after the *chArrAI* (intersection)?'

Now he really had caught our attention. That was precisely where we had lived some 26 years ago. 'You had a neighbour Habib who used to come to your house and play table tennis. I lived in that area and used to drop in as well.' A certain familiarity about his features began to form, like a camera shot coming into focus. The person standing before us was a man in his early 40s and we were trying to make the link between him and a skinny 15-year-old kid who used to drop in to our house all those years ago and ask for the stamps off our letters from

Australia. He laughed. It was distinctive and helped our recognition. He certainly knew exactly who we were and where we had lived. And as for calling me 'John', Afghans have difficulty with separating the first two vowels in 'Ian' and it often comes out as 'yarn' or something like that. On instantaneous reflection, 'John' was a good effort at remembering my name after such a long time (we lived in KArte ChAr from late 1983 to late 1985).

We started our introductions (or, it could be said, our reintroductions) once more. 'I am Daoud and this is my daughter Humaira. She is 11 years old.' We chatted about our respective families and then swapped phone numbers and agreed to catch up for a meal later. Anne and I walked home, gobsmacked at this chance meeting in a crowded bazaar. That we should run into a person we knew from that time seemed somewhat miraculous: it was not just that he had remembered us but, equally remarkable, as a young Afghan man, he had survived through so many years of conflict and war. He would later tell us of time spent in the army in Kandahar and also of a period when he and his family fled to Pakistan.

In this last week we went to Daoud's place for an evening meal. He led us back, past the Pul e Surkh bazaar and through narrow alleys to his house. Once there we were made comfortable and the introductions began along with the serving of tea and sweets. Daoud and Hamida have three children; a 12-year-old boy, Masi; an 11-year-old girl, Humaira, and a 15-month-old boy, MilAd. Hamida was busy in the kitchen and we would meet her later when the meal was served. Meanwhile the children came to spend some time with us, interspersed between jobs. Masi brought tea. And it was also, somewhat surprisingly, the 12-year-old boy, Masi, to whom the baby MilAd went to for comfort, clinging to his leg in the face of these strangers. Masi picked his younger brother up in a very natural way and, it seemed, in an action born of habit, kissed his baby brother on the cheek, comforting him while battling his own shyness before these new people.

The meal was ready. 11-year-old Humaira held an ornate metal jug and basin (together with hand towels) for us to wash and dry our hands. We sat down on toshaks, dense cotton-filled mattresses which serve as both furniture and beds. The meal was laid out on a plastic 'tablecloth' over the carpets on the floor. Kabuli pillau is a rice dish topped with slivers of cooked carrot and raisins and there are pieces of chicken buried in the mound of rice. Nan is always present (and welcome) and, on this occasion, other dishes, salads, beans and potatoes were also offered. Over the meal we got to know Hamida; an impressive person who works full-time for an organization that organizes and assists widows to make various handicrafts for sale to foreigners in Kabul and also for other export markets. Daoud uses his skills to market these to various organizations.

It was after dinner that the shyness of the children dissolved entirely. It started with Daoud, who we soon discovered is a bit of a joker. He told all assembled how a stranger (a fellow Afghan) had asked to take his picture down at Pul e Surkh the other day. The thing was that there was no camera in the man's hands. The man cupped his hands as though holding a camera and then in sequence simulated the shutter click with a sharp clap of his hands before completing the procedure with the now universally recognized raised arm, bent elbow and other hand slapped onto the biceps of the bent elbow. What it meant and why this 'picture' was taken, nobody knew, including Daoud. But the manner in which he told it had us all, including the children, rocking on our toshaks. Sometimes it is hard to put one's finger on why someone is funny. Daoud could certainly tell a story well. However, his high-pitched laugh, well sustained at the conclusion of each joke, invited enjoyment. And we did enjoy it. This was the second funny Afghan I had met in the last few months (the other being Mahmoud, the funny Pathan).

Then there was Anne's game with MilAd: she would place a hand towel over the child's head, who would then take a second or two to remove it, only to be greeted by Anne's 'boo', upon which the child would laugh so completely that he lost balance, followed soon after by a 'boomp' as he fell onto his bottom. The subject of 'tickling' arose, possibly because Anne introduced this as an enhancement of her game with MilAd. This is where I made my contribution to the evening's hilarity.

The Dari expression for 'tickle' is a tricky little number: 'qut ke taq'. The 'q' sound at the beginning and end of the expression is not one we use in English and can be best compared (by me at least) to a cat trying to expel a fur ball: that is, it comes from a long way back in the throat. The 'k' in the expression is more like our 'k' and comes from quite near the front of the mouth. Usually I can manage the 'q' sound quite okay, especially if there is only one at a time. The problem with 'qut ke taq' is that you have to produce two in quick succession separated by the front-of-mouth 'k'. As I practised my new-found vocabulary in front of the family, it is not putting too fine a point on it to say that I was mangling it, much to the glee of the family. In normal circumstances it would be culturally inappropriate for a 12-year-old boy to laugh at a guest. But listening to my attempts to pronounce 'qut ke taq', this was exactly what Masi was doing. Perhaps not with as much loss of self-control as exhibited by baby MilAd in his game with Anne, but, nevertheless, his rolling to one side, hands clasping stomach, appeared remarkably similar.

The war has claimed casualties in all directions: ISAF forces (including Aussie diggers), Taliban fighters, Afghan army and police, government officials and, yes, even foreign aid workers (our organization lost a team of ten people conducting health clinics last year in remote Nuristan). However, we were reminded on the BBC news this morning of newly released UN statistics demonstrating that civilians (ordinary Afghan men, women and children) far outstrip any of these other groups in terms of the numbers of those dead and injured as a consequence of this war.

Masi and Humaira popped in with their dad a day or two later to say hello; such lovely kids. Anne and I reflect on our recollection of Daoud as a scrawny 15-year-old kid on the lookout for stamps and now as husband and father in a wonderful family. In these few months we have seen threads of continuity; people somehow finding their way and surviving the vagaries of both war and poverty, leading and nurturing lives that can still produce love within and without their families.

Amsterdam

Posted on June 21st, 2011

The news which greeted us on arrival in Amsterdam on Sunday evening was very good indeed. Our friend and colleague Aziz had received his visa that very day at 2pm in Kabul (Sunday being a normal work day there) and was on a flight for Dubai and Amsterdam at 4pm; barely enough time to go home and pack a suitcase. We met him on Monday morning. He was tired and had been through a lot of stress but he had made it!

Last night we met up with and joined a 'delegation' of five Afghan physical therapists who are here for the first time at such a major conference. Aziz from the Physical Therapy Institute, Kabul, is a speaker (the first invited speaker from Afghanistan to a World Confederation for Physical Therapy conference). Del Afroze, the first female president of the Afghan Association for Physical Therapy (AAPT), is here to network with other associations (including the Australian Physiotherapy Association) to assist in the further development of the AAPT. Then there are three PT colleagues from the International Committee of the Red Cross (ICRC) ... From this group, Najmudin will be part of a panel discussion on the role of physical therapy in contributing to sustainable benefits for people in conflict zones and disaster areas.

Newcastle-under-Lyme

Posted on June 25th, 2011

The conference has come and gone. We are now in Newcastle-under-Lyme. 'Lyme' here refers to the ancient Lyme wood which overlooks this town in the midlands of England (not to be confused with the larger 'Newcastle' near the Scottish border). We are staying with more friends with whom we worked in Kabul many years ago.

We said our 'goodbyes' to Afghanistan when we farewelled our Afghan colleagues in Amsterdam the day before yesterday. My colleague Aziz spoke very well to an audience of several hundred about the ethical challenges of delivering healthcare as a physical therapist in Afghanistan and how they are endeavouring to equip their students in their training to reflect on these challenges.

It was a great joy to see how much our Afghan colleagues enjoyed the freedom of the conference to mix with and observe and hear other PT colleagues and to exchange experiences. They were very excited.

Epilogue

The dust of Kabul's blowing soil smarts lightly in my eyes,
But I love her, for knowledge and love
both come from her dust

Sa'ib-i-Tabrizi (from seventeenth-century poem 'Kabul')

The year 2014 was one of loss and handing over.

In April, Jerry, the paediatrician Anne worked with at CURE hospital, was shot dead by a rogue security officer at the front of the hospital. In July, Kaija Lisa was murdered in Herat. She was sitting in a taxi. A motorcycle pulled up beside it and a gunman shot her and her companion through the window.

In April, IAM handed the PTI over to the Ministry of Public Health and the Government of Afghanistan after a stewardship spanning thirty-one years.

I remember the coffin your mate Gerry made you, Paulo. It had handlebars, spoked wheels, a flashing light and your helmet perched on top. The group assembled to farewell you on the day were, judging by their laughter, well aware of your preoccupation with a certain family of magpies which lived in the trees along the cycle path between Willunga and McLaren Vale. You rode this path regularly to and from work and, just as reliably, these magpies were ready and waiting for you. I don't know how many strategies you tried in order to avert their strafing of you: cable ties attached to your helmet, a big eye stuck on your helmet facing skywards, a flashing light, full-throated swearing. You used to describe each of them to me in detail as they came and went: the strategies not the magpies. On each telling, amusement percolated my concern, colouring but not extinguishing it – I knew which of the two you most wanted from me.

The cycle coffin was a fitting vehicle for your final ride. If only we could have summoned this noble family of magpies for the wheeling out of your cycle coffin to the hearse, I was sure that a final dive-bombing might provoke some response from inside: knocking on wood, muffled swearing – anything would have been welcome. 'It might just bring the bugger back,' were my words on the day. But it wasn't to be. You would be dust within the next hour or two. But, my brother, the knowledge and love from that dust won't be easily blown away.

Now that I am near the end of this account, I imagine that you would want to know how I have changed. Did I, in the end, respond to Gerald's challenge, 'Ian, it is *you* that has to change'? I have no neat answers for such a question: there is no simple 'before and after' in all of this. But I can start with a change that is physically demonstrable and is with me daily. I have floaters in my eyes. They seem to drift back and forth across my field of vision like spider webs on a dance floor. My ophthalmologist tells me it is a degenerative thing. By way of encouragement he added, 'But your brain adapts and you will learn to look past them so that your awareness of them, and their capacity to irritate or annoy you, will diminish.' He's mostly right. Occasionally, if I focus on something for which there is a pale, homogenous background, such as when the sky divers are floating down onto our local beach at Semaphore, the waltzing spider webs are plentiful. But on the whole it is okay and I have learned to look past them. The other morning, however, I was driving alone and noticed how patchy my vision was: is it my eyes or is it dirt on my sunglasses? (Apart from my own contributions, Ocie, you often fingerprinted my 'sunnies' with a variety of substances.) On this day, it was my sunnies that were impeding my vision. Given that I was driving alone and thought that it was not a good idea to try to clean them myself, I concluded that I would just have to look past the marks. Then it came to me: that's what I do with my floaters, all the time.

In order to see, you have to look past. As an introvert I am always thinking about my thinking – it's probably one reason I was quite good at clinical reasoning. But it can become circular: I have probably spent too much time reflecting on my interactions with others, examining my beliefs and motives, rehearsing what I might have said or should have done, all with the purpose of deciding what to do next. Now that I have discovered the usefulness of looking past my floaters in order to see more clearly, I have also learned to dwell less upon my flaws and personal limitations: to look past them, not so much to excuse them, but so that they don't disable me. Periodically, however, I do have to focus deliberately on the state of my floaters, and other internal eye issues. I was given a card called the Amsler grid. It has a series of crossed, parallel black lines on it. I observe whether the lines on it are wavy instead of straight and whether there are blurry or blacked-out patches. I can therefore monitor the current health of my eyes. So, there are times for looking inwardly at my floaters and times for looking outwards past them. Likewise, I have concluded that self-awareness and knowledge, through introspection, is a good and necessary thing but only if it enables us to see past ourselves to others.

We started a community garden at the back of our church in Port Adelaide. In it there is an old native pine which bends to one side, at an angle of almost 90 degrees. Some felt that we should try to straighten it with some kind of ambitious staking. Others said it might be best to remove it and start with something else. After walking past it many times to get to other parts of the garden, it came to me that this bent pine is a metaphor of who we are and what we do. We are not here to straighten anyone up or out. And so our community garden is called The Bent Pine. It stands centrally in the garden reminding us that whatever flaws life has weathered on us, or in us, we can grow in a place where our particular asymmetries are still welcome. They may be more or less obvious but we can still look past them.

In Afghanistan, learning 'to look past' took the form of being able to see – a little better at least – what was on the other side of those 'curtains' which used to bother me so much. To do this I had to recognize the various 'invitations' that were offered to me in impromptu conversations with colleagues in and between classes, over shared meals and tea breaks, and via private disclosure. They were all forms of hospitality: a drawing of the curtains or an opening of the door – take your pick – inviting me, the foreigner, to enter the lived experience of Afghans. In one of the most hostile places in the world, therefore, I was given the opportunity to learn hospitality. I was always a foreigner, an outsider, a guest in Afghanistan. But, at the same time, as a teacher, each day and in each class, I was also a host. It became my turn to welcome others and offer them a particular safe and hopeful time and space. It was an exercise in vulnerability, for both me and my students, as we alternated between being guest and host to each other. Now, as a second-time teacher, I understand that whatever the content of our lesson plans we primarily 'teach who we are'.

I can see that the notion of not straightening anyone up or out is a funny message for a physiotherapist to proclaim, even when it comes from The Bent Pine. But it isn't really. Some of the best physiotherapy occurs when we support someone, even with their impairments, to meaningfully resume or even grow their participation in the world. Various patients over the years have said to me, 'I suppose you see people with problems a lot worse than mine. I shouldn't really complain'. And, Ocie, I *have* seen so many different patients with their individual trajectories of recovery or non-recovery. There were those whose lives were upended and irrevocably emptied out by seemingly common back pain, while there were others who lost limbs, or who were paralysed and lost control of limbs but were still able to re(dis)cover full and rich lives. My answer to such comments has for a long time been that I try not to compare patients and their problems. We each have to deal with what is on our own plates. And I think that I have to now apply this advice to myself.

In Afghanistan I was 'a stranger in a strange land', negotiating a landscape of unforeseen challenges and dangers. However, it was the feeling of being an outsider in my own land which proved to be more distressing. After returning from Afghanistan in 1987, it took me a long time to feel like I could fit in to life once more in Adelaide. I am not sure that I understand even now, some thirty-two years later, what 'fitting in' really means. Nevertheless, I see that I had choices and freedoms that many of the people I encountered did not. I think of the strangers and outsiders: 'the boy with no eyes' (and his father); my refugee physiotherapy student Nasima; the *campesinos* of *Ajoya* and their disabled children; the marginalized persons like Bobby, Novak, Freya and Marco who attended the BBC; 'Aunty Teddy' (my Dad's hidden mother); lost friends and colleagues like Tom, Dan, Kaija Lisa and Jerry; and the many, many Afghans I have gotten to know who still grieve for their families, their friends and the lives they used to lead, now so long ago, in a country that was at peace.

Each had so much to deal with – more than me, certainly. But Ocie, we must still take from our encounters and experiences what they offer us and try to live our lives as a response. We may become strangers or outsiders for any number of reasons, but we only become people who recognize and welcome the stranger by choosing to.

I continually come across other grandparents, Ocie, who are only too happy to talk about why we enjoy our grandchildren so much. It seems that being a grandparent is also a second-time kind of experience. Another opportunity to love.

EPILOGUE

A few days ago, on our regular Tuesday, you woke from your afternoon sleep. You had some molars on the way, pushing disagreeably through sore gums. You just wanted to be held while you woke up. I patted you gently on the back and spoke soft, gentle words to you. I felt your weight settle in my arms and your head relax and rest on my shoulder. Then, in this stillness, with a cadence almost matching mine, I could feel a little hand patting *me* gently on the back. And it was as if the future had learned from the past, even as the past held the future. And each spoke wordlessly to the other of hope and love.

Author's note

To protect their identities, I have changed the names of several people in this book.

Diaries

Kabul 1983

Ajoya 1993–94

Blog: Ian and Anne in Afghanistan. Wordpress https://anneandiane.wordpress.com/2011/02/

Notes

Part One: Kabul 1983–1987

Berger, J. & Mohr, J. 2015. *A Fortunate Man: The Story of a Country Doctor*. London: Canongate. (First published in Great Britain in 1967 by Allen Lane, The Penguin Press)

Winton, Tim. 2015. *Island Home: A Landscape Memoir*. Penguin Australia, p17

P.G. Wodehouse. 1953. *Ring for Jeeves*. London: Herbert Jenkins

Levinas, E. 1969. *Totality and Infinity: An essay on exteriority*. Trans. Alphonso Lingis. Pittsburgh, Pennsylvania: Duquesne University Press, p66

Orwell, G. 1946. Benefit of Clergy: Some notes on Salvador Dali. In: *Critical Essays*. London: Secker and Warburg

Richard Flanagan in conversation with ABC broadcaster Richard Fidler, regarding the background for his book, *The Narrow Road to the Deep North*. Conversations with Richard Fidler. ABC radio. Tuesday 19th November, 2013. http://www.abc.net.au/local/stories/2013/11/19/3894075.htm

Murdoch, Iris. 2014. The Sovereignty of Good. Routledge Great Minds series. Routledge: Abingdon Oxford, p91

Part Two: Adelaide 1987–2004

Kearney, R. & Semonovitch, K. 2011. At the Threshold: Foreigners, Strangers, Others. In: Kearney, R. & Semonovitch, K. (eds). *Phenomenologies of the Stranger: Between Hostility and Hospitality*. Fordham University. Retrieved from http://www.jstor.org/stable/j.ctt13x0brs

An accessible account of contemporary pain science by G.L. Moseley can be found at: https://theconversation.com/explainer-what-is-pain-and-what-is-happening-when-we-feel-it-49040 (Accessed October 10th, 2019)

Brooks, D. The Moral Injury. *The New York Times*, February 7th, 2015

Werner, D. 1998. *Nothing About Us Without Us. Developing innovative technologies for, by and with disabled persons*. Palo Alto CA: Healthwrights

Werner, D. 1992. *Disabled Village Children*. Palo Alto CA: The Hesperian Foundation

Lupe, the wildcat. *Newsletter from the Sierra Madre*, May 1987. http://www.healthwrights.org/content/newsletters/NL17.pdf

Marcelo and Luis. *Newsletter from the Sierra Madre*, December 1989. http://www.healthwrights.org/content/newsletters/NL20.pdf

Freire, P. 1972. *Pedagogy of the Oppressed*. Middlesex, England: Penguin books

The French philosopher Paul Ricoeur characterizes the challenges in achieving mutual recognition as 'a struggle against the misrecognition of others at the same time that it is a struggle for recognition of oneself by others'. See Ricoeur, P. 2005. *The Course of Recognition*. Cambridge, Mass: Harvard University Press, p258.

Part Three: Afghanistan 2005–2011

The paper referred to in 'An ordinary week in Kabul' is: Edwards, I., Wickford, J., Ahmad, Adel A. & Thoren, J. 2011. Living a moral professional life amidst uncertainty: Ethics for an Afghan physical therapy curriculum. *Advances in Physiotherapy* (now *The European Journal of Physiotherapy*), 13:1, 26–33, doi: 10.3109/14038196.2010.483015

Epilogue

Saib Tabrizi was a Persian poet in the seventeenth century. This poem is entitled 'Kabul' and is reproduced in Dupree, N.H. & Kohzad, A.A. 1972. An Historical Guide to Kabul. The Afghan Tourist Organization, Kabul. pV11

The expression 'we teach who we are' is from: Palmer, Parker J. 1998. *The Courage to Teach: Exploring the Inner Landscape of a Teacher's Life*. San Francisco: John Wiley & Sons

'Stranger in a strange land' is by no means a new expression. Moses was an outsider and named his son Gershom meaning 'stranger in a strange land'. See Exodus 2:22 KJV

Acknowledgements

Thank you …

To Barbara Washington, Howard and Jean Groome, Jane Edwards, Marianne Vreugdenhil, and Anne Edwards, who read the manuscript at various stages and offered valuable comments.

To Jo Holmes, whose original artwork, hanging on our livingroom wall, became this book cover. And to Amy Holmes for her work with Jo on the design of the cover.

To Margaret Hunter from Daisy Editorial, whose scouring of the manuscript provided consistency of detail and text less cluttered.

To Rommie Corso from Hardshell Publishing, who created the interior design and typesetting of the book and whose expertise brought it from an imagined existence to a published one.

To Mark Jones and Gisela Van Kessel, colleagues from the University of South Australia, who greatly assisted me in learning to become a teacher.

To my Afghan friends and colleagues, whose thirst for learning and persistence in difficult circumstances continue to inspire me.

To my family for your love and the joy you go on bringing to Anne and me.

And always to Anne, my fellow adventurer and love. Thank you.

Ian Edwards lives in the Port Adelaide area with his partner Anne and is a retired physiotherapist and adjunct senior lecturer at the University of South Australia. He has won local and national awards for teaching ethics.

www.ingramcontent.com/pod-product-compliance
Lightning Source LLC
Chambersburg PA
CBHW020318010526
44107CB00054B/1887